Wilderness in America

gROUNDWORKS|

ECOLOGICAL ISSUES IN PHILOSOPHY AND THEOLOGY

Forrest Clingerman and Brian Treanor, *series editors*

Series Board:

Wilderness in America

Philosophical Writings

Henry Bugbee

EDITED BY

David W. Rodick

Fordham University Press | *New York 2017*

Frontispiece: Henry G. Bugbee. Photo courtesy of Archives and Special Collections, University of Montana Library, Missoula, MT.

Fordham University Press has no responsibility for the persistence or accuracy of URLs for external or third-party Internet websites referred to in this publication and does not guarantee that any content on such websites is, or will remain, accurate or appropriate.

Fordham University Press also publishes its books in a variety of electronic formats. Some content that appears in print may not be available in electronic books.

Visit us online at www.fordhampress.com.

Library of Congress Cataloging-in-Publication Data

Names: Bugbee, Henry Greenwood, Jr., author. | Rodick, David W., editor.
Title: Wilderness in America : philosophical writings / Henry Bugbee ; edited by David W. Rodick.
Description: First edition. | New York, NY : Fordham University Press, 2017. | Series: Groundworks : ecological issues in philosophy and theology | Includes bibliographical references.
Identifiers: LCCN 2016050641 | ISBN 9780823275359 (cloth : alk. paper) | ISBN 9780823275366 (pbk. : alk. paper)
Subjects: LCSH: Philosophy, American.
Classification: LCC B945 .B761 2017 | DDC 191—dc23
LC record available at https://lccn.loc.gov/2016050641

Printed in the United States of America
19 18 17   5 4 3 2 1
First edition

to

Bruce Bugbee
Sally Moore
Ray Lanfear
Ed Mooney

Contents

Acknowledgments

The editor expresses thanks to the following:

Eldon H. Smith: For permission to reprint photograph "Bear Trap Canyon, Madison River, Montana";

The University of Montana: For permission to reprint photograph of Henry Bugbee;

Andrew K. Lewis: For permission to reprint letter from C.I. Lewis;

Gary Whited and Homebound Publications: For permission to reprint "Philosopher";

Oxford University Press: For permission to reprint "Wilderness in America";

University of Georgia Press: For permission to reprint excerpts from *The Inward Morning*;

The Estate of Henry G. Bugbee, Jr.: For permission to reprint "The Bugbee Nature Preserve," "For Henry," "A Way of Reading the Book of Job," "The Revolution in Western Thought: Another Step," "Nature and the True Artist," "Notes on Objectivity and Reality," "The Splendor of Rock Creek," "Letter from John M. Anderson," "An Interview with Henry Bugbee," "A Venture in the Open," and "Thoughts on Creation."

xi

The Hotchkiss School: For permission to reprint from the *Hotch-kiss Record*;

Albert Borgmann: For permission to reprint "Henry: A Tribute."

It takes many, many days to learn of what may and may not be in
   the river.
Let us wade right in and keep fishing where we are, with our
   fingertips
touching the trembling line. It is just in the moment of the leap
   we both
feel and see, when the trout is instantly born, entire, from the
   flowing river,
that reality is knowingly defined.

Now the river is the unborn, and the sudden fish is just the new-
born—whole, entire, complete, individual, and universal. The fisherman may learn that each instant is pregnant with the miracle of the
new-born fish, and fishing in the river may become a knowing of
each fish even before it is born . . . just in so far as this alert fishing
involves "abiding in no-abode," or the "unattached mind." If one
is steeped in the flowing river and sensitized through the trembling
line, one anticipates the new-born fish at every moment. The line
tautens and with all swiftness, the fish is there, sure enough! And
now, in the leaping of the fish, how wonderfully, laughingly clear,
everything becomes! If eventually one lands it, and kneels beside its
silvery form at the water's edge, on the fringe of the gravel bar, if one
receives the fish as purely as the river flows, everything is momently
given, and the very trees become eloquent where they stand.

—*The Inward Morning*

Introduction
Being in Nature: The Experiential Naturalism of Henry G. Bugbee Jr.

On January 21, 1953, the *Hotchkiss Recorder*—newspaper of the Hotchkiss School in Lakeville, Connecticut—reported:

> On January 14 with the temperature 10 degrees below zero, a foot of powdered snow, perfect for skiing, and with all three rinks open for skating, the Headmaster surprised the student body by declaring a holiday. Conditions were ideal and the day was enjoyed by every-one. The morning was sunny and clear, with the temperature rising gradually. Clouds appeared by mid afternoon and another three inches of snow began to fall. Many boys then went indoors to begin preparation for the mid-year examinations, ten days in the future.
>
> The holiday was in honor of Henry Greenwood Bugbee, Jr., '32, who has been awarded the first George Santayana Fellowship in Philosophy at Harvard University for the year 1953–54. Assistant Professor of Philosophy at Harvard since 1948, Dr. Bugbee is interested in the metaphysics of responsibility. During his fellowship he will be pursuing this interest at book length in journal form.
>
> In announcing the holiday the Headmaster regretted the fact that Henry Bugbee, an ardent outdoorsman, could not be in Lakeville to enjoy the ideal winter sports conditions.[1]

I first heard the name "Henry Bugbee" in 1986 during a graduate seminar on Martin Heidegger. Following a discussion of the mystical-poetic aspects of Heidegger's later thought, one student posed a question concerning what possibilities, if any, remained for

1

the discipline of philosophy as traditionally conceived. Silence fell over the classroom. The professor responded by offering an example of "a philosopher who moved to Montana and took up fly fishing." I approached my professor after class in order to learn more. At that moment I became acquainted with the name "Henry Bugbee."

Bugbee's philosophy defies traditional academic categorization. Calvin O. Schrag, professor emeritus of Purdue University, once lamented that Bugbee was one of the more marginalized philosophers of the twentieth century, while the late Willard van Orman Quine of Harvard University, world-renowned analytic philosopher and logician, described him as the ultimate exemplar of the examined life. Bugbee's most recognized work, *The Inward Morning: A Philosophical Exploration in Journal Form*, consists of a series of journal entries. Bugbee's writings are remarkably different from anything written in twentieth-century American philosophy. Albert Borgmann, longtime colleague at the University of Montana, has remarked on more than one occasion that the two greatest books in American philosophy are Henry Bugbee's *The Inward Morning* and John Rawls's *A Theory of Justice*.[2] As an undergraduate, and already aware of the need to overcome the limitations of formal philosophical writing, Bugbee acknowledged: "Certainly anyone who throws his entire personality into his work must to some extent adopt an aesthetic attitude and medium."[3]

The purpose of this book is to remove Bugbee's thought from relative obscurity, making it more accessible to the wider public. Beginning with an introductory account of Bugbee's "experiential naturalism," the development of his thought is traced from student writings in Part I to select published writings in Part II, followed by heretofore unpublished writings in Part III. Part IV consists of an in-depth interview conducted during the twilight years of his life. The book concludes with a rich collection of appendixes that are intended to shed light upon the unique person Bugbee *in fact* was. The end-in-view throughout has been to allow Bugbee the opportunity to speak in his own words and, when appropriate, through the words of others: those both familiar with the man as well as with his philosophy.

Who Was Henry Bugbee?

Outside of a small cadre of American philosophers, little is known about Bugbee. Henry Greenwood Bugbee Jr. was born in New York

City in 1915. He attended the Browning School and Hotchkiss before enrolling at Princeton in 1932 where he graduated with high honors in philosophy while competing at the varsity level in crew. His undergraduate thesis, entitled "In Demonstration of the Spirit," bespeaks a life-long concern with understanding the depth and contour of everyday experience. As Bugbee notes in the Prologue:

> Throughout these chapters a certain attitude will take on form; hitherto I have been wont to think about it as my general philosophical outlook even though perhaps it takes in a more complete acumen of philosophical experience than formal Philosophy usually accepts. [I]ndeed I feel the limitations of the latter and set forth the former by preference as an interpretation of the universe.[4]

Bugbee headed west to pursue graduate study in philosophy at the University of California, Berkeley. His studies were interrupted for a period of approximately four years from 1942 to 1945 while serving as commander of a 137-foot navy minesweeper in the South Pacific during World War II—an experience significantly affecting his philosophical development. His doctoral degree was awarded in 1947, following the defense of his dissertation "The Sense and the Conception of Being." Bugbee taught for a short time at the University of Nevada at Reno and Stanford University until 1948 when he accepted a position at Harvard University as assistant professor in the Department of Philosophy. Bugbee accepted the position knowing full well that the Harvard approach to philosophy would chafe against some of his deepest philosophical commitments.[5] However, when reflecting years later upon the Harvard experience he noted: "[My time at Harvard] was wonderful. I think it is one of the greatest breaks I've had."[6]

Given his preference for experiential reflection over formal writing, Bugbee was denied tenure at Harvard for reason of insufficient publication. This fateful event helped to contribute to the publication of *The Inward Morning: A Philosophical Exploration in Journal Form* in 1958.[7] Like Thoreau's *Walden, The Inward Morning* is a reflective meditation upon what it means to live and *to be* in the world, day-to-day, in such a way as to reflect integrity of meaning and purpose. The preface reflects upon the process of the book's composition:

> As I would put it now, the guidance of meditation, of the themes received in meditation, is the fundamental feature of the work;

and the themes of meditation live a life of their own. . . . It was my work to attend upon such themes, in the very rhythm of daily life; to follow them where they might lead.[8]

Bugbee accepted a teaching position at the University of Montana in 1958. He retired in 1979, remaining active in the Missoula community for as long as his health permitted. It is important to note that Bugbee published only nine or ten journal articles over the entire course of his academic career. While this might appear to be a paltry sum according to today's hyperaccentuated standards of professionalization, one must remember that from the time he was an undergraduate Bugbee sought to maintain as much transparency as possible between "the life we lead and the philosophy we believe in our hearts."[9] His approach was radically peripatetic: one must move about in the world within which *we* live, think, and act while remaining alert that "there is no surer criterion of truth . . . than the utter clarity and delight in the commonplace, just in its matter of factness."[10] To make his case, Bugbee drew upon the distinction Paul Tillich made between "experimental" and "experiential" verification:

> [I]t is not permissible to make the experimental method of verification the exclusive pattern of all verification. Verification can occur within the life process itself. [Experiential] verification has the advantage that it need not halt and disrupt the totality of a life process. . . . The verifying experiences of a non-experimental character are truer to life, though less exact and definite.[11]

Situating Bugbee within the American Tradition

Situating Bugbee's philosophy is no easy task insofar as his approach to philosophical reflection is deeply experiential and resistant to summarization. Reflecting upon the course of his philosophical education, he acknowledged:

> Since [my] earliest days of philosophic study, I have remained concerned with the works of philosophers . . . as helps to the understanding of experience. I study the works of philosophers out of an interest which subordinates theory to understand-

ing. . . . It will be ever important to me to give attention to technical philosophy but I will never be able to take technical philosophy as the ultimate phase of a reflective life.[12]

This is not to say that "technical" matters were never a concern. Bugbee's doctoral thesis, "The Sense and the Conception of Being," despite its intent to offer an "experiential" metaphysics, remained, in the end, an abstract affair and, from the perspective of the author, somewhat of a failure. After roughly a decade of reflection, Bugbee reconsidered his doctoral thesis in the following terms:

[The Sense and the Conception of Being] left man out of account, and, in so doing, falling short of a philosophy of action. . . . Those days give me the courage now to continue this endeavor in terminal reflection, not as a termination of anything, but as a renewed endeavor in understanding finality more maturely, in rounded human terms.[13]

Philosophical reflection need not begin with technical jargon, indubitable foundations, metaphysical abstractions, or any "meta-level" order of discourse; philosophical reflection must begin with a consideration of *things themselves*: "[L]et the sense of being reaffirm its significance in human experience."[14] Leaping trout in Montana, the chapel bell ringing in Harvard Yard, a kamikaze pilot crashing into the South Pacific now become intensive indices of the extensive panorama of being. The question remained whether "the profession" of philosophy—what William James so aptly referred to as the "Ph.D. Octopus"[15]—would be willing to tolerate an experiential approach of this magnitude?

The publication of Bugbee's book by the defunct Bald Eagle Press in 1958 did more to champion the experiential possibilities of meditative reflection for American philosophy than anything heretofore written in the American philosophical idiom. For this reason *The Inward Morning* remains an "underground classic" in philosophical circles. Gabriel Marcel in his introduction to *The Inward Morning* points out the spiritual topography with which the book is concerned:

Henry Bugbee and I inhabit the same land . . . illuminated by a light of its own. . . . Since this is a spiritual light, however . . . we do not occupy fixed and distinct positions which might be plotted on a well-defined map . . . [W]hat we have to deal with here is a spiritual itinerary.[16]

Bugbee's Experiential Naturalism

Referring to Bugbee's thought as "experiential naturalism" will undoubtedly raise some objections. I agree whole-heartedly with Thomas M. Alexander when he writes:

> I am tempted, like Dewey, to use the familiar—too familiar—term "naturalism," except that it, too, has probably been poisoned beyond redemption. As noted, it commonly is taken to mean that nature is whatever "science" says it is . . . Those who proclaim [this] sort of naturalism tend to exhibit what John Herman Randall, Jr. once called "nothing-but-er" philosophies . . . If the term "naturalism" could be rescued from its reductionist associations, it could be used.[17]

A nonreductive naturalism:

> [R]aises the question of the *being* of Nature. Now this inquiry may remain focused on "what there is." . . . The result is a metaphysics of "things" thought of as an aggregate of determinate objects of cognition. . . . An ontology of Nature must be open to the variety of modalities and the mysterious depths of Nature lest it lose itself in a "thing-metaphysics."[18]

Bugbee's philosophical approach may be viewed as a kind of experiential naturalism insofar as it recognizes the need to address beings experientially on their own terms, within the natural context out of which they emerge, in an effort to see what can be revealed once beings are beheld in their own light: "The theme [is] simple enough, indeed it [is] the theme of simplicity: Things say themselves, univocally, unisonously, formulating a tautology of infinite significance."[19] This is no mere "armchair" exercise or any kind of action-at-a-distance. Experiential reflection is a demanding peripatetic activity occurring only to the extent one is, to use a nautical term, *underway*:

> [M]y philosophy took place mainly on foot. It was truly peripatetic, engendered not merely while walking, but *through* walk-

ing that was essentially *a meditation of the place*. I weighed everything by the silent presence of things, clarified in the racing clouds, clarified by the sound of hawks, solidified in the presence of rocks, spelled syllable by syllable by waters of manifold voice, and consolidated by the act of taking steps, each step a meditation steeped in reality.[20]

One of the unfortunate consequences of modern philosophy, including naturalisms of the reductive type, is the tendency to balkanize *"ought"* from *"is."* Given this separation, how is it possible for the acting agent to inhabit any stance in the world other than one of sheer contingency? Philosophical solutions that attempt to reconcile *"ought"* and *"is"* range from claiming that "ought" cannot be derived from "is" (logical empiricism), to claiming that "ought" must be located at a level other than the empirical (deontology).[21] The value of Bugbee's experiential naturalism lies in its ability to circumvent these academic distinctions, allowing the possibility of discerning the eternal amid the temporal.

For example, events occurring at critical junctures in life oftentimes take on universal significance, indicating a "once-for-allness" about them. Events of birth, marriage, and death call "attention to the being of the self and life as a *whole* . . . away from the parts and details of life."[22] At such moments "life as such and the purpose of living come into view at points where decision affects the direction and destiny of life *in its entire cycle* and not just in one aspect or part."[23] Bugbee refers to such profound experiences as "moments of obligation." Obligation indicates a "deep interest and absorption . . . *from* a spirit by which [we are] invaded from within."[24] The experience of *being-obligated* points to an objective referent through which "a light dawns upon us in the light of which we become enlightened in our relationship with [beings], as they dawn on us as given-in-that-light."[25] The fact that we often find the strength to face adversity with a sense of courage and resolve far outstripping physical capacity implies "a basis in [our]selves deeper than anything we can muster and confer upon us by decree . . . that moment in which we may find immediate incentive and confirmation from within [our]self for complete commitment in action."[26] These crucial moments of destinate decision[27] make it clear that there are not only problems *in* life but also problems *of* life; namely, the problem of seeking and finding the basis upon which we depend for our being and purpose.

Authentic experiences of obligation "demand [of us] to be and to act consonantly with the felt universe."[28] The moment of obligation is a reflexive, "double-barrelled" experience—as William James and John Dewey liked to say—of centripetally awakening to one's centrifugal immersion in a world of being. Things previously seen *per speculum et in aenigmate* become encountered "face-to-face"—*sub specie aeternitatis*—within purview of the eternal, beholding things anew as if for the first time:

> We become *reflexively* mindful of ourselves as rooted in a source of life wherein we become decisively animated—sponsored evocatively in a way underlying our very responsiveness. Our awareness of this *is* essentially reflexive. . . . [L]ight dawns upon us in the light of which we become enlightened in our relationship with them. . . . And in that Johannine light one may come to meet them anew.[29]

The *Being* of Nature

Experiential naturalism of the Bugbeean kind, or any other kind of naturalism for that matter, remains abstract without *nature*: the creatures, mountains, air, waters, and land that we absolutely depend upon for our being and existence.[30] The fact that nature is considered not only the source of existence but *being* as well may strike some as anthropocentric puffery. I hope it is by now obvious that our natural habitat is essential for physical survival—both individually and as a species. What is not so obvious is whether mere perpetuation of life-function through physical survival, even under the most luxurious conditions, should provide the be-all-and-the-end-all according to which the goals and purposes of humankind are oriented and shaped. We must approach the natural world "appreciatively," outside the lens of utilitarian calculation. As Bugbee indicated, nature houses the potential to *be instructive*—as connoted by the Latin verb *in-struo*, meaning to be "in the process of formation."[31] Instruction in this sense does not refer to any type of programing or social engineering. Experience is rich in disclosive potential, leading to an awareness of things exceeding parameters of material causality. When a person is experientially impacted, a *mental* response of some kind occurs—an image, a sensation, an idea, or a thought. Qua mental (*Geistigheit*), cognitive responses elevate the subject into the realm of spirit (*Geist*), revealing a centrifugal reservoir of possibility. At the spiritual level, life gives birth to something more than itself.[32] When a quickening of consciousness occurs, a new idea is engendered, offering potential for both transition and transfiguration. The human capacity for increasing the scope of reflection is the cognitive side of mystical experience—a grafting of flesh onto spirit. Polyphonic perspectives stand to be revealed. As Emerson indicated, "Let a man fall into his divine circuits, and he is enlarged. Obedience to his genius is the only liberating influence."[33] Spirit reveals itself reflexively through limited acts of self-disclosure, leading to a heightened consciousness of self. Similar to the way in which Bergson likened the self to an uncoiling of a coil, self-realization is an experience of burgeoning unity, as we become implicated within larger unities and synthetic wholes. Our cognitive capacity for increasing the scope of reflection is similar to what Aristotle referred to as contemplation, an intellectual activity allowing one to become *theómorphos* or more "godlike." In Bugbee's words,

> We become authentically ourselves in the image of the divine and on the strength of the divine. This implies that we come to know ourselves in being ourselves and I think in a very precise sense: We are strictly as nothing in and of ourselves. Of all creatures, we must *know* our creatureliness and accept it in order to be as the creatures we really are. . . . Now this means two things: It means that considered in and of ourselves we are of no account and impotent. It also means that we are able to be in the image of being, which is no *thing* at all.[34]

The Sublime as "Our Daily Bread"— Thoughts on Finality

"Give us this day our daily bread . . . ."

The experience of the sublime conveys a mysterious sense of the "wittingness of ourselves and things—together—in the mode of finality."[35] Bugbee's conception of finality is best captured through concrete events of witness and testimony. When Job cried out for understanding from the depths of anguish, he asked one of *the* perennial questions: "*Why hast God forsaken me?*" A compelling silence ensues—the why-and-where-to-fore of divine justice resists anthropomorphic reckoning. It is interesting to note how the Western Apache language recognizes *specific* conditions when it is *necessary* to refrain from speaking—situations in which participants perceive their condition to be governed by relationships mysterious and unpredictable.[36] Silence prepares a space for deeper reconciliation, allowing illumination to break through and to "light-up" what stands in the clearing.[37] Out of the depths of such numinous silence, Job's sense of justice becomes ecstatically transfigured in light of faith in the eternal possibilities of experience. As Bugbee recounts:

> And the story seems something like this: as we take things, so we have them; and if we take them in faith, we have them in earnest; if wishfully—then fantastically; if willfully, then stubbornly; if merely objectively, with the trimmings of subjectivity—then emptily; and if in faith, though it be in suffering, yet we have them in earnest, and it is really them that we have.[38]

The togetherness of things in modes of finality is an event of co-articulation: subject and world fused through an act of *réceptivité réflexive* [reflexive receptivity]—a dynamic combination of *recueillement* [receptivity] and *accueil* [release]:

> *Reflexive* receptivity . . . is necessarily twofold: It embraces receptivity to beings given into perceptive attention and the engagement of our concern with them; and it embraces receptivity in the radical reflexive engagement of attentive concern "from within." The former is a matter of responsiveness to . . . the moment of the reception of beings in the life of spirit. The latter is a matter of "responsiveness in, upon, and from . . . this is the moment of recollection in the life of spirit.[39]

Finality experienced to this degree culminates in a sense of homecoming—a feeling of reconnecting with Being in its intensive unity:

> This, so far as I can tell, is the theme which unifies my own life. It enfolds and simplifies, comprehends and completes. Whenever I awaken, I awaken into it. It carries with it the gift of life. And it lives in the authenticity of every authentic gift, every true blessing confirms it deeper; it is always with me when I come to myself.[40]

The experience of finality—in the Bugbeean sense—is not intended to be a "death-bed conversion," but a profound revelation of existential meaning occurring in time: "what we know in our bones . . . [while] witnessing events being born out [*in statu nascendi*] of the eternal meaning that 'explained them.'"[41] Bugbee's philosophy celebrates what Heidegger referred to as "*die Pracht des Schlichten*" [the splendor of the simple] here and now.[42] Insofar as "we are sensitive to the absoluteness of our situation, we live in a dimension of meaning which is the depth of our experience—we live in eternity."[43] The American writer Annie Dillard beautifully captures the experience of eternity holding forth in time:

> Here is the fringy edge where elements meet and realms mingle, where time and eternity spatter each other. . . . [W]e have less time than we knew. Time is eternity's pale interlinear, as the islands are the sea's. We have less time than we knew and that time buoyant, and cloven, lucent, and missile, and wild.[44]

Bugbee's Legacy

Sadly, methodological orientations such as Bugbee's remain foreign to the arid landscape of contemporary philosophy. The danger lies in what Alfred North Whitehead referred to as the "fallacy of misplaced concreteness"—the tendency to give priority to the most refined *results* of experience at the expense of the more original ways in which things appear—a tendency to prioritize "mind" over "heart." The American philosopher Elie Maynard Adams referred to the cybernetic character of the contemporary world as a "sabertooth tiger civilization"—"the saber tooth tiger developed great tusks as effective weapons in combat, but perished because they obstructed its eating."[45] Ontologies in pursuit of noetic autonomy resemble "tusks" through their inability to access the vital source of nourishment upon we depend as a species—sources underwriting our being *and* existence. Unlike the saber-toothed tiger, we can change our course.

The legacy of Bugbee's philosophy lies in its ability to serve as spur operating in the Socratic sense of a "gadfly," awakening us from dogmatic slumber. His philosophy speaks to layperson, student, and philosopher alike by conveying a sense of the panoramic reach of experiential reflection—as if to say "*this* is what the love of wisdom truly *is*." Bugbee's philosophy also serves as a reminder of what philosophical reflection, in the most comprehensive sense, is *meant to be*—an Ariadnean-like thread indicating "a central strand of meaning capable of bearing the weight of all the disparate moments of *our* life."[46] As a former student vividly recalls:

> With his silvery hair, bronze complexion, and tall lean figure, he was a mysterious and somewhat commanding presence in the room. I remember him wearing a grey and white long-sleeved flannel shirt, cotton pants and mountain boots. . . . He didn't speak often, but when he did, he left a deep impression. . . . His sentences, with their complex vocabulary and multiple subordinate clauses, undulated . . . visually choreographed by constant hand gestures and changing facial expressions. In speech and mannerism, he seemed at once fascinating and mysterious. . . . There was something vital and deeply exploratory about everything he said.[47]

As Thoreau stated at the conclusion of *Walden*: "Only that day dawns to which we are awake. There is more day to dawn. The sun is but a morning star."[48] May the light illuminating the life and work of Henry Bugbee continue to serve as a guide along the circuitous path of reflection—a path he helped prepare.

Student Writings

In Demonstration
of the Spirit (Selections)

Every time I retrace the course of my reflections since "their beginning" in my undergraduate years I discern as central this preoccupation with [the] "somewhat absolute" in experience.[1]

Bugbee earned a bachelor's degree with high honors in philosophy from
Princeton University in 1936. His thesis, "In Demonstration of the Spirit,"
was directed by Warner Fite. Regrettably, little attention is paid to Fite,
but it was Fite who instructed the young Bugbee on the significance of the
personal perspective.[2]

"In Demonstration of the Spirit" exhibits a striking religious tone.
Three of the four chapters begin with biblical epigraphs and the epilogue
concludes with a quote from *Saint Paul*: "To this effect I have not spoken
'with enticing words of man's wisdom, but in demonstration of the Spirit
and of power: That your faith should not stand in the wisdom of men, but
in the power of God.'" The salutation "Amen," immediately followed by
Bugbee's signature, leaves a sense of witnessing a "demonstration" of profound significance in terms of the author's spiritual development.[3]

The thesis criticizes academic philosophy's failure to address "the crying need of the whole man." Bugbee's "final word" indicates a degree of
insight well beyond the ken of a twenty-one-year-old:

A final word—you will realize that my efforts, while wholly
tentative and probably quite inadequate, represent a most serious
and valuable attempt to think my way out of the particular situation
in which I have become vitally involved. I hope to accomplish more
than the fulfillment of certain requirements, for a good deal of my
future depends upon what may be considered Philosophy. If it is the

strictly limited pursuit—in regard to method—which it may possibly turn out to be, then I am afraid I will have to break the confines of the medium, for images and a full conscious life beckon me more than their purified reflection—ideas.

The thesis also appeals to the need to engage experience reflexively, questioning the dualism of "self" and "world." The problem with "dualisms," is that we simply don't experience *life* that way:

> When we place our ears close to the stream of life we do not hear a ticking of segmented consecutive instants but rather a constant hum, a mingling of harmonies interposed by epoch changes in key and imperceptible blends from one orchestral movement to another.

Reflective experience is interpenetrative—a *logos*, or unifying thread, pervades every act of comprehension. Experience is also *compelling*, rendering it possible to move beyond phenomenal knowledge to an experience of "things-in-themselves"—not as "bolts from the blue," but as an experience of such degree that the numinous aspects of existence become recognized as something necessarily participated in by everyone. The British philosopher C.E.M. Joad[4] helped Bugbee to appreciate intuition's potential for yielding awareness of dimensions of reality recalcitrant to logical reasoning. Intuition is a personification of spirit:

> This, then, is the unique character of consciousness, whereby many elements are combined within a unified personality . . . and thus the Spirit represents the supreme embodiment of both the one and the many, an integrally logical manifold of infinitely diverse particulars. Such is the logic of personality, and it must furnish the basis of any living philosophy.[5]

The thesis also captures the relationship between de facto and de jure dimensions of experience: "Moral Philosophy must start at the other pole, first of all with one's own moral experience, and from a careful attempt to get at the meaning of this it will perhaps be possible to infer what that of others may mean." Bugbee referred to this as "listening with a brotherly ear."[6] The problem with existing forms of ethical relativism is "I have yet to hear of a single solitary human who acted as if he believed this true of himself." Moral experience reveals a constellation of issues oriented around *my life*. What at first glance may appear as a series of aporia, upon further examination indicates traces of enduring facticity. The perennial nature of moral questions offers a clue to the universality of moral experience. Each person irrevocably instantiates value while living in the world—valuation [*estimato, ergo sum*] precedes knowledge [*cogito, ergo sum*]: "The individual personality is in the widest sense the expression of morality . . . Hereby we identify the locus of moral value within the core of the human soul, and this constitutes the essence of consciousness in general." If the self is wrested from the context of concrete moral action, it mortifies into abstract, lifeless existence—a formal agent or cipher divested of existential reality: "That the moral problem in general has remained relatively constant in the memory of man I will suggest is also corroborated by . . . every man not completely anesthetic to the central perplexities of life."

~

Prologue

I sit down to rearrange my ideas in the form of a thesis with some reluctance and trepidation. It cannot fail to reflect the uncertainty and ambiguity with which I am at the present moment assailed. For this reason, then, it will primarily represent an attempt to clarify and evaluate certain aspects of experience about which I have always felt a predominant concern; it will embody a problem, a conflict confronting every attempt to analyze human nature, and one involving, to some extent, every kind of Philosophy, but particularly that part employed in value theory.

The first chapter will try to analyze the field of consciousness and determine how knowledge of the most significance to us as humans may possibly be attained; it will examine the approach of Philosophy and suggest what other approaches might be; whatever the method, however, it may be considered conceptually, and thus falls within our scrutiny. It is my general suggestion that such questions as this are of ultimate importance and must be brought to bear compellingly on the modern mind, which in a typical sense seems directed toward different ends. Specifically, I believe Culture to be of more philosophical importance than Science, and this does not seem the predominant opinion,—hence the additional timeliness of the question. To illuminate the nature and opposition of these traditions, it will be a primary necessity to deal directly with their respective sources to be found in the nature of consciousness itself. Here I find a dichotomy of experience, as have many others, which produces one of the most fundamental and evasive problems ever to persist. Many great Philosophers have been deeply troubled by it, and each of us in turn must cope with it in himself.

While the first chapter will outline various types of knowledge in general, the second will attempt to analyze moral experience, and taking this as a branch of value experience consider how it may be treated from the different standpoints already indicated . . .

Throughout these chapters a certain attitude will take on form; hitherto I have been wont to think of it as my general philosophical outlook even though perhaps it takes in a more complete acumen of reflective experience than formal Philosophy usually accepts. Now I have my doubts, and I see that my notion of what constitutes Philosophy may possibly undergo a change. Possibly it is not the all-inclusive subject I have cherished as my own. Then what is my attitude, perhaps more aesthetic than philosophical? If it is aesthetic to try and reflect ones' spiritual growth and the full power of consciousness by the most imaginatively convincing means, a means most nearly reflecting the personality as it really exists for us, and if Philosophy would exclude this practice, than indeed I feel the limitations of the latter and set forth the former by preference as an interpretation of the universe. What I will develop, if indeed it may be deemed Philosophy in the last analysis, represents a sort of Personal Idealism, and I intend to expand this throughout, depending largely on the logic of my own personality for continuity. The first chapter will serve an introductory purpose in discussing method, which in turn will be adapted to the subject of our approach, namely consciousness . . .

A final word—you will realize that my efforts, while wholly tentative and probably quite inadequate, represent a most serious and valuable attempt to think my way out of the particular situation in which I have become vitally involved. I hope to accomplish more than the fulfillment of certain requirements, for a good deal of my future depends on what may be considered Philosophy. If it is the strictly limited pursuit—in regard to method—which it may possibly turn out to be, then I am afraid I will have to break the confines of the medium, for images and a full conscious life beckon me more than their purified reflections—ideas.

A Preliminary Account of Consciousness

Eye hath not seen, nor ear heard, neither have entered into the heart of man, the things which God hath prepared for them

that love him. But God hath revealed them unto us by his
Spirit: for the Spirit searcheth all things, yea, the deep things of
God. (Cor.—I. I, 9-10)

Philosophy has always claimed a close acquaintance and judicial relations with the various kinds of experience, its purpose being to
examine fundamental relations of these and fit them into a whole.
To what branch of experience does it bear the closest resemblance?
Well, at one time certainly religion at least furnished the subject
matter. But with Modern Philosophy the major concern has persis-
tently and increasingly been directed upon our knowledge of the
external world; I do not forget men whose scope was broad enough
to include an examination of practically every branch of experience,
particularly Spinoza, or Kant, or Hegel. Nevertheless the problem of
knowledge has been ever more narrowly focused to bear upon the
world of Science. The object of knowledge is the 'material' object,
and the other 'objects' external to subject which come within the ken
of the latter are obscured to this extent; I will not say forgotten.
    It is the same with a large preponderance of value theory these
days, and I will illustrate the point. On the highroad the other day
I noticed a series of advertisements assuring the reader, and the ad-
vertiser, that "Posters show the news of America's values." These
would be chiefly economic, and next hedonistic values. This seems
to symbolize a situation which is rapidly becoming acute. To cite
a striking instance of the tendency, look around even in the broad
cultural center like Princeton and note the majority interest in spe-
cialized education among the practical and abstract sciences; I think
an explanation may be found for this in the wider demands of an
industrialized, even mechanized civilization. This is probably more
true of some European countries where cultural interests are treated
as secondary, if not really superfluous. Those things which actually
should come first in a man's purpose and plan of life are relegated to
moments of luxury snatched from 'the serious business of modern
life.' Certainly you will agree that we are held closer by economic
fetters today than ever before. Men live and die under continuous
fear for their practical security, and it is small wonder that in their
struggle they should grasp hopefully at Science to subdue adversity.
To the extent that Science fulfills such expectations it commands
the reverence once extended even toward deity itself. As I intimated
at the outset a great deal of this spirit has likewise crept into the
'critical sanctum' of formal Philosophy. I discern much the same

predicament in both contemporary life and Philosophy which led
Rudolph Eucken to exclaim, "In the face of the starry firmament
without what has become of the moral law within!" Moreover, "beneath the comfort and splendor of our modern life runs an undercur-
rent of pessimism regarding the value of life itself."

That Science virtually sets the type and topic for an alarming
amount of Anglo-Saxon, if not other current Philosophy as well, I
will indicate by referring to a few such movements which appear
typical.

First of all Psychology, which up until a relatively few years ago
was a branch of Philosophy, has now become identified with Physiology and Pathology. I do not deny that the brain is concomitantly
correlated with whatever else consciousness may be; but if any experience is to be trusted, perhaps it is that of self-consciousness,
and manifestly we do not find physico-chemical processes upon introspection. Consciousness is essentially unique in that it cannot
be represented in the Spatio-Temporal dimensions of Science, nor
can we understand it by an exclusively behavioristic approach, if
for no other reason than that such observation fails to take account
of a tremendous amount of data rendered inaccessible by the very
nature of the case. There is more than idle humor in the saying that
upon entering the Psychology Laboratory you check your soul at the
door. The tests administered therein rely largely for their accuracy
upon a steady and uninterrupted chain of stimuli and reactions; if
the subject stops to conjecture or think and lets his consciousness
function intelligently upon what he is doing, then what can this
mean for the recorder? It is the same with aptitude tests, if time is
consumed in reflection, then the student is indeed to be tabulated
among the stupid. I find fault not only with the human Psychology,
but also the animal division of the Science, for it fails to see the animals' consciousness as he sees it. Mr. Fite has suggested that a parallel experiment be practiced on the psychologists themselves. Like
dogs, they will be singled out and exposed to an unprecedented and
unpremeditated situation; the dogs will conduct the investigation,
and it will attempt to see how long it takes the human to discover
that the scent of, say, aloes leads to the goal. If the man stops in
bewilderment, or out of weariness, hunger, fatigue, or for any other
reason, then the dogs will nip at his limbs, nor shall he have time to
think. Such a caricature may be used to score a good deal of modern
Psychology in general, in so far as it considers its experiments as
measurements of consciousness; I do not deny that physiological

data are the very important results to be obtained, and that they have a bearing upon psychological data, but to identify the latter with the former,—well, it is significant of the scientific trend flowing into Philosophy.

Probably the most complete adaptation of Philosophy to scientific method is represented in the movement known as Logical Positivism. For exponents of this view the criteria of all Reality are founded in Symbolic Logic, and this in turn is based on mathematics. Thus the ideal of philosophical dialectic would eventually be formulated in terms of mathematical equation; but furthermore this is the only way according to the position in which the philosophical situation can be interpreted. In addition to these fundamental principles the determination of meaning in every field of practice is based on the scientific method, so that Ethics is to Moral Philosophy as abstract is to applied mathematics, and this parallel might be drawn in all the branches of Philosophy. Like the mathematician the Positivist is essentially monistic, and like the practical scientist he is a pluralist. In any case he is above all scientific and nothing means anything to him that cannot be verified in a public field of reference. I don't deny that any of these views have a particular significance, but the trouble is they can't get beyond the mechanical affairs in which they are involved; they are dealing with only a part of reality from a single point of view, and this aspect, as I shall try to show, is not even the most important consideration of human beings. But as to the departmentalization of consciousness, in particular for philosophical purposes, this seems to me a grave error, for we don't experience life that way, as I will eventually try to show.

I have enumerated several views which I consider typical of a tendency in philosophical and public opinion, and my own attitude is more or less diametrically opposed to it. Would I, then, recommend that the data of Science be cast aside as irrelevant to Philosophy? Not at all—Science serves its purpose to an undeniable degree of effectiveness, and it must bear out a certain correlation with Reality to predict and achieve such verifying results. But surely you will begin by agreeing that significant experience is not confined to the categories of Science. Before I get through I want to suggest that the more an experience transcends or interpenetrates categories in general the more significant it may be. This will be made a point of contrast between the broader type of aesthetic experience and the more restricted scientific type. In this respect I will suggest that the former offers more valuable data for Philosophy than the latter; it would be a mistake, however, to hypostatize either aspect of Reality to a position of exclusive importance over the other; it is the business of Philosophy to supplement if possible such varied aspects and approaches to what may be real, for the chances are that any persistent interpretation of the situation is in some sense or other true.[7]

Of almost equal demand upon the attention of Philosophy, along with the general acquisition of knowledge, is the function of evaluation; that is, we reflect particularly upon what is of significance to man; whether there may be any ultimate goal which shall culminate this existence; and while on the road what is worth while picking up and cultivating, what shall be cast aside or ignored; supposedly, in so far as a man is able, he governs his life and at least his thought by his choice or preference in such distinctions as these. Such questions I deem of ultimate consequence, and so they are defined ipso facto; on what kind of experience may such an understanding of life be based? Not, I maintain, on scientific experience, but rather on a generally moral, religious, or aesthetic appreciation of Reality. The crying need of a man is a faith fostered in the latter spheres of human nature, for herein the soul is perpetuated beyond the chains of Time and Space, thereby achieving such salvation as is humanly possible. This type of experience is, moreover, more intensely real and empirically verified than any other conscious visitation upon human existence. Having definitely placed our subject matter within this problem of ultimate significance, the problem of value experience, I now propose that we examine how an understanding of such experience is possible.

That understanding is possible rests on certain remarkable unique characteristics of consciousness perhaps most adequately symbolized under the faculties of memory and imagination. In the function of these powers we may begin to see what differentiates the forms of consciousness from mechanical Reality; compare ideas for instance with mechanical facts: the latter by themselves remain haphazard, opaque, and thus meaningless; but of ideas we must say that those of successive moments are bound to interpenetrate if the idea of any one moment is to have any meaning.[8] This, then, is the unique character of consciousness, whereby many elements are combined within a unified personality, and thus the Spirit represents the supreme embodiment of both one and many, an integrally logical manifold of infinitely diverse particulars. Such is the logic of personality, and it must furnish the basis for any individual living Philosophy.

Possibly to use 'logic' in this sense is to take some liberty with its conventional connotation, but it is my opinion that 'logic' may be applied to any principle of structural unity whether it be manifested in a series of concepts, or a work of art, or a human personality. Thus Logic is a system of rational propositions which organize the structure of Reality according to strict implications. In our value theory, then, we will necessarily rely upon the medium of Logic to develop the meanings implied within our interpretation of experience and render them to some degree determinate within an objective whole. Now we come to a point upon which I am reluctant to decide, namely; as to whether the medium of logic (and of Science) is the only method recognizable as truly philosophical. I will not conjecture one way or another at present; but however necessary this conceptual frame work of Philosophy may be to the assimilation of knowledge, for the understanding of value experience I feel an additional requisite must be satisfied. In order to grasp the true meaning of values we must somehow enter into a sympathetic experience of them even at the time when we would assess them through logical observation. All Philosophy is composed of various attitudes of one type or another, and these are instituted from various points of view, removed as it were from the current of life to a position of observation. As I have already indicated, this is necessary for the sake of coordinating and clarifying our knowledge within the widest possible perspective. Nevertheless, this approach when practiced to exclusion even on one's own value experience fails to realize the true meaning of the situation. Hence I will suggest not only as a necessary supplement but as an absolute prerequisite to the understanding of values some sort of internal approach which will veritably vivify their significance. Each of us within himself has faith in some sort of life as valuable to him either in that it is good, or friendly, or pleasurable, or profitable. Yet when we try to justify these beliefs in an objective scheme of Reality, it seems inevitable that our efforts will culminate in an insecure skepticism. That this is true in the field of morality I will offer in the next chapter.

This general question with which we are dealing seems to embody a fundamental paradox; we know that certain values exist and they are corroborated in our very lives, yet any nominative statement of what they may be has never yet succeeded in developing more than the meaning of the question itself without answering it; so we have come to a state where we no longer expect such answers, and even to regarding the possibility of such an ultimate meaning of Reality as our religious an moral experience might suggest with outright incredulity. In this sense we are foundering in more of a quandary today than perhaps ever before, and so it goes; but at that every age has probably been an age of unrest and perplexity for those who have lived in it.

When Kant dealt with the limitations of knowledge, it became necessary for him to divide experience into the categories of noumena and phenomena; knowledge in the philosophical sense is confined to the latter; that is, of the objects of knowledge we are confined to their appearances, their externals, from which Philosophy attempts the reconstruction of Reality. His Moral Philosophy is not based, however, on this kind of experience, but rather on a fundamental conviction of noumenal Reality, and throughout the *Critique of Practical Reason* bears out this noble strain of faith. The value experience with which I am concerned is of the noumenal character; it transcends phenomenal knowledge, and yet in a sense it must be 'known.' Strictly speaking the method by which we may experience the reality of noumena is not purely rational intelligence, and therefore as I have suggested it is necessary to base our Philosophy upon a deeper understanding; for this I see no alternative and I shall proceed to analyze the nature of this necessity.

It has been previously mentioned that logical, or scientific method must pursue a restricted course. In dealing with the object of knowledge the extensive meanings discernable are objectified into a fixed and uniform connotation which supposedly denotes and defines that to which they refer. Relations between these concepts are regulated by the principles of strict implication. Now it is my opinion that if we are to understand persons and personal values, they cannot be calculated in such fashion. We must somehow get at experience itself in a sympathetic manner, and our interpretation must make use of variety and shades of suggestion accompanied by imaginative insight. Thus even metaphorical meanings must be considered as essential to our grasp of such reality. For our purpose in value theory it is desirable, moreover, to consider experience in a different light from that afforded by the criteria of logic, if we would determine when we actually have a significant experience. I do not deny that the coherence and correspondence of such data, their consistency within the philosophical whole, contribute largely to their verification. But in our personal relations we are apt to satisfy the demands for validity along different lines. Here we feel ourselves in the presence of something real; the assimilation of truth may be likened for instance to the gradual discovery of significant music and not a mere wandering association of tones in Brahm's C minor Symphony.[9]

Repeated acquaintance with something of such aesthetic value, or with people in moral relations, and other similar situations stimulate the receptive consciousness to an awareness of a compelling meaning, and this in turn is richly developed in the vistas of the imagination. Here, I maintain, is the ground upon which the comprehension of reality, and especially of values is rendered possible. I do not say this is the philosophical recognition of truth, but it does render possible the understanding even of things in themselves to a degree and furnishes the basis for faith in noumenal experience.

Perhaps it will appear that I am likening the recognition of such aspects of Reality to some sort of revelation bordering upon mystical intuition, but at least for the extensive purpose to which I will employ this symbol or concept of Intuition, I cannot consider it to infer any such revelations occurring like "bolts from the blue." So far as I know intuitions like all organic things do not explode in consciousness ex vacuo, but rather bear the fruition of seeds planted and cultivated in the field of our previous experience. Opposed as I am to definitions, I think it advisable to give an introductory explanation of what I consider to be an intuition; "it is the immediate and relatively adequate apprehension of any object of awareness as a unique particular—an apprehension in which all pertinent knowledge is digested, and in which the object is known in its relation to a wider reality with imaginative insight and emotional intensity."[10] Thus it represents the deepest type of experience from which knowledge can be derived, and for the understanding of values such unique, concrete, full-bodied conscious relations constitute its very essence. As Mr. Joad puts it in his recent defense of reason, value, and a *Return to Philosophy*, intuition is capable of exhibiting to the minds' awareness aspects of reality which are inaccessible to the logical reason.[11]

In addition intuition thus interpreted most completely typifies consciousness as the experience of unity in plurality, and it is this synthetic realization of life which constitutes the soul and substance of Philosophy, and particularly the possibility for an evaluation of life. This should become clear with a little reflection upon our relations with persons, and more specifically those of intimate and long-standing acquaintance. How is it that we most clearly understand what a friend may be and what he means to us. Is it by withdrawal to an attitude of observing his behavior and determining the logical implications of his objective characteristics? Or it is through eventual sympathetic insight that we become a part of the other's interests and almost make his life out own by the accumulation of all relevant conscious experience into an imaginative whole, which then for us is his living personality, his inner logic and meaning. Ultimately this type of relation may multiply in intensity to consummate probably the most significant and complete consciousness of Reality that is humanly possible. Take this type of experience as it furnishes the very root and life of the Christian Religion. The understanding of what brotherly love means is a knowledge embodied in the experience itself. In the face of a strictly scientific or rational approach to such a problem as this one cannot fail to recognize a skeptical misunderstanding, such as that which is becoming increasingly evident among the majority as time goes on. I suppose I never understood myself what this concept of Christianity could mean—until by chance I really found it through Handel's *Messiah*, and the last movement of the Ninth Beethoven Symphony (among other sources of the intuition). Alone by means of such intermediary penetrations of consciousness into the realm of significant experience does it seem possible that formal Philosophy may approach the inner sanctum of the soul with true understanding.

As I proceed in this interpretation of intuition it will appear that I am stressing along with its depth of divination its equally broad synthetic capacity for fusing various types of experience; I will develop this aspect more full in relation to aesthetic experience, but at present it will be seen in addition that intuitions may combine more completely than any other form of conscious understanding the various cognitive, conative, affective, and 'hedonistic' elements which are always present in any given experience. Upon careful introspection the inadequacy of abstract departmentalization and atomism in describing consciousness must become apparent. When we place our ears close to the stream of life we do not hear a ticking of segregated consecutive instants but rather a constant hum, a mingling of harmonies interposed by epoch changes in key and imperceptible blends from one orchestral moment to another; so again we may come nearer to the situation by entering into ourselves with a sincere consciousness of what actually takes place, as it takes place, and this would not be to the negligence of what may be gained from the attitude of critical observation. What I advocate throughout is a sympathetic imaginative insight into the understanding of the agent, fortified by what can be learned from the more protracted and remote speculations of the observer. Intuition fosters knowledge at its best in the culmination of these two approaches. A Philosophy, then, which is to recognize the nature and value of consciousness must above all represent the ever augmented acumen of a man's entire personal experience. Considered in this light Philosophy becomes more than an outfit of systems with which a certain academic minority professionally invests itself, to discard them by the fire and bedside,—but rather the reflections of everyman, however adequate or persistent, with which he pursues the entire course of this life.

It is quite possible that my attitude will seem distinctly informal and rather more inclusive than most conceptual reconstructions of Reality. It may also be argued that the concept of intuition, upon which it relies to such a large extent, covers a multitude of intellectual sins. I will not deny that either of these implications is inferable to some extent, but on the other hand they do not recriminate the true sense in which I have employed either Philosophy or 'intuition.' The former I have identified with the 'world view' which tosses and tumbles through the wakeful hours of every individual. The more highly developed attitudes and reactions to life are certainly more comprehensive and probably increasingly significant; but on the other had the refined conception of the universe must indulge itself in such full and organic conscious relations with reality as I have attributed to intuition. In the latter, then, it must be clear that I do not offer an excuse for mental laziness or inaptitude, or a blind retreat in the face of skeptical despair. I do not offer a 'solution' at all, but merely try to bring out an actual and fundamental means by which life may be preserved in Philosophy, one which is above all empirically corroborated. If ours be an attempt to reproduce in our consciousness, and particularly to recreate and appreciate the value of the universe, it must not be an exclusive procedure, but rather an inclusive, expansive, and suggestive experience of Reality. To receive and remake this Reality with selective attention, weighing one aspect against another within a generic whole, this is the procedure involved in the theory of value, and this judicial function in turn singles it out as distinct from the more photographic strivings for 'ordinary' knowledge. Thus for our purpose the need to get into the spirit of personal, moral, religious, or aesthetic value experience is absolutely imperative. Ultimately we cannot assert or deny the existence of noumena, for they represent a phase of Reality outside that of definition of phenomena, but if they do not exist life is meaningless, that is, it has no significance; the fact is, very few if any act on this assumption, and furthermore experience would seem to corroborate the fact that some such noumena exist. If Philosophy is to determine the significance of such experience, its inferences must be grounded in some sort of intuition of the type which I have outlined.

Now we have come to the very heart of our problem: is this grasp of noumenal Reality which I am advocating knowledge of an experience, or merely that experience itself? This I conceive to be the ultimate question to be asked of Mr. Fite's distinction between the agent and the observer. Have we not admitted that the latter is confined to phenomenal intelligence and that these in turn are the bounds of all knowledge? Then how is it that we 'know' the noumenal beyond a certain faith nurtured by direct experience? Is this 'knowledge' actually the experience of the agent, and nothing more? If this be the case then my contention would amount to an insistence upon a more complete empirical orientation than is possible from the more or less remote point of view of the observer.

To try and get at the bottom of this it is first necessary to analyze the knowledge relationship. Some sort of representational theory would seem to be the very constitutive principle, and at least the regulative assumption warranted by any instance of relation; that is, there must be two related elements pre-supposed to exist somehow independently of one another. The process is thus essentially one of a passage of certain aspects of an object into a conscious subject; even within the subject, as Kant makes clear, there is the ego as subject and as object, so introspection will be seen to differ from the more 'objective' approach of experimental psychology not on logical grounds, but actually only in that it has a more complete manifold of relevant data on hand. A good many of Mr. Fite's distinctions between subjective and objective rest merely upon such a gap between various sets of facts. Is it possible, nevertheless, that the subject may at times virtually envelop its object almost to the point of becoming identified with it? I have suggested that such a possibility exists and remains essential to the understanding of values, and in order to see how, I will have to recast once more the notion of consciousness. It is essential that we regard it as a unit and not an aggregation of distinct functions. I have already mentioned that all experience has certain aspects which are fundamentally merged in any given phase of conscious time. For our purpose we cannot consider consciousness now as purely conceptual, now as distinctly perceptual, or affective, or conative, etc. Like Kant, Mr. Fite also drives the same point,[12] from a different direction. Consciousness functioning as a unit is essentially at all times a consciousness of something, if this be considered a "purely rational" procedure then we get the foundation for traditional or phenomenal knowledge. But when consciousness involves all of these 'faculties,' as if in a single act of understanding, then the subject consciousness may indeed incorporate the object—also consciousness; experience of this sort is characteristic of human life functioning most comprehensively as a whole through imaginative insight, thus becoming aware of itself through itself after the manner of intuition as I have described it. By virtue of this fact consciousness is most truly one in many, a vital interpenetration of meaning, and these in aggregate form the integral and vital motif of human existence, the variations upon which are found in individual personalities. Personality is thus the concrete embodiment of human values and experience, and these in turn are understood in the essence of their conscious being; that is why our theory of value must be able to participate in the organic continuum of the entire spirit with the proper sympathy of imagination, this rather than to regard consciousness purely through the 'categories of thought,' for above all these categories of thought are inadequate to noumenal reality. That is the case in the moral problem I will shortly undertake to demonstrate.

Meanwhile let us sum up the kind of attitude I have been developing, and the ends I have held in view. My interest is manifestly in persons, the consciousness whereby they exist, and I have held these to constitute the primary elements of Philosophy. It follows most naturally that I should adopt a kind of Personal Idealism as the central theme of my exposition, though this is neither Subjectivism, nor does it deny that Science is also a valid approach to Reality; but I stress the more ultimate importance of noumenal Reality and the questions centering more specifically around the meaning and value of human existence. As an approach to these problems I have above all tried to denote the functions of consciousness as a unit most self-expressive to the understanding in intuitive experience. This approach represents the culmination, assessment and evaluation of our reflective experience as embodied in the most significant moments of our conscious time. Herein the past is sifted and absorbed in the present, and the growth of personality prospers. Intuitions may be recognized as the guiding experiences in every field of human endeavor, even in Science and Mathematics; like proof, intuition is never ultimately adequate, and in fact proof itself may be finally reduced to a series of telescopic intuitions more or less conclusively inviting agreement. Such is this preliminary account of consciousness, which I have tried to render in close accord with the signification and import of personal experience.

A Brief Analysis of Moral Experience

Let no man deceive himself. If any men among you seemeth to be wise in this world, let him become a fool, that he may be wise.

Probably our primary concern as human beings is with some sort of moral life; and the difference of opinion and approach to this problem is ultimately as varied, I suppose, as persons are themselves. The Relativists have seized on this astonishing fact with avid interest and a supremely self-conscious sense of the important revolution they have once for all effected in the field of Ethics. The latter in turn has become the field of Mythology, Anthropology, Physiology, and the vast tradition of False Hopes and Illusions has been leveled before this general scientific onslaught. It is my purpose to oppose this tendency, at the same time pointing out certain aspects of moral experience which are often overlooked, and which pertain to this exposition I am aborting from an embryonic philosophical attitude, or conscious way of life.

To institute my criticism I will cite as significant a notable predisposition on the part of the Relativist to accept as the object of his scrutiny the moral experience of almost anyone but himself. The more remote and impersonal these data may be, the more they reveal the true character of morality as he sees it. An analysis and comparison of customs and habits accordingly demonstrates that whatever people think it makes no difference; they are merely functioning as units in an environment governed by cause and effect, or stimulus and response. If this be the case then our function as philosophers could be ideally performed by some sort of gigantic sorting and adding machine which would roll up a facsimile of the universe of experience tabulated according to the classifications of the various mechanized series constituting Reality. It will be my contention that Moral Philosophy must start at the other pole, first of all with one's own moral experience, and from a careful attempt to get at the meaning of this it will perhaps be possible to infer what that of others may mean. That persons and this essential aspect of them are in fact understandable also implies that they are actually to a large degree alike. To my mind the individual personality is in the widest sense the expression of morality, and thus our understanding of people of all times, ages, cultures, and creeds relies on the fact that certain elements of morality remain more or less constant throughout. That this is the case I will also attempt to show.

One of the most difficult and crucial questions which Ethics involves is the problem of freedom. All exhortations assume that a man is capable of governing his choice, and responsibility of all kinds rests on some similar conception of the efficacy of consciousness. Yet if there be any moral standards, or duties, or obligations imposed, as it were, upon the individual, wherein lies his freedom in the face of compulsion? Attempted solutions, although often developing the meaning of the situation the more they get to the roots of it, are still more apt to uncover a most obscure and confusing paradox to which there seems no actual resolution. Any number of theories accomplish this much; Bosanquet's principle of self-government through the General Will furnishes an excellent example of freedom attained through obligatory repressions. Perhaps the most discerning and provocative of these interpretations is that developed by Kant, for whom Duty actually implies freedom of the will. The moral law is a law of the ideal, or what ought to be and not one of nature. In his terms freedom is the ratio essendi of duty, while duty is the ratio cognoscendi of freedom. If we are to learn what freedom means, however, it is not to be acquired through ordinary or phenomenal knowledge. This intelligence is rooted in the noumenal nature of man, and the most reasonable interpretation of our moral experience must assert the reality of this nature—rationally conceivable but based upon moral faith. Hereby we identify the locus of moral value within the core of the human soul, and this constitutes the essence of consciousness in general.

I am inclined to agree with this explanation though I am not in a position yet to grasp the full significance of Kant by a margin of much study. His analysis of moral experience seems incontrovertible on one point, however, i.e., on the locus of value. Moreover, if consciousness is the expression of anything it is in its essence the apotheosis of freedom. This view I will oppose to the current contention that all action is at bottom conditioned by mechanical factors. Determinism is the result of an external and scientific approach, while the moral approach, as I shall suggest, is through sympathetic insight. The information of Science is of interest to our observations upon various aspects of experience, but it fails to grasp more than the externals of the situation, and morality is not a question of this sort.

The Relativists, and for that matter the Determinist, since the two are often identical, may explain the ends attributed to man and the corresponding incorporation of them into his life in terms of environmental conditioning as evidenced in custom and evolutionary cycles of conduct; he may invalidate all the notions and hopes which have sanctified the innermost purposes of men; he may even pronounce life meaningless apart from a blind casual nexus, whose principles apply down to the last particle of Reality. But I have yet to hear of a single solitary human who acted as if he believed this true of himself; others may be explained in terms of stimuli and responses, but who thinks of himself as acting apart from the motive, or purpose, or reason that he has in mind. His actions are essentially sui generic. Certainly the vast influence of environment must be recognized, and no one upon any reflection at all would think of himself as an isolated individual, but on the other had in the maze of interlocking consciousness there exists the individual matrix of personality, and from this source every man believes some sort of unique and fundamental reality to emanate, the expression of *his* life, freedom, imagination, and personality. Thus the individual is both generic and specific, or as I have said before, one in many.

I venture to add that the scientific observer in Ethics who has found 'in the real situation' the manifestation of an impersonal universe must also conduct his own existence only on the basis of some conception of value,—perhaps because he feels that in Science rests the salvation of man and the solution for his needs; furthermore his practice enables him to support not only some pastime of relaxation, but also a home—the chances are—founded upon certain family relations. These, I maintain, bespeak his moral philosophy rather than his professional theory of the universe. If some sort of devotion, and I take it for granted that this is the case with most anyone, shall shape the course of his life, then certainly this is the very moral essence of his being. That widely diverse yet intensely similar state of consciousness designated by the term 'love' will thus be seen to sum up the most fundamental of all moral relations, one which has predominated throughout the complex variations of human existence.[13] This is the first fact based on experience which should come to anyone when confronted with the arguments of Relativism. That the moral problem in general has remained relatively constant in the memory of man I will suggest is also corroborated by the fact that the great works of art based on human nature, such as those of Sophocles, Euripedes, and Shakespeare, have ever struck to the core of every man not completely anesthetic to the central perplexities of life. Along these lines I think we begin to see that Relativism and the behavioristic approach are merely scratching the surface, if the missing the mark of morality altogether; yes, they are dealing with a different set of facts, and to develop the meaning of this proposition I propose a little examination of some of the theories which they have 'invalidated.'

From the Ethics of Plato and Aristotle, the Epicureans and Stoics, down through the great Christian era to Hobbes, who set everyone to thinking again in traditional philosophical circles on the problem, the Utilitarians, Moral Sense Philosophers, Kant, Hegel, and Bosanquet, or Bradley, to mention a few at random, the divergence of view is apparently as wide as that of the respective environments in which they lived, and in fact as the different people they were. Even the hedonistic argument which has prevailed perhaps more evenly in some corner of Philosophy than any other doctrine of morality shows a striking variety on the annals of its exposition. Well, doesn't this all overwhelmingly back up the position of the Relativist?

No. It merely makes me suspicious of the phenomenal approach to moral value. It certainly seems plausible that no conceptual norm of morality will stand the polemic of time and experience, let alone that waged in the hands of Logic. Yet because all these men failed to establish the ultimate end of life conclusively will they be seen now as immoral, or else as seeking for something which never existed? May I suggest that this is a crucial question, for it will be my contention that any man has lived a moral life who has done what is humanly possible to emulate what he most earnestly considers to be honest and just. Despite the platitudinous appearance of this statement, I feel it will be seen to accord with the opinion of every age and people. From all indications Plato, Aristotle, Kant or Hegel, any of them were particularly noble men. Their tremendous accomplishments alone necessarily attest to the conclusion; even that villainous creature Thomas Hobbes was probably not a hopelessly evil personification of man in the state of nature.

Many of these theories which on first glance appear to contradict one another may eventually be reduced to the same position. For instance Epicureanism, or enlightened Hedonism, and Stoicism in the end reconcile themselves to the same course of action. Even the modern Stoic Kant, who seems so unique among Philosophers, may serve as the ultimate guide for the supposedly more pleasure-loving Utilitarians,[14] and who could have been more distasteful to him than were they in their approach. Of course very few act on pure pleasure motives anyway in their most significant decisions as moral beings, that is without relying on some other ultimate conception of value for qualitative distinctions between pleasures. I merely mention this in passing to suggest how often people develop a theory of human action without realizing they actually imply entirely different motives in their own actions. In any case, however, whatever the point of view adopted, it is moral for the man who sees and acts upon it with sincerity and understanding. Our effort as moral philosophers should be to see it from his point of view,[15] and then it will be possible to extract some meaning from the general history of opinion on the question. The Relativist is quite right in arguing that these various normative standards are meaningless—from his unsympathetic position—but the morality of the past must have more significance than this, I maintain, for among other reasons we ourselves exist in the past. Indeed I can begin to see very well what many of these various expressions men have offered have really meant; primarily they have represented a sincere belief based on their own particular noumenal experience. Seen in this light Moral Philosophy is more than a shuffling of words with an eye for their consistency, it stands for an attempt necessarily participated in by every one, by which some unity of purpose and integrity of character comes into being. This is above all recognizable in personal relations, where matters of constancy, friendliness, honesty, sympathy and understanding, courage, and thoughtfulness are what count. Likewise within the individual personality it is above all essential to preserve freedom of spirit and self-respect; in comparison with this nothing else matters. As Mr. Fite has said, "the last thing in immorality is to fool yourself;" that is, to segregate your consciousness into separate compartments, "keeping from the left hand what the right hand doeth," is the undermining of character and the integrity of consciousness. The more one travels rough shod over this moral consciousness the more numb and insensitive to his own freedom a man becomes. Thus above all the will perseveres the unity of a moral personality, and this is the principle of his being; in other words his innermost self imposes order and purpose upon a chaos, and this is the teleological autonomy of the soul. Such I take to be the meaning in part of what Kant had to say, and it constitutes the essence of moral experience since men have begun to function with intelligence and understanding.

Even as I progress with this exposition I am aware that perhaps I will be mistaken for setting up in turn some sort of conceptual norm as to the Absolute of morality, after admitting the impossibility of such a formula. No, I am just trying to indicate various aspects of moral experience, which I have reason to believe are universal. For knowledge of what such experience is, in itself, I must refer one to his own moral intuitions. And to understand the morality of philosophers as well as of any who have gone before us, we must attempt to reconstruct the essentials of the times in which they lived and the personal problems with which they were intimately concerned. It is interesting and often enlightening to abstract the principles they formulate apart from their lives and weigh them in the contemporary balance of our own times, but if we are to understand the particular moral significance of their lives it is a prerequisite that we get beyond what they said into the motives upon which they acted as concrete individuals. In accord with the universality and fundamental persistence of human nature, I venture to say that the moral man of one generations would be essentially a moral man in any age, and in so far as we are able to judge what kind of man another may be, we must be potentially capable of the same experience ourselves. The Relativist makes few attempts to recognize this medium of sympathetic insight into the more experiences of the past in passing his judgment; likewise the behavioristic approach fails to deal with the situation as moral, but only with the most outward appearances of morality. On the other hand the essence of the question boils down to the finding of an objective moral value, one which is real and intrinsic within our noumenal experience. That some intrinsic value of this kind exists is more than a fact, it is an experience and the recognition of it is the constitutive principle of personality, or conscious being.

And now it will appear that I have again committed myself to a fundamental dualism, of noumena and phenomena; is this distinction founded in the relation of knowledge to experience? As I have previously implied the knowledge relation implies a duality, we will call it between subject and object. I have further identified consciousness in general as consciousness of something, and this is an experience, which in turn may become the object of future experience as in introspection. Knowledge of the self, however, would not be through immediate consciousness, although any given instant of conscious experience possesses a strong cognitive element but rather through the latter mediate type of experience; thus it is a knowledge of appearances of phenomena and can never fully reconstruct its object, as it is in itself. We have taken it for granted that moral experience of some kind is universal, and have discussed certain aspects of it as universally similar. We have determined the object of moral consciousness or experience as identical with the inner unity and essence of conscious being, of noumenal Reality. There are then three factors as it were involved in the process of understanding moral value. First that of moral experience, then the noumenal reality of which it is an experience, and third our phenomenal analysis and intelligence of the experience. The intermediary moral experience is the basis for moral faith, and as I shall indicate of moral intuitions as well. Intuition as I have employed the term is not to be confused, however, with the immediate experience, but rather represents in the ideal the most consummate and complete phenomenal intelligence of noumena that is possible; or, to put it differently, intuition is both potentially and actually the most sympathetic and understanding reconstruction of value experience known to man. This implies at the start that an intuition sums up an unusually complete set of data, recalling at the same time much of the full conscious intensity of direct moral experience. The intuition furthermore represents a synthesis of relevant knowledge and the residuum of experience of all kinds with a bearing upon the function of consciousness, bringing into play the full power of consciousness that is called upon in the immediate experience of noumena itself. I have hoped that this description of the role of intuition would make clear the possibility for a more adequate philosophical apprehension of value experience and the noumenal reality which constitutes its object. An approach to Moral Philosophy which is purely analytic without at the same time enjoying these essential and unified synthetic recreations fails to give an adequate interpretation of Reality. In the particular case of noumenal Reality such reflective metamorphoses of the situation represent the only approximation to a just reconstruction of moral experience. In short moral intuitions have ever formed the basis for real understanding at the heart of friendship, love, and moral relations in general. Thus it will be seen that the true function if Moral

Philosophy is exercised in guiding the activities and mutual interests of men in everything that is expressive of true intelligence, honesty, sincerity, sympathy, integrity, and broad mindedness. May I venture to intimate, the, that even those who have extracted elements from moral experience, such as Duty, or Happiness, and hypostatized them as the ultimate object of moral experience, are more apt to have had a real insight and understanding of noumena, being more intimate in their theory with the actual meaning implicit in the actions of men, than many of our modern Relativists, or Behaviorists, or Operationalists, or Positivists are capable of. The phenomenal acquaintance with noumena through rigid scientific method is ultimately destined to a skeptical position in all value theory. Our philosophy must ultimately rest upon the most adequate and plausible interpretations of the situation which will satisfy to some degree our critical observation on the one hand and our direct experience on the other—call them in general acts of reconstruction[16] to fit Reality, but in value theory more fittingly acts of reasonable faith.[17] In my opinion intuition affords the only relatively final experience of understanding which meets Reality through the combination of these approaches in its own likeness. This is above all significant of our attempts in moral philosophy.

The Sense and the Conception
of Being (Selections)

As I put it years ago in my doctoral thesis, reality makes its stand
here and now in existing things.

Bugbee defended his doctoral dissertation, "The Sense and the Conception of Being," at the University of California, Berkeley on January 25,
1947. Prior to this important event, his graduate study had been interrupted, in 1942, after he volunteered for service in the United States Navy.
He was deployed to the South Pacific at the rank of lieutenant, commanding the minesweeper *Y319*. Naval service kept him from graduate study
for four years. Back at Berkeley, he overcame any previous sense of writer's
block that he had with regard to his dissertation. He once recalled that
upon returning from sea duty he felt that he could sit down and do the
work that he had had difficulty doing before.[1]

"The Sense and the Conception of Being" does not offer an extensional
metaphysics of Being in the classical sense of Aristotle's timeless study of
being qua being. Being is fundamentally experiential, something *sensed*
as opposed to conceptualized.[2] Bugbee insisted that formal metaphysics
fails to capture the experiential immediacy and compelling directness of
Being—dimensions "formal" structures struggle to register.

The dissertation was signed by Jacob M. Loewenberg, Stephen C. Pepper, and George P. Adams.[3] The reader is immediately struck by the degree
of emphasis placed upon the natural world as a source of the experience of
being:

> This dissertation attempts to work out the meaning of being,
> not merely as abstractly conceived, but as it arises, through special
> awareness of the *presence* of things in their definiteness . . . . If it

38

should be asked how to proceed and what to attend to if we were
to encounter being, face to face, perhaps no better answer could be
found than by attending to the stars, the living air, the moving waters, the earth, the stretch of forests and deserts, the wild creatures
in their alertness and grace, the myriad things great and little to be
seen and heard and felt and meditated upon . . . The world of the
sense of being is vivid with the infusions of sense perception.

Bugbee attends to the way things are disclosed experientially as we
encounter a world present as meaningful and indubitable—"inviolable
before any attempt at theoretical or conceptual reduction." The failure of
philosophical conceptions to deal directly with experiences causes these
conceptions to "wash off," resulting in the preponderance of verbal dis-
putes so endemic to contemporary philosophy.

Bugbee's approach eschews any goal of formal completeness, choosing
instead, to chart a course in search of experiential first principles:

> The focus of metaphysical attention is not characterized by a
> direct stretching and extension until it blankets an all inclusive
> situation, but rather by an intensive analysis of the concrete world of
> our experience until those of its features which are ultimate . . . are
> elicited into view.

Bugbee addresses the question of being *intensively*, seeking a sense of
ontological continuity existing prior to conceptual differentiation:

> Being is undifferentiated; there are no degrees of being, no
> qualitative shades no islands of being, no differential relational
> systems. . . . [Being] is infinite, not in the sense of indefiniteness,
> but in the sense that the categories of limitation are not germane . . .
> Such is the ontological wholeness of reality. Being is absolute.
> The extensive wholeness of reality is founded on an intensive
> wholeness.

Being is intensively present throughout experience. Unity and multi-
plicity have a common origin—Being: "It is the *presence* of things in their
definiteness which occasions the sense of being." An intensive metaphysic
views Being as, to some degree, pre-reflectively given *at once*. A nascent
sense of completeness accompanies any experience recognized *to be*
incomplete.[4] The implications of this insight led Bugbee into the farthest reaches of experiential philosophy: "The basis for the metaphysical

perspective of any actual or possible situation must be at least theoretically accessible in any . . . situations that *are* accessible to us." Lived experience becomes a vital source of metaphysical speculation. Paul, a main character in Norman MacLean's *A River Runs Through It*, expresses an intensive conception of Being when he states: "All there is to thinking . . . is seeing something noticeable which makes you see something you weren't noticing which makes you see something that isn't even visible."[5]

∽

The dissertation attempts to work out the meaning of being, not merely as abstractly conceived, but as it arises, through special awareness of the *presence* of things in their definiteness.

This attempt is oriented in the first chapter by a critical reexamination of the possibility of empirical metaphysics. Ultimately we must be told what kind of a world it is that either precludes or permits some fundamental, comprehensive understanding of its nature; therefore, criticism of the metaphysical enterprise must be viewed as revision of it from within; one does not repudiate this enterprise without repudiating his position as a knower in and of the world, reflecting its nature in the way he does or does not know it. The primitive metaphysical concepts of relation, insularity, quality, dynamicity, and being are suggested as a basis for defining the possibility of empirical metaphysics, but the first four are developed only sufficiently to afford the necessary conceptual content for discriminating the meaning of the crucial context of being.

The second chapter presents the meaning of being as experienced by bringing what is here meant by being into the focus of direct and immediate apprehension. Human interests and persuasions *not* conducive to the sense of being are used to set off this distinctive mode of experience and the cosmocentric attitude which it engenders.

In the third chapter the sense of being is analyzed in terms of three major "conditions" fulfilled in the experience: "Impact" and "poise" designate two; the third is indicated by asserting that the sense of being is a form of value experience. The significance of this assertion is brought out through an analysis of the parallel notions in Aristotle and Spinoza, of contemplative happiness and the intellectual love of God, respectively. The foregoing analysis of the sense of being is then elucidated by exemplifications from the field of art, with special reference from the field of art, with special reference to Bach, Gregorian Chant, Brahms, Sibelius, Charles M. Doughty, Chekov, and Melville.

The fourth chapter formulates the meaning of being as an abstract conception. The concepts stated in the first chapter are used to demarcate it; major contributions to the conception of being by Parmenides, Aristotle, Spinoza, and Kant are examined; the term "being" is fixed in its employment here as synonymous with "existence" abstracted from a temporal connotation. Grounds for distinction of differences of degree or kind of being are critically rejected. With respect to being, any situation is whole, self-sufficient, self-contained, absolute. The standard of factuality presupposed in the possibility of empirical knowledge reflects the epistemic aspect of the conception of being; the standard of integrity reflects its ethical aspect; and as Spinoza has shown, being is correctly understood as an object of religious experience.

The Sense of Being

In the conscious experience of any situation there is at least a latent opportunity for the sense of being to develop. For wherever there is anything at all to reckon with, there is being. On every hand something definite confronts us, something commanding attention, something to lay hold of and adhere to in experience; something pertaining to which descriptions, assertions, judgments, and actions are in order. It is the *presence* of things in their definiteness which occasions the sense of being.

In all our conscious relations the factor of presence in awareness is inescapable. Yet the presence of whatever is present can be taken for granted, quite naturally and tacitly, since it is a *sine qua non* of the awareness. To the extent that there is nothing exceptional about it, there is no reason why it should achieve recognition in the focus of our attention. We are normally concerned with the particular definiteness of any situation, be it qualitative, relational, dynamic, material,—whatever its peculiar and distinct constitution may be.— In so far as there is nothing peculiar, particular, rare, strange, disjunctive, complex, singular, dynamic, or distinct about the factor of presence in all presentations, there is no reason why it should be easily distinguished or become the occasion for a special response. From this standpoint we might liken the factor or presence in our presentations to a monotonous undertone, given whenever hearing takes place, and so thoroughly concealed by our complete habituation to it that the most attentive and discriminating listening could scarcely be expected to discern it.

On the other hand, whatever is present is always a definite *presence*, and when a situation impinges forcefully enough, where its peculiarity, distinctness, even strangeness become impressive, and the definiteness asserts itself to effect the profound captivation of our sensibilities, then and there attention is drawn to the very presence of such definiteness. Where situations occur that occasion deep interest, intense wonder, reflective digestion, the stretching of our capacity for emotional assimilation, where our faculties for appreciation are engaged at a peak of sensibility and concentration, when we rise with strength to a challenge, there and then the sheer presence of what we have to cope with is enforced upon us. Yet on such occasions this presence is received most often still at a level of absorption. We become steeped in it, rather than directly aware of it through a special selective experience. Thus for the most part the sense of being remains but a nameless and inarticulate undertone even where it is a strongly felt component of experience.

Our problem in connection with the sense of being is threefold: to work upon this "undertone" of experience until it rings out clear and pronounced and discernable; to determine what the condition of the sense of being, as a distinct and selective mode of experience, may be; and to explore as exemplifications of the sense of being some possibilities of its cultivation and expression.

There are many human interests, persuasions, attitudes, and preoccupations not in themselves conducive to the sense of being. Perhaps it would be just as well to single out and cast off some of these things at the start, as we would discard clothing that might hamper us before plunging into the sea.

We have noted that our direct concern with specific situations is usually focused upon particular characteristics, properties, relations, materials, processes, and complexes of these, exhibited in the situation. In most walks of life this concern is also predominantly practical. There are many ways of being practical, but the preponderance of them actually seem to limit concern in the situation where a practical interest is at stake to those features of the situation which may be used and manipulated with an ulterior end in view. Thus, as we know so well in America, one plants his foot on one foothold while his eyes are already anxiously seeking out the next, and so on. In this way one can go on being practical, eminently so, and let the universe pass him by, just as one can speed up getting from here to there to the neglect of the country lying between. Narrow practicality can give neither the time nor the imaginative room for the sense of being. And all of us are narrowly practical much of the time; it is a species of myopia dictated by the particularity and the urgency of certain of our needs. Thus, for instance, hunger, thirst, or acute bodily distress may capture a life within the confines of a miserable animality. We should also note, however, that where suffering fails to blind or sour or embitter the sufferer, experience and an attitude congenial to the growth of the sense of being may stem from it, far transcending a narrow practicality. But such occasions come about as they may, we do not deliberately seek them.

There are also many ways of minimizing the effectuality of things in imparting the sense of being. One can, within limits, avoid taking the world on its own terms. The mobility of our bodies is only surpassed by the facility of our minds. If we are confronted with cold, we provide for our warmth. If the light is glaring, we shade our eyes. On every hand we modify and manipulate our environment so that we may be satisfied by it, so that ease and comfort surround us, so that the conditions of our daily living are tamed down to provide for a relatively smooth and unobstructed flow. There are all the various opiate entertainments to insulate us against the shock of an idle hour with at least ourselves to face. If one is beset by loneliness, why there are people all about, aren't there? We circulate freely among them, choosing our friends. We build our communities, and where those communities are large and highly concentrated, almost no object can be encountered there that does not appear as directly subservient to human convenience and taste. The very sky over our cities is a utility, and city parks are overgrown flower-pots. Where we see the power of human ingenuity and artifice writ so large, where 'nature' is exhibited in the guise of the servant man, is it any wonder that our attitude and approach toward things is so largely anthropocentric?

While man busies himself with his own world, with things as assimilated to his needs and tastes, he is constantly defining a sphere of familiarity, congeniality, and equilibrium in which he can move with confidence and complacency; in short, an egocentric world. Some succeed so well in this that *the* world almost never makes itself felt as an intruder in *their* world. There are, however, two lines of least resistance which we practice in the face of recognized intrusions. One is to avert the eyes as soon as possible. The other is to acknowledge the intrusion, but to avert the eyes with the sanction of a dogma or an unexamined faith. One can, for example, cling tenaciously to the belief that even the most inscrutable occurrences and the most remote reaches embody a purpose or a constitution congenial to man, so in the face of an intrusion on his world, a man can go his way as before. We buffer the accesses to our minds, as well as those to our bodies. In so far as such procedure leads to complacency and exclusive anthropocentricity, or worse, to egocentricity, it offers infertile ground to the seeds of the sense of being.

Among thinking men there are tendencies which we will do well to guard against, if we would foster our present purpose. There is the anarchy of the analytical mind which lays about itself with such critical distinction that in the end it exhibits only its own keenness and splendor, and is receptive to little more. There is the "disillusioned" learnedness which ends by viewing every positive situation as problematical, and so transcends any incentive or preparedness to receive, much less to interpret the world on positive terms. The enlightened agnostic looks for the deceptions and the saving graces in the ways others have sought to approach reality; he is ready for all comers on this score. But he is not the man to approach reality himself, and he is certainly not one to expect reality to approach him. And yet, where agnosticism also bespeaks a deep appreciation of the mystery of reality, and of the partiality of human understanding, as with those agnostics who are mystics at heart, we may suspect that something close to the sense of being may rule the experience and the attitude of the agnostic. It is the sterility of agnosticism that is objected to here, not its tolerance or its sensitivity. But to the agnostic our importunities would seem to ask that he become a child again, when he has grown to man's estate.

Indeed there must be something almost childlike in the approach to a sense of being. The sophistications of the man of taste or of the aesthete, no less than those of the analyst and the categorizer and even of the learned, would only obscure the approach, unless one sees beyond them. Not only are the simplicity and directness of the sense of being childlike; there is also something about the experience which makes a man only a child, consumed with wonder, receptive, yet not of question nor of answer, alone and yet at home with all the sticks and stones and stars that he can see. But while to the child the world may appear to center around himself, to *this* child, that a man may become, the world is the center of itself, and it includes him.

The sense of being implies the transition from an egocentric to a cosmocentric point of view. And the latter view inevitably places man as but a child in the universe, introducing a humility and a receptiveness into his position which are neither forced nor assumed, but the natural concomitants of that position.

To set aside the ways of the practicalitarian, the authoritarian, the dogmatist, the aesthete, and academicist, is not to narrow the field of empirical encounter which we are attempting to demarcate. Thus, although neither scientific nor practical interests are directly disposed to concentration on being, still, the sensitive and reflective investigator or agent may encounter ample circumstance which may lead him to such experience.

One would imagine that it must be hard to step back from the microscope or the telescope, or from an experiment or an operation, however familiar one may be with what is encountered there, without at times being transfixed with wonder at the sheer presence of what is revealed, made immanent through the observer's absorption and fascination. However remote the moment of hypothesis may be from the moment of observation, or however completely the moment of observation may be permeated and directed by the moment of hypothesis to which it is subservient, it is difficult to see how scientific procedure in its application throughout could fail to yield a very deep impression of being through the factuality of the world dealt with; for the objective situation must be adhered to in any investigation, however much the facts may remain in question, however amenable they are to manipulation or assimilable to artifact. Thus that curiosity exercised within the precincts of science is a special case of philosophical curiosity, and the wonder that must grow through engaging in the scientific enterprise is potent with a kind of wonder, bordering on reverence, that is philosophically fundamental. This is not reverence for science, but for what science is getting at, and steeping itself in. It is not the experience of design, order, purpose, or evidence of 'mind,' that is meant here, however; undoubtedly such experience may be impressive, and may be interpretatively confused with the experience to which we now refer.[6] It is an experience of being that is meant here, of the presence at all of reality in its definiteness, of the unanalyzable and utterly unaccountable factuality of anything whatsoever that may be discovered, including design, order, purpose, or evidence of mind, or anything else discoverable. It is the experience of that to which either a genetic or a teleological approach would be quite irrelevant.

In the vast realm of practical affairs, the activities in which we participate almost always involve in varying measure interests which are more than practical in the narrow sense caricatured above. If we denote as practical those activities which are primarily concerned with accomplishing an end, not itself consummated in the activity in question, such as the manufacture of goods, provision against the needs for food, clothing, shelter, health, the processes attendant upon 'making a living,' the removal of sources of pain, discomfort, worry, and the like, it is obvious that such activities do involve far more than an exclusively utilitarian interest. This situation may be symbolized by the demand for beauty exacted of the useful, and by the fact that philosophers, artists, and pure scientists sometimes make a living through their chosen pursuits.

But let us consider a clearly practical man, say a farmer. His approach to the soil is eminently practical; his interest and attention are fixed upon working the soil for what it will produce to requite his basic needs, either directly or indirectly. Yet if working in the soil is not satisfying to him in itself, if the quality and the fecundity of the soil do not constantly enrich him by more than the products which are yielded for his use, that man may well not even succeed at farming. So with the worker in wood, in metal, in textiles, and so with the fashioner of houses and machines; such is the element of artistry in all artisanry. Thus it is almost impossible to be a good salesman unless the dealings with people which the job requires are founded on an interest in the people dealt with that far outreaches the desire to sell them something, and a natural facility for cultivating personal response. Thus transportation may mean far more than getting from here to there to the person transporting or transported.

In fact every utilitarian interest is shot through with extrautilitarian interests, apart from the investment of energy toward ulterior ends. It is, moreover, an ineluctable condition of practical success that we must appreciate the situation which we hope to use for what it is, to an extent which will render our operations relevant and therefore feasible. Manufacture, production, the utilization of anything whatsoever for any purpose, are dependent on a minimal recognition, understanding of, and adherence to the conditions imposed by an objective state of affairs. Our ability to control any situation and work our purpose upon it is indeed a measure of our knowledge of that situation, as men have recognized in practice since early in their exercise of control, and as Pragmatism has more recently discovered. In fact any attempt to realize ends presupposes an appreciation of the state of affairs preconditional to success which must be as unbiased as possible by the very interests served by this appreciation.

However practical the enterprise a man may be engaged in, therefore, it should afford some opportunity for a growing realization of the significance of existence; for the obdurate objectivity of whatever confronts him in his undertaking receives an emphasis proportional to the compulsion with which that objectivity is imperiously asserted by the situation at hand. His 'situation' may be macroscopic or microscopic, his data may be pre-analytic or post-analytic, his approach may be relatively pre- or post-interpretative, his environment may be cosmopolitan or primitive, so long as the force of that objectivity is not lost on him. Wherever a man gets in and takes hold of something, with persistence, sensitivity, curiosity, receptiveness, imagination, and some degree of reflectiveness, he is moving toward a sense of being. This movement is not necessarily intentional, however, and where it leads to the occurrence of the sense of being on a wide scale among men, the strangeness, inarticulateness, namelessness, and the dissociation from particular interests, all characteristic of the inchoate experience, readily account for its loss in the private wells of consciousness and in the public shuffle.

In the regular course of our lives the moments and occasions for the sense of being are most often unanticipated and unpredictable.[7] Indeed their force and effect is to a large extent contributed by their unexpectedness. A man may be eating his supper in the twilight hour, weary with the concerns of the day that has passed, and suddenly, clearly, with utter purity, the quiet notes of the song of a single bird penetrate to him and transfix him with the twilight and the stillness of the hour. Yet a whole chorus of birds might twitter their hearts out, or that same bird might sing again and again, and the sound might register only as a mildly pleasant, or possibly inane undertone or interlude in the prevailing attention. Or one may hopefully await, say the song of a linnet, only to hear it as an anticlimax, devoid of any special significance. Yet the three notes of the linnet's song can say more of being than many a page written on the subject.

Sometimes the rare and uncanny phenomenon, flashing into view, will limn the mystery of existence, as when to the unsuspecting mariner appears the masthead glow of St. Elmo's fire, a fugitive, luminous center in the sea-storm's obscurity. Such is the little detail that intrudes upon the empirical foundations of great scientific hypotheses, some discrepancy so slight, or so infrequent perhaps, as to have passed long unnoticed, yet so freighted with import as to require an entire revision or vast supplementation of the world of hypothesis upon which it intrudes. The very *existence* of such a detail is underlined by the momentousness of its discrepancy, as compared with its apparent insignificance, or the possibly accidental manner of its discovery. In proportion to the consequence of "if it were not for that fact there . . . ," the import of factuality is now insinuated, now thrust upon us.

Who can avoid the same sort of impression when he reviews the ruling part played in his life by the little events, the casual decisions on minute affairs, the accidental factors, and the unobtrusive contingencies, which, if barely noticed upon their happening, seemed utterly inconsequential? Thus we move from the rare to the realm of the most commonplace sort of phenomena. Any old everyday occurrence, if viewed reflectively, can be seen to wear the stamp of being; it has its own finality, its own presence, and its own factual weight. The weight of the factuality of the commonplace we may feel in the retrospective backhand when the commonplace is seen to have usurped an uncommon role. The presence of the commonplace slips upon us unawares, even as the roar and bustle of the city saturates the city-dweller, to be revealed to him only occasionally, perhaps in the dead of night. And the finality of the commonplace is like that of going to sleep, waking up, going to sleep, waking up, and then, one day, just going to sleep. Being is really an unusually commonplace sort of affair. It is not surprising that we are only seldom impressed with it, and that such occasions are largely inadvertent and even less susceptible to artificial cultivation. We must recognize this as an important limitation imposed on any effort *to go about acquiring* the sense of being at first hand . . .

The sense of being is a face to face encounter with the *presence* of things. And because in their presence things are manifestly on the common plane of being, they are in a sense universal; therefore the sense of being is a walking with simplicity and alertness into the presence of this universe. It is not the discovery of a question or of the answer to a question; it is an absorption in, a reception of, a feeling and a thinking of a clear and distinct perception of being. The relative immediacy of the experience does not exclude from it the culmination of a great deal of careful thought and previous perception. The experience is neither vague nor occult in its profundity. Its inspiration to reverence does not exclude variation with immense humor. It is an experience that transcends the vulnerability of a life, the bondage of a soul, the impoverishment of a mind, the particularity, the permanence, and the change in a world. Such is the experience *in kind*, represented in terms of a climax of attainment to which we approximate in varying degree, and through the matrix of far less concentrated experience.

Before we go any further with our exposition of the sense of being, let us now attempt a concrete approximation to the inner point of view of the experience. Let us take, for example, a mountain landscape and try for a glimpse of our subject matter through this very normal sort of medium. Let us pick a particular place, on this near-vertical thrust of rock, some two-thousand feet reached clear into biting air, among the northernmost of those mountain tiers which rear in relief a rigid spinal column through western North America. Crouch for shelter against this drifted bank of snow. Now, let us look abroad.

A great half-circle of bleak and jagged horizon lies visible before us. There upheave confrontingly those abrupt gigantic masses. Upwards they sweep from timbered girth, steep up the grassy barrens, still up fragmented slides, till rimmed in solid matterhorns and chiseled into glacial crevices, these mountains unbelievably tower; self-defined, self-contained in the chill-grey sky. Tilt for tilt and cleft for cleft they vie far into the distance for possession of the air, carving out atmosphere into captive spaces bound in between. Over and weathering all in its ceaseless blast rushes a planetary wind. And far below traverse the streams; they too in watery course will be voicing the voice of this wind: that same, hollow, forest-filling voice, which drowns our hearing where we stand. Listen . . . And what do we hear? What but the self-wrapt sounding?

Clouds laden with snow drive hard before the wind. Swirlingly, they descend and stream off the mountain tops. In behind each rock, and here behind our shelter, whispers the portent of a new coming in the land. Hark we longer where we stand and there to the spot will the makings of thought be congealed and frozen. So let us down into the valley, walled in on every side, hemmed by the dark spruce and pine, and tented over withal,—there to await the coming.

As the waters of the Red Sea billowed over Pharoah's followers, so now the clouds envelop the hosts of trees. And as that multitude of indentities upon a time ceased struggling and settled in the embrace of ocean calm, so each thing which had stood out, crying in resistance to the wind, now lapses and is lost in a pervasive still.

Bird, bush, mountain, animal, stick, and stone,—each is left to itself, alone, as in that timeless slumber. The wildness is sealed in
silence.

What steals through the land with a motionless coming? What
blanches thus things visible, blotting mass and form, absorbing their
very thinghood? What in this obscuring is hushedly revealing? What
but the pure and secret presence that is snow?

Quite of a sudden, with the evening, it is clear. Things start magi-
cally from their privacy and again manifest a world. Fine and sharp
is their pronouncement under the blue, like the pure heralding of
many horns from afar. But remembrance of snow's meditative silence, too, lies heavily upon them. As if in the completeness bestowed by a self-knowledge, this world now shines forth fully and
limitlessly, accentuated in the light which it intensifies. Ere this
light fades into night, what stands out so clear and distinct? What
but the absolute presence of things, transfigured through the presence of snow?

And now by the night reflecting, we bank our fire against this
snowbound world, midst these pallid starlit forms. As if all those
points of light strewn across the winter-clear sky were brought to
a concentration therein, so glows with a livid heat the heart of our
fire. And from the stillness of its central glow radiate regions of avid
flame, reaching out to consume the forest's yield, transforming the
dark shapes of logs into the molten inwards of fire. Thus in the very
rage of change, there is poise.

Our fire dwindles and retreats within itself. Yet another light, and
a stranger one, spreads from behind yonder peaks to the north. What
sun or moon may this be, to creep from over Arctic slopes? It is the
aurora borealis.

Steely shafts and flying beams explode from over the horizon; vi-
brate, dilate, and hurtle off on cosmic path across the sky. Whence
came these mute chords of light struck on high? They are but mir-
rorings from a land of perpetual ice and snow.

As the storm resolved in silence, as the snow hushed us in, as
the fire withdrew, so recedes the wondrous light. Now in the frozen
calm of night, there is peace.

Where shall we turn in nature, and pushing hard, come up against
aught but being? Where shall we seek, if at all, in search of the
rounding out of things? Beyond the ends of the earth, beyond the
river sea, beyond all seeking and finding? Shall we think that things

ultimate and absolute retreat before our advance, till we are lost at every turn? Can we suppose that things fail to disclose themselves in earnest, lurking aloof behind the scene of a phenomenal drama? Is there then no finality about the world for us to discern? Must all decisive reckoning wait upon the revelations of that mythical Judgment Day?

But what is this and every day if not a Judgment Day? What drama could fail to involve things in earnest? What is this, palpable in our grasp, if things fail to make a stand before us? Beyond our farthest seeking and finding, what can be added to the completeness of *being* there, that is not also here, lying within reach of our finding?

It is through the sense of being that we come to apprehend the earnestness, the self-sufficiency, the ultimacy, and the finality of reality. Looking deep and again into the eyes of things, do we not read there of wholeness and poise, the plenitude of being?

Before the compelling mystery of existence propounded through the sense of being, the spectre of the unknowable is exorcised. A meaning of the natural is acquired in the experience which banishes the possibility of anything supernatural, or extra-natural. This does not imply the denial of a place to anything which, in fact, has a place in the world; but in the sovereign demesne of being there are no privileged characters, no subversive elements, no opposing factions, nor any encroachments from the outside. Being is both cosmic and one-dimensional. That is why the existence of anything in particular is more than anything particular, namely cosmic participation. That is why the existence of anything temporal is more than temporal, namely eternal. At the level of the sense of being the presence of things reveals to us *evidentially* the wholeness, self-sufficiency, uni-dimensionality, simplicity, and eternity of reality as being. To a man endowed with the normal capacities for sensation and understanding, and with a normal bulk of experience behind him, it is the silence with which the world sings to him that articulates being empirically as well as anything else.

The sense of being engenders an attitude appropriate to the disclosures of the experience. This is fundamentally a cosmocentric attitude, by virtue of its recognition of the universality of the ontological status, and of the absence of priorities or centralities within that status. It is reconciled to the inscrutability of the universe, in so far as being is simply accepted and must fail to yield intelligibility in the form of intention, purpose, cause, or the manifestation of anything other than being. Thus it must be incapable of regarding the universe fundamentally as either benefactor or malefactor, creator or creation, as a fostering power or a design. It perceives that the realm of ignorance must share a common plane with the realm of knowledge. It is an attitude which is open to evidence as the decisive factor in knowledge, since it views any possible situation as a definite situation, standing on its own feet in nature, therefore, such as to be inherently capable of yielding evidence. In this last respect it is an attitude that no one seriously questions in his dealings with nature.

At this point the sense of being places us on the threshold of philosophy. We have passed over this threshold in making conceptually explicit something of the attitude, the empirical origins of which we are now examining; thus the complicity of the sense and the conception of being is acknowledged by anticipating here the theoretical treatment of being to follow. The point is that the sense of being *is* the threshold of philosophy. It gives us something to think about requiring philosophical thought: the recognition of a reality to which that thought is relevant.

With his unmatched appreciation of first philosophy, Aristotle put his finger on both the logical and empirical occasion for philosophy in his assertion: "It is owing to their wonder that men both now begin and at first began to philosophize."[8] Over and above wonder at any particular situation, as such, is the wonder at there being anything at all, a wonder therefore relevant to anything at all, a wonder that bursts upon us with the realization of the meaning of being in reality, a meaning without which the notion of a reality is meaningless, a meaning which must be imbedded in reality if the thought of reality were possibly to occur to us. It is through the sense of being that the most profound wonder of reality is borne in upon us, disclosing the object requiring speculative understanding of us and guaranteeing the relevancy *of the very attempt* at such understanding. It is the sense of being discovered, persevered in, and acted upon by those early speculators in terms of both the concrete and the abstract which guides them beyond the attainment of simply poetry, bad physics, and elementary mathematics, to the first beginnings of first philosophy. Thus it is not surprising to find in Parmenides a direct approximation to the formulation of the conception of being, inadequate though his formulation may be.

Viewed in this light, philosophizing is not merely the indulgence of an inclination disposing us to the pursuit. It is the fulfillment of an obligation to understand the world in positive terms which is born of our relations in the world; and through the sense of being this demand for understanding is asserted by reality recognized in its wholeness, the wholeness of being, and therefore as calling for philosophical understanding. Philosophical perspective on any particular situation depends on such a basic understanding, which *begins* with the recognition of being.[9]

The peculiar aptness of the notion of wonder applied to the sense of being can be grasped from an incidental observation of Aristotle's in connection with the nature and development of philosophy. He says, "for it seems wonderful to all who have not yet seen the reason,"[10] a point that would be applicable to anything seeming wonderful. In the context of this remark Aristotle discusses wonder as involving a recognition of ignorance, and consequently a motive to escape from ignorance, upon which the pursuit of knowledge for its own sake ensues. Accordingly he interprets knowledge with a strong emphasis on the role of explanation, understanding the causes of things, the "reasons." Thus, when he reiterates: "For all men begin, as we said, by wondering that things are as they are,"[11] we may inquire appropriately: would the achievement of the philosophical goal imply the dispelling of the original wonder?

There are, no doubt, many ways of dispelling wonder. Essentially they would seem to be ways of assimilating some specific situation encountered to a context or to contexts in relation to which it may be relevantly and coherently understood. Thus the strange may lose its wonder for us upon our habituation to it. Thus the isolated phenomenon is accounted for and no longer strikes us as remarkable in so far as we are able to discern its relation with some particular temporal antecedents which bear on its occurrence, or with some special consequences that hinge upon it; we wonder still less about it if we can discover some motive embodying purpose contributing to the phenomenon.

As we grow up our ideas of the contexts in which phenomena do occur become expanded and fixed; they become more adequate to the comprehension of whatever comes along, so that we recognize a dream for a dream, or a fantasy for a fantasy. And life is robbed of much of the wonder of childhood.

In the context of ideas and beliefs we become acquainted with those procedures of explanation employed in showing what an idea or belief presupposes or implies.

All these are ways in which explanation is accomplished or habits are formed which tend to expurgate wonder. Yet the sense of being suggests a wonder which must grow, rather than diminish, in proportion to the attainment of the philosophical goal that is breached by the experience. There is no explanation for being, and it is in this sense that our wonder "that things are as they are" is fundamental and final. This wonder may be viewed as substantiated by a kind of absolute ignorance, if ignorance means failure to find a reason, a cause, purpose, logical ground, or wider context in terms of which to render its occasion intelligible. On the other hand the occasion for this wonder is nothing obscure; it is only obscured by our high degree of habituation to it, and by its independence of the common focus of our attention.

If we may digress, then, to enforce a point implicit here, let us note a legitimate sense in which we might say that there is no reason for anything at all, in so far as anything at all is viewed as participating in the universe of being. There is that about the existence of whatever may exist that there can be no accounting for, no "raison d'être" to explain. This is to define the profound unintelligibility of reality in a way that has nothing to do with our lack of knowledge of particulars as particular. It is not to imply an attitude of philosophical despair, however, for it also points out accurately the kind of intelligibility that remains possible with reference to being, namely, the positive apprehension and conception of things, qua being. This is the same sort of apprehension which qualifies the formulation of all our knowledge as, in the last analysis, descriptive. The fact that things are as they are, whatever they may prove to be, establishes the standard of relevancy for knowledge by both acquaintance and description. A definite situation is not only presupposed by all our efforts to determine what any given situation is, the efforts arise and the attempt at determination is relevant only because there is an occasion and a referent for them that stands on its own feet . . .

Once we have fixed the gaze of our inner eye on the ineradicable wonder of being, the role of imagination in fostering the development of the sense of being assumes noteworthy significance. A grasp of this role seems essential to balance the distortedly flat and passive and naïve-realistic-seeming aspects of the experience, as so far depicted in our analysis. Neither acquaintance nor description, where being is concerned, are effortlessly, passively, unimaginatively acquired. Although the sense of being is a tremendous act of *acceptance*, that very acceptance is an act of spiritual creation. To know the world we must build it in the mind, we must realize it ourselves.

What has this wonder, then, to do with imagination? Perhaps it is quite contrary to Aristotle's meaning to take our cue in answering this question from this suggestive remark of his, that "even the lover of myth is in a sense a lover of wisdom, for the myth is composed of wonders."[12] Yet even in the myths, the legends, and the fairy tales of our childhood, in the fabulous worlds early lit by imagination's light, just there are sown seeds of the sense of being. Our dreams and most outright fantasies, no less than our most sober thoughts and perceptions, contribute variously in the growth of these seeds. For here in the realm of our dreaming and imagining we learn to create and recreate liberally all that strange definiteness, marvelousness, and mystery which are, after all, not inappropriate to the presence of reality. At the very least our susceptibility to the sense of being is thereby enhanced.

But the complexity of our subject here demands careful analytical treatment. Let us consider first the dream.

Notwithstanding its fictitious character, the dream world takes matters into its own hands; within the brackets of oblivion and wakefulness that surround it, it asserts itself with all the compulsive objectivity of the real world, but with an objectivity doubly enforced in so far as the dreamer may view himself as a participant in the events of the dream with all the helplessness of a spectator. Within the dream objective presence is often asserted with an intensity seldom matched outside the fastnesses of dream experience. Perhaps we carry with us into the dream a sense of what can and what ought to happen in reality, and of actions which we would normally consent to, a sense which is outraged by the happenings which parade through our dream, enforcing our credulity in the incredible, to a point where the grip of the impossible may become so violent as to shock us into wakefulness. On the other hand we may swallow the impossible without any stress or protest, reveling in its naturalness, especially when we do not dream ourselves to be direfully threatened or discomfited. Viewed *ab intra*, the dream packs a terrific punch. And how profoundly the dream world immerses us in the image of reality, self-contained as it is, suspended in itself, absorbed, and mantled in slumber. Its presence is purely artificial, and yet *ab intra*, there's nothing artificial about it.

Viewed *ab extra*, what an excellent foil the dream is to genuine perception and coherent thought. Surely the context of experience that marks the dream down for merely a dream is set forth in relief for the reality which it is with a clarity and distinctness and a conviction about it, that must be lacking to it, but for being a world to which one may awaken from fantastic dream, or, simply, just from a sleep. If reality were itself some sort of comprehensive dream, a public Wonderland, as some have mused it might be, it could practice no deception on us through the distinction that arises between the real and the dream world. But for the fundamentality of this experienced contrast, the meaning of existence in reality would be far less clear to us.

The phenomenon of dreaming is no less amazing than anything dreamed. It offers to a man the most penetrating glimpses of the independent stranger that so largely is himself, not only by discovering to him the unsuspected in himself, but also through the unsummoned conjuring of his dream-consciousness, asserting a life of its own, with which he has nothing to do in so far as he is asleep. Then too, so often do dreams occur, to leave behind them only a faint, blurred trace, that one seems in remembrance to be finding just a hint of another man's dreams. One may well never cease to wonder at his dreaming, that elusive life of his at which he may not quite catch himself.

The fact is, dreaming allows one to see himself in the third person, on a plane with other creatures apart from himself. It thrusts him to the brink of his self-ignorance and forces on him the impression of regions there that escape familiarity, remain opaque before introspective scrutiny, and baffle surmise. Appearing out of the vast and confounding darkness of his nature, the dream peculiarly illumines to a man his own presence in reality, his own independent existence, his own incorporation in the realm of being, with the same flash and stroke that pronounce to him his own immense obscurity. The dream introduces us to the sense of being through ourselves as no overt phase of self-consciousness can, by showing us to ourselves as strangers.

Perhaps the kind of conscious access we have to ourselves lends itself to ready misinterpretation, of the kind for example that Descartes yields to in his assurance that conscious activity is primarily a deliverance of the self to the self, as foremost and most trustworthy among conscious deliverances. Consciousness is primarily a thing-consciousness, is it not? The locus of the self of which one is self-conscious, is in the residuum of thing-consciousness, and therefore self-consciousness is a derivative form of thing-consciousness. This self is but a transparency through which the shadows of things are manifested.

To symbolize the situation, vision does not take for its object the organic process of seeing, or the media of vision, but the thing seen. Likewise if we attempt to focus attention on the self that participated in the act of vision, again we encounter the thing seen, as remembered, thought about, and assimilated to a mass of residual impressions and attitudes of like object-attentive origin. As we turn now from the dream to a consideration of imagination, it will help us to bear in mind just this point, that even imagination, as conscious process, is inevitably a derivative form of thing-consciousness, and therefore if we push our inspection of imagination *in concreto*, we must always come up against this or that imagined, rather than the imaginative process.

In contrast with the dream, however, as well as with sober thought and perception directed on reality, our imaginative excursions do not so readily take us in. Indulgence in the play of imagination can be notably fast and loose and imperious. We exercise a freedom in shifting imaginative awareness about and a control over its contents which emphasize the arbitrariness and the independence from constraint of the imaginative process. The fantastic distillations and compoundings that result so often in the process proclaim the fictitiousness and factitiousness of the work of imagination. There seem to be no limits to what we may imagine, since imaginative room expands the more freely we range in it, and imaginative power grows the more practiced we become at invention.

Are we not libertines with our verbal constructs? Who has not traversed the way from sense, through logical nonsense, to the utterance of sheer mental or vocal sounds, signifying to say the least, little? Who does not revel in relaxation from the immediate, the here and now, in the command of the there and then, in the aimless wandering of reverie, in the escape from the pressing, in the delight of images that fly in the face of reality?

In its irresponsible aspects imagination gives us all the release from reality required to permit the assumption of responsible relations with it as an alternative. If we had to deal with the real thing directly all the time, the earnestness of reality would be deadly, and we would be so absorbed in it that we would be unable to withdraw to any point of vantage from which to regard that earnestness in the light of contrast for what it is. Imagination stands between us and the world in such a way as to prevent the world from swallowing us up.

On the other hand, harking back to the point stressed in connection with imagination as a mode of consciousness, even the most

outright hoboing of human consciousness subsists on a minimal re-
quital of the organic needs of conscious activity. Imagination has its
substance, which the world conspires with the person to provide,
even to the farthest reaches of imaginative life; if at some advanced
stage in this creative conspiracy either partner were to drop out,
imagination must evanesce through a vanishing punctiformity. Total emancipation from the world would constitute the annihilation
of consciousness. The solipsist has given us a prescription for this,
but does he succeed in taking it? It is indeed a deadly prescription.

There is nothing like running away from the world in imagination to teach us that we cannot leave the world behind, to reveal to
us the minimal and primitive roots of consciousness in reality. Unless imagination attempts to repudiate seriously its debt to reality,
however, it may never discover its indebtedness.

Take the centaur, as a classic example of the figment of imagination. The centaur is as purely imaginary as any creature of the imagination could be, yet its umbilical connection with the shape of real
horses and men is obvious. No doubt the Jabberwock and the Snark
provide tougher hunting, but we are entitled to some confidence in
looking for them in the same general hunting ground.

Imagination turns out to be as highly complex as it is fugitive.
While at times listless and lethargic, again it is driven with passion. While on occasion it is undisciplined, again it is subservient
to the quiet guidance of directed thought. It is constantly infused
with the elements of sensation. It is mnemonic and reflective as
well as creative. And where it strains for expression of the voice-
less life of the spirit, its work is inspired with purpose, method and
meaning which always have their relevancy, their cores of sense,
their centers of improvisation, even though these be subject to vast
misinterpretation . . .

A great deal might fruitfully be said still on the complicity of
imagination with all phases of conscious life, and on its limiting and
definitive characteristics. The term "imagination," as a descriptive
term, must be handled guardedly, lest it lead us to assume some sort
of faculty or organ or entity for which there is not the slightest psychological warrant. The exact nature of conscious life in its imaginative phases and nuances must pass largely unexamined here. We
have drawn out only enough of a sketch to allow us to put our finger
on the role of imagination in the sense of being, and the significance
of imagination in the development of the experience.

For our purposes here, then, it is suggested that we reflect upon imagination as the pioneer of knowledge. This is to single out those imaginative processes bent upon understanding. To understand a situation we have to be able both to represent it and to misrepresent it to ourselves. We have to approach it with questions; the formulation of those questions, and the initial representations from which we begin to carve out our answers to them, is essentially creative imaginative work. At the frontiers of understanding we explore the deliverances of experience with alternative interpretations which require of us the imagination to pose, if we are even to begin to understand the situation to which the deliverances have reference. It is just because we are always confronted by a definite situation to be understood by a selective discrimination from within envisaged alternatives, allowing for passage from the implicit to the explicit idea, from the confused to the clear and distinct and coherent thought, and permitting plenty of opportunity for being mistaken,— that intelligent apprehension of the nature of things is possible.

In pioneering the frontiers of understanding imagination places the hands of the mind on the definite presence of reality. Thus underlying all scientific and practical intelligence, as well as artistic creation, imagination performs a thundering philosophical service. It gives us an implicit grasp of being wherever we drive at an intelligent adjustment to any situation. In pursuing a disjunctive approach to reality at any point, imagination lays hold of the definity of reality. As an assumption of the attempt to understand, however, the definity of reality remains quite tacit in the case of most undertakings; the conceptual tools of logic lay it bare. That definity makes all the difference between talking sense and talking nonsense, whatever we may be talking about, as Aristotle has clearly shown.

It is too far-fetched, then, to suppose that any man of intelligence, any man who has worked long and hard at the frontiers of understanding, can not fail to possess something of the wonder, the natural humility, the reverence and integrity that stem from the sense of being? For is not the sense of being a primordial empirical root of intelligence?

PART

II

Published Writings

A Venture in the Open

Bugbee appropriated the phrase "inward morning" from Thoreau in order to convey the experience of radical reflection:

> There is this bathing in fluent reality which resolves mental fixations and suggests that our manner of taking things has been staggeringly a matter of habituation. Metaphysical thinking must rise with the earliest dawn the dawn of things themselves. And this is the dawn in which basic action, too, comes into being. It is earlier than the day of morality and immorality.[1]

The luminosity of inward morning is a result of "venturing in the open."[2] To venture in the open is to live in a way as connoted by the German verb *"untersuchen"*—to literally "seek among" things, probing their capacity to reveal more inclusive radii of meaning. To venture is to occupy a bipolar site where subject and object are no longer divided, "at once referential and reflexive, reflexive and referential."[3] The luminosity of inward morning is "original"—ontologically autochthonous: "appear[ing] as that which dawns and *is* in the dawning."[4] Venturing into the open is most exacting work and not devoid of risks. Bugbee explains:

> For five years I have been writing in an explanatory way, gradually forced to recognize that this was the case and I must accept it, along with the professional consequences. My task has been to learn to write in a vein comparable with what I can honestly say in the act of trying to discover what I must say. It has been a precarious business. I have found myself thinking quite differently from the majority of

men who are setting the style and the standard of philosophy worth doing.[5]

Bugbee wrote "A Venture in the Open" for the 1958 International Exposition sponsored by UNESCO and held in Brussels, Belgium. The conference addressed topics such as the criteria of reflective judgment, the experience of *la durée historique* [historical duration], and the relationship between rational and the nonrational approaches to philosophy.

Venturing is a requirement for living a reflective life, a winding and wending path that remains:

> In essential continuity of human life, brought out through endur-
> ing encounter, we are liberated from that otherwise overwhelming
> incubus which weighs upon the actualities of human affairs. Our
> ventures no longer hinge on their success or failure. . . . They are
> grounded . . . in that which nothing can destroy, on the strength of
> which we may transcend—and so become ourselves, for as long as it
> may be given to us to live.

∾

Prefatory Note: For six days early in the summer of 1958, during the International Exposition at Brussels, a "Colloque Orient-Occident" was held there. Thirty participants with diverse professional back-grounds but convergent reflective interests were invited from coun-tires of the East and of the West by our Belgian hosts. The six days were devoted to discussion of themes which had been proposed for the occasion. Our written contributions were prepared for the re-cord of the colloguim in retrospect upon the discussions that had taken place, and with such selective emphasis as each participant might deem appropriate. The following essay touches in particular on three foci of the colloguim: (1) "criteria of reflective judgment," (2) "la durée historique," and (3) the distinction and correlation, repeatedly invoked during the discussions, between "the rational" and "the non- (or 'extra'-) rational."

The expression, "the Same" which figures in this essay should be acknowledged as a naming of the grounding of a truly destinate existence which seemed to me particularly fitting at a time when I was absorbed in reading later works of Heidegger. (HGB)

Again and again the considerations made vivid by Monsieur Lam-billiotee at the beginning of our symposium come to mind with a sense of practical urgency: the unprecedented increase of peoples; the rate of technical development, so fraught with ambiguous import; and the acuteness of our plight as peoples thrown together more and more. The International Exposition, as the setting of our meeting, enhanced this atmosphere of practical urgency in which we met. How did our symposium answer to the demands of an occasion keyed to such practical considerations and pervaded by such an atmosphere of practical urgency?

At times our reflections seem to have taken a programmatic direction; and at times each of us may have felt that our discussion was not sufficiently to the point, in view of those sharply etched features of our current situation on Earth from which we started. Yet the basic character of our discussion seems to have been that of a reflective exchange on reflective themes, involving us in a declaration and interpretation of our own basic attitudes. In weighing the significance of our symposium, then, I find this question of especial interest: How can reflective life, and the relationships we establish with one another in sharing it, be consonant with the urgencies of our practical situation, especially in so far as reflection mindful of the latter nonetheless is not primarily directed to the solution of practical problems?

I see the answer to this question along two related lines suggested by our experience in the symposium. First, I believe that we brought to pass, in a measure, the kind of human relationship in which the future of man is decisively touched; something that goes deeper than the engendering of amicable feelings. Second, in and through this relationship, I believe that we are able to approach the kind of mutual reflection in which thought itself assumes the character of decisive action.

The more I have thought about our meeting and reviewed our discussions, the more I have been struck by the sense of enduring encounter with so many who were there. Now such encounter between persons seems to me to put thought in its place; not to make it of incidental importance, but to provide us with a stand in which we are more able to take the measure of what is thought and said. The more we called one another out in the open of living speech, the more we declared ourselves in direct encounter with one another, the more our thought testified to the heart of our experience bearing on the themes discussed—the more we could feel ourselves subject to the touch through which thought itself becomes a fundamental and decisive human deed.

It is from this experience of our meeting that I would like to offer retrospective comment on some of the themes we discussed.

In any undertaking of real concern it is natural to raise the question as to how we may be sure that we are on the right track. It is a question of judgment, and we try to answer it by formulating *criteria of judgment*. We try to formulate the conditions under which a man may trust in what he is thinking or doing. Human reflection in every civilization is perennially concerned to define such conditions, to develop basic criteria of judgment of relevance in the appraisal of thought and action. On this theme of 'criteria' to which we addressed our attention I find our meeting itself the fruition of thinking and acting. Criteria are themselves situational and attitudinal. They are a function of our situation and our mode of being in it. The criteria which occur to us and develop into governing considerations grow out of the way we assume our existence in our situation. Therefore criteria cannot assure us that we are not arbitrary in what we think and do. They must themselves share the questionableness of our very existence, and require to be distinguished from methodological and procedural rules.

I am not suggesting, however, that relevant criteria of thought and action are impossible. But I would suggest that they tend to arise as enduring forms of presence of mind only as we give ourselves with constancy into the reality of relationships entered upon and renewed in earnest. Then our situation itself tends to lay hold upon us, summoning us to be wholly present within it. Then presence of mind emerges as a function of the unique occasion to which we give ourselves. Then we are bound anew to that Same which comes to us, in which we—and therefore our minds—can meet. Such was the reality of our meeting itself, as I read it now, and sense in it a possible measure of what we thought and said.

If enduring encounter is of criteriological relevance—even to the point of emerging as a fundamental condition in which thought and action can be free, it is no less significant for the interpretation of *"durée historique."* What distinguishes enduring encounter is that we become bound up in it with destiny which is ours to participate in fulfilling. Since historical continuity is essentially that of destiny to be fulfilled, its meaning cannot be discovered and disclosed apart from our taking it upon ourselves and affirming it in a way we assume our existence. It cannot be clear apart from that sense of solidarity with the generation of men to which Canon [Charles Earle] Raven bore unmistakable witness at a memorable point in our discussion. Times of encounter are times of destiny, and through them the meaning of temporal existence is established. If they are enduring it is because they partake of the one life in which we may all actively share, in which they prove themselves enduring through their evoking, strengthening, and confirming the fundamental commitment of which we are capable. They lead us on and out of ourselves.

In essential continuity of human life, brought out through enduring encounter, we are liberated from that otherwise overwhelming incubus which weighs upon the actualities of human affairs. Our ventures no longer hinge on their success or failure, nor upon ideals or values proposed for realization or attainment. They are grounded, in so far as they are grounded, in that which nothing can destroy, on the strength of which we may transcend—and so become ourselves, so long as it may be given us to live.

Yet from this we lapse. From this we fall away. In this we prove failing, and the very thought of it becomes vague. Our actual existence is surely, for the most part, ambiguous. And it is a faithful reflection on that ambiguity to pose the issue for an interpretation of *"durée historique"* as that of conceiving the possibility of our "overcoming time," just as Mr. Dhingra did in his introduction of the theme into our discussion. What we have to distinguish are the aspects that time and historical continuity can hold for us, depending on the way in which our existence is assumed.

Monsier Abel has provided us with a very direct and exact statement of one aspect which time can assume, and of which we must take account:

> For those immersed into the reality of things, who live according to what is happening at any moment in the world, considering the fundamental differences which exist historically between this or that civilization or who was born in this or that country, this appreciation of time differs from the things that certainly interest the intellectual who has time, leisure, and comfort to indulge in free and pleasant speculations, but for the man who lives in real time, number and space are precisely the settings of this cruel reality.[6]

This statement precisely suggests a mode of existence which breaks into two correlative phases, each of which presupposes the other as its necessary counterpart. On the one hand there is "the reality of things" into which man feels himself to be plunged, to which he is attached. These things are constituted as "in themselves," posed "objectively" and indifferently over against a "subject," who can only suffer, in the end, the dominance of that "objective order" which he struggles, meanwhile, to control in behalf of his interests and needs.

Existence assumed in these objective-subjective terms renders time accordingly, now as inherent in an objective order of successive events, now as time feels for a subject for whom reality reduces to such an order. The interests and needs of the subject prompt control of "objective reality," and "objective reality" appears precisely in those terms which invite and implement the possibility of control. As this equation works itself out with time, however, the controlling subject is bound to fail; he is haunted by that inevitable failure; and the human lot takes on more and more the guise of fate. The course of an existence so assumed can only culminate in our undoing. Thus time becomes that demonic power through which "objective reality" temporarily indulges human life only to disown it utterly. In so far as we live plunged in the actuality-of-things-so-construed, dependent on what transpires in these terms, then time and space are indeed the backbone of "this cruel reality" to which Monsieur Abel alludes, and thoughts on the meaning of time in different civilizations must surely seem matter for rather idle speculation.

Yet not only thought but whatever else we may undertake loses point in the end, if the continuity of historical existence is essentially that of a fate. And the appreciation of this fact, as we suggested in the legend of the life of Gautama Buddha, is often the point of departure for most urgent speculation. But how simple, unmistakable, and eloquent the testimony has been of those whose meditation on this predicament has indicated the possibility of its resolution! In so far as we do not disown what we meet on our way, but can affirm it with our being, reality tends to confirm us in this. "Nature," persons, institutions, people, events: they become bound up and bound into a destiny which is that of communal life, and at the same time uniquely and unrepeatably for each one of us to fulfill. Of life appreciated in these terms I remember a saying which I heard from Mr. Nikam some years ago: "If in this thy faint heart fail, bring me thy failure."

If it is our mode of existence, then, upon which discovery of the meaning of time and historical continuity depends, I hope I have suggested that our concern does not accordingly lie with "subjective" as opposed to "objective" meanings of time, but rather in transcending these interdependent and correlative meanings.

I believe Monsieur Abel is right, however, about the possible irrelevancy of thinking in determining the meaning of time. One might think till Doomsday and never transcend alternatives couched in terms of the correlation of objectivity and subjectivity. Thinking of itself cannot be decisive. Or more fundamentally stated, a man "of himself" cannot decide the matter. Perhaps this point is nowhere stressed more clearly than in the annals of Zen Buddhism.

Finally, it seems to follow that we cannot strictly speak of "the bondage of time"—and in that event freedom cannot mean at all "a timeless state." Rather, both bondage and freedom must be construed in terms of the way we assume our existence, and with due recognition of the fact that in the way existence is assumed we are for the most part liable to misconstrue them both. On this point the *Bhagavad Gita* seems particularly suggestive in its emphasis on "the sense of ego" and "attachment to the fruits of action" as the nerve of bondage. These companionate phrases seem to signify accurately that *from* which freedom is to be interpreted as obtaining, in the aspect of "freedom from." It is from this that we may become free in time, and in so far as we do, space and time no longer threaten to freeze life in its tracks, we no longer suffer mere insular individuality amidst a world of "things-themselves." "Space" becomes a recognizable abstraction relative to the concrete reality of a place that owns one, where a man belongs, to live and to die. And time is the amplitude within which existence is pledged to affirm the eternal meaning of what may come to be and pass away. That meaning, ever depending on the Same, but only uniquely discovered in being done and confirmed in faithful life—as the meaning of the beings we encounter—is the essence of historical continuity and of a free life.

At this point it may be possible to suggest how either a predominantly thoughtful or predominantly active way of life, carried through decisively, may come to one, as the *Bhagavad Gita* suggests that it may. I should like to develop this suggestion now in order to comment on the discussion of "the rational" and "the extrarational" which kept cropping up in our meeting.

If it is meaning that requires to be worked out in life, then even a predominantly active way of life cannot be decisive except as a working out and confirmation of the meaning of the beings we encounter. But that is precisely the concern of a thoughtful life, the way of which is predominantly that of meditation. Therefore we might say that decisive action is itself essentially meditative, and the more clearly to be appreciated as such the more it is recognized as a way of "renunciation and devotion" (to employ these further terms from the *Gita*).

On the other hand, a predominately thoughtful way of life cannot become decisive without assuming an essentially active character, in that the meaning with which meditation discovers its proper concern can only be discovered as a meaning to be done, and done by a man with the whole of his being. Therefore we might say that decisive meditation is itself essentially active, and the more clearly to be appreciated as such the more it is recognized as a way of "renunciation and devotion."

Since neither meditation nor action can be carried out decisively under the domination of the sense of the ego, however, it is characteristic of either, in so far as it is decisive, that it is as if it simply came to pass; in a sense one does not know what he thinks or does. In being truly oneself, it is just that old "knower" and "doer" from which one is free. Not that discrimination dissolves; no, it becomes fluent and freed from fixation. Not that interest dies, no, it becomes freed from obsession. Not that the beings one encounters are drained of reality; no, they become freed from the abstraction of existing "in-themselves" even as they are affirmed in their independence. What they are is what they may be affirmed to be in that enactment of their eternal meaning through which creation dawns upon us—in so far as we accept our part in this.

If the rationale of our existence is to be taken in this vein, as served in active meditation and meditative action, then we may understand how the two images of Buddha referred to by Mr. Malalasekara[7] are both necessary, and necessarily of the one Buddha: the Buddha must be seated on the lotus, and the Buddha must be walking; but the seated Buddha is walking, and the walking Buddha is seated. Meditation is active, and action is meditative. "Reason" is essentially active; and action is essentially rational. That is why either the way of meditation or the way of action, carried through decisively, come to one and the Same. But as Mrs. Mehta said of *karma yoga* (the way of action), it is only carried through decisively as a "way of renunciation and devotion," and the same would be applied to a thoughtful life. Accordingly, the essential unity of thought and action could only be discovered in and through renunciation and devotion, in a way of assuming our existence for which no method of thought or of action can substitute, or even serve as a guarantee.

Concrete reality can only be that of awakened life, in which the rationale of existence is simply done.

The sleep and fantasy of reason is that it may never awaken into concrete reality, missing or failing its own essentially active character: that character through which it dawns on one that *responsible existence* is the defining of concrete reality. Then reason succumbs to the perspective of knowledge about things—as if that were final, and remains fundamentally at a loss to take account of action understandingly. Reality is reduced in principle to the "objectively known," "the objectively knowable"; and active existence, devoid of rationale, lapses into "subjective life," whose "values," for all that may be said in their defense, remain the reflection of *de facto* interests and needs. A merely subjective life must feel itself gratuitous and ineffectual in the end, even if it ranges the keyboard of feelings to the heights of spirituality.

The sleep and fantasy of reason is to relinquish—all inadvertently, no doubt—the rationale of human existence as requiring to be *done*, even in a thoughtful way.

The sleep and fantasy of reason is that it may never awaken into concrete reality, missing and failing its own essentially meditative character: that character through which it dawns on one that responsible existence is the *defining* of concrete reality. The action succumbs to the play and interplay of wants and needs, satisfactions and frustrations, of liking and aversion, which of themselves presume to the status of *raison d'être* of active existence. The sleep and fantasy of action is to relinquish—all inadvertently, no doubt—the *rationale* of human existence as requiring to be done, even in an active way.

And so it is that the rationale of existence may be appropriated as the concern of reason unawakened to its own essentially active character; while action, unawakened to its own essentially meditative character, perfectly corroborates the reading of action which reason is likely to accord to it. So it must seem from the standpoint of a self who arrests himself in a merely individualized existence. But meetings such as ours suggest that we may be drawn out of ourselves in the power to rise into encounter with one another. Then we may come into that vein of personal life in which we share actively and thoughtfully in working out that meaning of existence through which we discover again and again that we have to do with one another essentially. Such experience is neither rational, nor extra-rational, nor a synthesis of the two, in the terms which this distinction is likely to suppose; it transcends those terms and confirms the unified character of human life, in which reasonable action and active reasoning come to be one and the Same.

What I have derived from our symposium above all is a more accurate appreciation of the world which may be brought to pass through men, in so far as we stand forth into the open in which our encounter with one another becomes fundamental and enduring. It is not ours to suggest a program to cope with the practical urgencies of which we remained rightly mindful in our reflections together. It was ours to go to the root of the urgency in action and reflection alike. It was ours to declare unmistakably the irrelevance of optimism and pessimism alike in the face of an unknown future. It was ours to suggest a foundation of hope and faith more ultimate than either our needs or a practical perspective can of themselves provide or confirm. Such a work of reflection can become of the nature of the deed itself through which genuinely communal life is brought to pass on Earth. It may also clarify the more-than-practical character of those actions through which alone even the most practical exigencies of our situation can be met.

Thoughts on Creation

"Thoughts on Creation" was written in 1962 during a brief period when Bugbee was teaching at the Pennsylvania State University. Moments of inward morning occur through the grace, generosity, and majesty of creation.[1] The world exists in a state of *essentially* dynamic configuration:

> [The] world essentially can be only in coming to pass; it cannot be conjured with as extant. World is, if you will, always in the building, being forged, to be done; it cannot lapse from dawning and formation. . . . Thus, to be in and of the world would be to be in and of continuous creation, and to abide in the world would be to abide in no fixed abode.[2]

To be reflexively self-aware requires active participation as both patient and agent in the dynamic process of creation's coming-to-pass. Participating in creation is "not a matter of destination and linear movement."[3] Participation is an elevated level of *experiential* reflection rich in sensory and intellectual content. Appropriating notions of "problem and mystery" and "primary and secondary reflection" from Gabriel Marcel, Bugbee notes:

> Here we may put the point by availing ourselves of a term of Marcel's: Action and reflection on the point of action are both *meta-technical*, over and above whatever technique may enter into them. And for convenience, let us use a similar term, and say that they are both meta-objective in the sense that they move in a dimension of meaning over which we cannot exercise the power of representation and control that obtains with respect to things in taking them as objects.[4]

73

Throughout the course of day-to-day living, our primary mode of relating to the world is mainly functional. Marcel refers to this way of existing as "primary reflection"—things are abstracted from their wider context and represented in terms of function served within a chain of efficient causality—"doing this in order to obtain that." Despite location within a causal network, things experienced from a merely functional perspective appear fragmented and incomplete, indicating a condition of ontological deficit—a sense of metaphysical disquiet Marcel referred to as *exigence ontologique*. The shape-shifting countenance of appearance mollifies the naive observer but, as Marcel reminds us: "Life completely transcends the categories of biology [and] infinitely transcends my possible conscious grasp at any given moment."[5] Existence oftentimes bespeaks a sense of mystery unable to be captured in canonical speech or ratiocinative categories. Problems, on the other hand, occur in specifically defined contexts in which they can be "solved." A problematic situation requires the subject to take an exterior position vis-á-vis the problem "at hand"—a strange perspective in which the subject somehow removes itself from the very circumstances under consideration. What gives the self the ability to inhabit a "non-problematical" sphere? Our egocentric orientation is unable to account for the obdurate and inviolable source of *that* through which the problem is constituted. What is the source that gives meaning to the self, allowing the self to consider itself separately from any problem? This source cannot come from the self! Sands begin to shift beneath our feet. According to Annie Dillard, this feeling is akin to the experience of a tightrope walker who, "as soon as it looks at its feet . . . realizes that it is operating in mid-air."[6] Invoking Marcel's peripatetic ideal of *homo viator* as a permanent mode of human wayfaring, of *being* in continuous state of vigilance, Bugbee writes:

> Even what is taken as given for explanation, or as the most minimal and secure disclosure from which discursive thought can warrantedly proceed, is taken, and taken discursively. If not so taken, it cannot provide either a point of departure for explanation or evidence, i.e. the *data* for knowledge. Judgment can have no access to unjudged disclosures.[7]

Perhaps in so far as myths of creation tell of special events, they do so almost reflexively. This speaking, this uttering, this primordial thinking of the coming into being of things and man, this placing of all that is in the world: is not this speaking, this uttering, this thinking a participation in the coming to pass of that of which such myths tell? So construed, at any rate, myths of creation tend to disclose that of which they speak; the mists and emerging grandeur of the morning of creation play *in* this very speech. Here speech itself seems to find its origin and meaning, bursting forth decisively. It is not that there is, or once was, creation and subsequently a telling of it, by means of speech imported for the occasion and of an origin extraneous to the occasion told. No; primordial speaking and thinking cannot disavow the origin they would acknowledge in myth of creation. They reflect upon that which they bear witness to, realize, and fulfill. Yet the speaker, for all his part in this, remains anonymous, even though man may appear as in some way central in the creation told.

In narrating a story, myths of creation seem to have to do with events in time, with coming to pass. We have begun to recognize how they may tell of special events. Yet what appears to be special about these events is that they are world events. In them world is coming to pass, and coming into being is coming to pass. The events narrated seem to yield an appreciation of being in time and of all things implicated in temporal existence. And the point seems to be that being in time somehow "has an origin"—that all things implicated in temporal existence *derivatively* enjoy such being as may be theirs. The being of beings in time is somehow bestowed upon them, and the bestowal of being here in question seems indissolubly linked with the coming to pass of the world. World and the being of beings in time thus appear alike as of one and the same origin.

Before turning to the element of origin invoked in myths of creation, let us consider how world is suggested in them. The suggestion, as I venture to read it, is that world essentially can be only in coming to pass; it cannot be conjured with as extant. World is, if you will, always in the building, being forged, to be done; it cannot lapse from dawning and formation. It appears as that which dawns and *is* in dawning. So world does appear as world-without-end, and creation with respect to world is continuous creation. Hence the feel of creation is one of fluency and constancy, one of opening out and opening up, one of gathering up and growing together of things and events to enter into the this ongoing ever-forming of world. Thus, to be in and of the world would be to be in and of continuous creation, and to abide in the world would be to abide in no fixed abode.

Turning now to the element of origin invoked in myths of creation, we have every reason to be especially careful. For what is being invoked is invoked as divine, as birthless and deathless, as the ever-so, the self-same, the fundamental and ordaining power. Here, if I were to say that we are hard put to it to know what is in question, I would think it very reasonable of you to smile—providing you don't smile too sardonically. Yet, is the point that the divine is very, very difficult to know and such that only very, very few come to know what is in question—if, indeed, the invocation of divine origin of creation is not what we speak of today as *merely* mythical? Or is it the very tone of primordial speech of creation that must instruct us in listening to its imagery? Is not the divine more like what is to be discovered in this very act of speech, responsively echoed in the hearing of our hearts? The divine is there, animating that speaking, and to be marked, if at all, in a ring of authenticity and a tone over which simplicity itself presides. That is the divine, inexhaustible in power: utterly simple, presiding, gathering, disposing, revealing Presence—calling forth the very speech, imparting the very gift of speech, in which the being of beings of consummated, acknowledged, confirmed. Then things are the things of the world that is coming to pass and address the hearing heart as divine speech.

Creation is indeed a story to be told, and in the telling of it, it is with reason that divine power is extolled. Myths of creation reflect the fact in the primordial doing of the deed. Where this sort of telling occurs, the reason for it appears in and with the telling. In myths of creation, creation seems to be claiming speech as its own proper and revealing dominion.

But how many things stand with us nowadays in thinking and speaking of creation?

Sometimes it seems to me that to bespeak creation comes so naturally and spontaneously that it is what all naturalness and spontaneity do: Whenever and wherever they occur, they bespeak creation. As we put it, there *is* something creative about them, whether wittingly so or not. And it is, above all, of actions and of people in action that we have come to think when we think of creation. There is even a tendency to think of creation preeminently, though not altogether exclusively, in connection with those actions we typify as artistic. Not too many for whom the meaning of creation has been thus focalized wend there way back—or on—to a renewed or new appreciation of the primordial themes of creation: coming into being, coming to pass of world, and divine origin. I will not attempt here to follow up at all the direction indicated by Whitehead through reflection on "aesthetic experience" to reinterpretation of reality. Nor will I attempt to discuss those great essays of Heidegger's which seem to me to go so far in opening up this direction of thought.

What I wish to do now is to suggest that it is our part in creation which presently calls for reflection and that we may come at this task by reconsidering the possible meaning of *creatio ex nihilo*. It is the *nihil* that establishes this story as essentially pertaining to ourselves, as well as all things, and in a way peculiar to ourselves.

The way to willing participation in creation seems to be a dialectical one. It is not at all a matter of destination and linear movement towards it. Whatever we distinguish as pertaining to this way is likely to be implicitly involved with contraries. What has appeared thus, now appears so, and thinking does not necessarily stabilize the shape-shifting countenance that appearance wears. But I will speak of nothingness in three distinguishable senses which seem pertinent to the theme of *creation ex nihilo*; without suggesting, I hope, that I mean to describe "something having a nature," with fixed and discrete properties to be elicited and recognized as such.

First, there is the nothingness known as such, say, in dread and despair—such as Kierkegaard deals with so carefully. Second, there is the nothingness known to renunciation, so central in Buddhist thought and there called *sunyata*. And third, there is the nothingness of being, in the sense that being is not a being at all, as Heidegger makes the point—so central in his thinking.

Now in entering upon a development of these three senses in which creation seems to involve "nothingness," I believe we must be explicit about the standpoint from which we must think and speak and the language in terms of which our thought can move. There can be no talk, no proper thought, in this matter that does not presuppose the standpoint of care and move in the language of care. Nothing and being obtain for care, and it is essentially being of which care stands in need; and being comes to care as calling upon it. Our lives are in essence vocational, however long we may be in realizing it. Perhaps I would say that it is quite impossible to speak without interpreting at least implicitly what is called for and what it is to be called upon. "Philosophically stated," one cannot help begging the question, and explicitly, when it comes to talking of being and nothing. One can only help to beg it appropriately. This, I confess, I have no assurance of doing, yet I will do my best, tending to follow my master, Eckhart, in the way the question is begged.

That is, I shall speak of creatures and of creaturely being in a way that presupposes that decisive mode of care in which renunciation, or "disinterestedness," is pivotal. Implied in this presupposition is the impossibility of forcing it upon anyone, for care only *is* in this mode willingly, by utterly free consent, and not otherwise. As the *Tao Te Ching* suggests, reasoning in this mode of care, however firm it may be, cannot contend.

As in Hindu and Buddhist thought, it must be an early part of our story to take account of the great illusion into which our senses, intellect, desire, and will are likely to plunge: It consist in taking the ten thousand things as if they *were* in and of themselves. Now of creatures thus construed Meister Eckhart seems to be talking when he says that creatures of themselves are mere nothings. Their really being something, their "suchness," is in their being taken as creatures; I would almost say, in their being permitted to be, in being *as* creatures. Thus the irony of the illusion to which I refer is that, in tending to treat things as if they were beingful in and of themselves, we reduce them to nothings. In a way this is equivalent to washing our hands of them—treating them as if they *had* being and could well enough go their own way without us.

But what is this way of construing being implicit in taking things as if they *were* in and of themselves? Is it not that being and care are in utterly contingent, accidental relationship? Being is independent of care. If so, in what way can care work out the equation of its relation with things whose being whose being appears in the guise of inherent independence of care? It would seem that care must alternate between two correlative positions with respect to things and others: Either it can assert itself and seek to impose itself or it can acquiesce in what may be imposed upon it. Care then takes itself to be free and independent in so far as it has its way with things, and any possible dependence in which it may stand must seem to it a threat to its freedom and independence. And death entering into the life of care to qualify it as mortal is all that is needed to lock care in an utter impasse, in that it must come to feel itself as bound to fail. Being must seem to tolerate care and ultimately reject it with inscrutable indifference. Dread anticipates the crisis of futility, when nothingness seizes the heart, and care comes consciously to despair.

But through precisely such happening, and not otherwise, is selfhood potentiated, as Kierkegaard says. And precisely through such happening we are cast out of illusory proximity with things and put in relationship with what-is *as a whole*, or better, *in toto*. A pall of nothingness falls between us and everything; it is our relationship with *everything* that is radically in question. Only in so far as this happens can we can we really come to put the shoe on our own foot, as it were, and come to realize that *our* being is somehow pivotally in question with the being of all things. "At this point" care is got ready for an examined life, when it feels itself essentially in question even as it questions and lives in question. Care awakens to itself as somehow responsible for its way of taking things and may well be imbued with suspicion that as it takes things, so it has them, yet precisely not in the sense that it can at will confer on things the fundamental aspect which they assume for it. Thus everything about the situation of care tends to a dialectic and irony on which tragedy and comedy alike may strive. And what do the most trenchant tragic and comic dramas tend to show? Is it not that we are somehow responsible for the way in which things appear to us without being able to determine how things appear at will? Do not these dramas study appearance in intimacy with modes of care? And do they not tend to suggest that care cannot absolve itself of the way things appear to it, so that if appearances come to wear an illusory aspect, as in disillusionment with them, then care must acknowledge its part in illusion and know that part as delusion?

At this phase of our story the situation of care seems to be something like this: the being of things can no longer be dissociated from their appearing and the way in which care discovers them. Care and being have essentially to do with one another. Being is no longer that to which care may take itself to be accidentally abandoned. The questionableness of being is now also the questionableness of care. The meaning of being becomes care's own undertaking. We may say that the stake in the venture is both the self and the world. Thus, as Tillich points out, in so far as self-loss may attend to the venture, this is also at the same time world-loss. But in the course of speaking of creation and the story that may be ours to tell of it, we have already said as much: Namely, that the coming to pass of world and our coming to be as selves are essentially related: we participate in this as selves. World, in turn, seems to come to pass only through our participation in it as selves, and this is ultimately a matter of free consent on our part, by coming to pass through us.

Can we now say what the situation of care implicitly is, with respect to being? I think we must try, in that the very predicament of the self must implicitly foster whatever, by way of resolution, may answer to it. I would say the situation is implicitly this: Care and being are "promised" to one another. In consonance with being alone can care be confirmed in its being. We become authentically ourselves in the image of the divine and on the strength of the divine. This implies that we come to know ourselves in being ourselves and I think in a very precise sense: We are strictly as nothing in and of ourselves. Of all creatures, we must *know* our creatureliness and accept it in order to be as the creatures we really are. Our true dignity consists in our ability to acknowledge that considered in and of ourselves we are nothing. Now this means two things: It means that considered in and of ourselves we are of no account and impotent. It also means that we are able to be in the image of being, which is no *thing* at all. The free consent to be as nothing in both these senses is what I understand by renunciation. And what is it that renunciation is renunciation of? Simply of the claim, I think, to be in one's own right. Care cannot entitle itself to be nor can it issue the title of anything to be, no matter how benevolently disposed by inclination care may be. In renunciation, so construed, care is not being "heroic" but essentially matter-of-fact. In so far as care is prepared to give itself up, then it is prepared to receive all things. In doing so, it makes room for things to come into being and does not block the mutual access, so to speak, of things and being, consummated through one's willing participation in this. In thus receiving all things into itself, care recognizes them as divine gifts, for so they are in creation.

If these gifts are not to be disavowed, care must be willing to part with them; they cannot be owned; they cannot be claimed; they cannot be clung to; and when departed, they cannot be sought. The continuity of participation in creation is in uninhibiting restraint, forbearance, a continuing receptivity, an evenness in arrival and departure, way beneath the fluctuating surface of events. Otherwise stated, we may say: Receiving is parting, and parting is receiving; renunciation is the receptivity of care—receptivity, that is on the part of care. Such is the Valley Spirit of Tao and the poverty of spirit of which Eckhart speaks. There is nothing in all creation to which care may make fast; but in so far as care will agree to this it embraces all creatures as creatures, participates in all creation, and abides in no abode.

There is one parting pertinent to the possibility of participating in creation in our own time, especially here in what we may still call Christendom, and I see it as a parting of special historical relevance to us, nowhere more clearly indicated than in a remark of Meister Eckhart's in which he explicitly speaks of a parting that is last and highest:

Man's last and highest parting occurs when, for God's sake, he takes leave of god. St. Paul took leave of god for God's sake and gave up all that he might get from god, as well as all he might give—together with every idea of god. In parting with these, he parted with god for God's sake, and yet God remained to him as God is in his own nature—not as he is conceived by anyone to be—nor yet as something yet to be achieved—but more as an "is-ness," as God really is. (*Meister Eckhart: A Modern Translation*, R. B. Blakney [New York: Harper & Brothers, 1941]: 204)

The story of creation is an ontological one: indeed, *the* ontological one. But we may surmise what the discovery, the disclosure of being may presuppose. It presupposes radical and willing acceptance of creatureliness on our part. It demands no less and no more of us than ourselves. Perhaps the blessing of mortality consists in this, that as mortality grows upon us it strengthens in us the intimation of what is demanded of us—no more and no less than ourselves. Perhaps this is the one thing we need to know; somehow, unmistakably, unerringly conveyed with the possibility of being as a self, and it must be conveyed as a demand as inescapable and it is incomprehensible and beyond our capacity to bear. Then, in so far as—in spite of ourselves, very likely—we are led, trapped, surprised into moments of unconditional assent and free consent in a mortal existence, we begin to discover the meaning of creation and of coming into the world as men; and the possibility of our part in this, as agents of creation, dialectically insinuates itself into the human will. Now one lives in question: Who is he, really? Does he really will what, somehow, he knows he must will? Namely, as Kierkegaard suggests: one thing. But what would one will in willing one thing? We might say, with Kierkegaard, the Good; or, with Buber, whatever in fact one is *able* to will unconditionally and with the whole soul, by way of contrast with double-minded, equivocal, and only seemingly decisive, namely *insistent* willing. But what is it one wills in so far as he wills univocally and decisively? It must be something unutterably simple that one wills in willing one thing, so simple, perhaps, as to seem like willing nothing at all; and that is just being. To will one thing is being patient of creation, to be willing to be with all creatures as creatures, even as the most creaturely of creatures oneself.

One really does not know what is happening, or what he is doing, or where it will lead. But perhaps it is not necessary to know, any more than it is necessary for us to live forever. What is really necessary is what really comes to pass. And it will come to pass, whether we are willing to or no, but not in a sense that we can make out independently of care. For care is what we are, and creation uniquely involves us as agents of creation in what necessarily comes to pass. If, as Thoreau says, we may learn to love the darkness no less than the light, we shall know that we do not live in vain and that what is necessary is not imposed upon us as a fate. It is simply and eternally to be done.

Wilderness in America

"Wilderness in *America*" (1974) constitutes Bugbee's most sustained reflection on the importance of wilderness: "ponder[ing] anew the potential significance [wilderness] might yet hold within the shaping of our destiny as a people."[1] Technological advancement and increasing bureaucratic intervention has led to the neglect of "the attenuated heritage of the wilderness tradition in America."[2] Wilderness, as primordial, speaks to us from a depth beyond "subsumption to human enterprise . . . and its voice will be heard anew only as we come in decisive forbearance into its presence."[3]

Bugbee draws attention to the possibility of a "more radical reckoning" vis-à-vis nature. In keeping with Bugbee's radically experiential orientation, experience of nature must exhibit *both* referential and reflexive axes: "One [must be] brought to realize that one is held in the embrace of what is proffered in its being proffered."[4] Bugbee offers this powerful account of the symbiotic relationship between wilderness and humankind:

> Together, the perceived and the perceiver enter into the working
> of the world. . . . In wilderness the partnership of man and nature
> dawns on our surmise—prior to all undertaking and use to which
> nature may lend. . . . A two-fold authorization, or sponsorship, of a
> pledging of ourselves in the relationship may obtain: At once salient
> in attention, there is the reach of nature as given—primordially
> given—yet given at the same time in *a receiving of the given reflex-*
> *ively sponsored from within a depth underwriting our ability to*
> *respond.*[5]

Echoing Thoreau, our task is become duly instructed in the majesty of nature. If our instruction goes deep enough, implications will be lifelong—

"destinate," as Bugbee liked to say—because "nature is with us more surely than we know."[6] But nature will be able to instruct us only if it is acknowledged and appreciated in its own right and on its own terms.

~

During recent months my reflections on wilderness have been worked and reworked through participation in hearings concerning the disposition of areas and rivers in the Northwest which might still be conceived wild. Attending to the testimony of hundreds, and attempting to formulate my own, I have strained to discern both the actual significance wilderness may hold for us in manifold ways and, more deeply, to ponder anew the potential significance it might yet hold within the shaping of our destiny as a people.

These hearings themselves have brought out a wracking incongruity of relatively recent origins: When Thoreau wrote "that in Wildness is the preservation of the World," he surely was not thinking of Wildness as being yarded and bounded in specified preserves. Yet more and more, of course, we have been forced to conceive wilderness lands under the rubric of conservation.

The deliberations of Thoreau's Westward Walking was not that of an excursion into an area *set aside* to remain in its natural state. The "West" he signified did not remain by man's decree, subject to regulations aimed at preserving it from human onslaught, or to quotas of scheduled access. "The unexplored forests and meadows" but for which he thought "our village life would stagnate" still sufficiently abounded *matter-of-factly* to obviate their holding tenure under the aegis of planning and deliberate disposition. Thus the recreative tonic of wildness was not about to be bottled and labeled as a recreational resource. And matter-of-factness in the style of human venturing amidst wild places was not yet massively invaded by self-consciousness searching for "the wilderness experience," even though eulogies of natural beauty and sublimity were popular among the cultivated.

Most widely, in Thoreau's time, the appeal was to venturesomeness, to setting out anew, to a break with convention in which life might have been constrained if not falsified, to exploration and discovery rich in promise of new beginnings and firmer foundations, to a testing of mettle in which a man might find himself and inherit a dignity proper to him. Wilderness offered invitation and opportunity for active undertaking on which the person might thrive and even communities might be founded. Its call was that of rallying men to enterprise, to work that might befit them, to a life to be instituted in conscious affirmation and not one merely acquiesced in as a matter of course.

Whatever one may say of the significance wilderness thus formerly assumed in this country, or of what came of response to its appeal to active engagement, we may note that its significance lay squarely in the mainstream of men's lives; and if not directly so with many, at least sufficiently so to become widely acknowledged and traditionalized in such a vein.

With the advance of the technological area and of bureaucratic management of human affairs, what is now left of *de facto* wilderness areas still does not present itself to some within the attenuated heritage of the wilderness tradition in America as continuous with human enterprise. The formerly seismic passion seems to linger strongest with those whose life's work is carried out in closest proximity to wilderness lands—"the back country," as it were. Out of their understanding of themselves in their work, these people tend to avow as an inalienable right the accessibility of the land to human enterprise and livelihood. And I think that to them the denial of this assumed right goes far deeper than an economic threat. One suspects that to them this denial seems maddeningly frivolous, an offence to manliness, and a contradiction of the significance which the land assumes at the center of a lived working relationship with it. You will perceive I am not talking about corporate interests or calculating exploitation, but about an attitude to be discerned in the passionate voices raised by individual persons close to the land—*against* the setting aside of wilderness sanctuaries subject to restrictions. However numerous or few these persons may be, it seems worth pondering the basic question they propound: the dilemma concerning wilderness in our time. If one respects their attestation that the land is to be truly met in the mainstream life and accordingly warrants unilateral accessibility of the land to human enterprise, one knows full well the attrition of what remains "undeveloped" to be expected under the ever-mounting demand for diminishing resources. This land too will be made captive to the dogma of multiple *use*, and those who cling so fiercely to keeping the land in the ambience of man's work in the world will awaken one day to their own irretrievable loss: the source of their very passion. Yet alternatively, in setting wilderness areas aside as inviolate, does one not inadvertently attenuate their very significance by removing them from the mainstream of life? Already in the very speaking surrounding the alternative, even among its fervent advocates, one may sense contradiction of the matter-of-factness but for which we fail to "stand right fronting and face to face to a fact"—in Thoreau's sense. As he warns, indeed,

> Very few men can speak of Nature . . . with any truth. They overstep her modesty, somehow or other, and confer no favor. They do not speak a good word for her. The surliness with which the woodchopper speaks of his woods, handling them as indifferently as his axe, is better than the mealy-mouthed enthusiasm of the lover of Nature. Better that the primrose by the river's brim be a yellow primrose, and nothing more, than that it be something else.

Yes, discretion in speaking is called for. Perhaps discretion would *preclude* trying to "speak a good word for nature." Yet wilderness may bear upon the possibility of discretion in speech—even upon the speaking carried on afar, in the far-flung sprawl of cities upon the land. From of old, in traditions vastly antedating that of the enterprising spirit in which our American forebears tended to respond to the land, a more deeply heeding attentiveness in the wilderness found sponsorship therein for a speaking that might yet hold for us commanding resonance—such speaking as one may hear, for example, in the Voice from the Whirlwind, on which Melville's ear was trained.

Speaking is potentiated in a listening through which we find ourselves addressed. From of old, genuinely destinate speech, awakening speech, seems to have come forth bred of the address in which wilderness played no small or accidental part. The very silence, the solitude, and the infinite manifestness of the place being germane to the speaking that might be called for—especially in those junctures of the lives of people from which men were singled out *in withdrawing to that distance* of the mainstream of life from which they might recollect themselves and submit to being placed in radical question. There, in turn, they knew themselves to receive life anew—as given to them. With all this, which no man made, given in foreverness— the measure of the hours, of the generations of mankind—in ancestral memory and progeniture.

Wilderness, it would seem, may lie closer to the whence of speaking than to the thematization of a speaking about. And deeper, then, than enterprise may fathom the significance thereof. For it would be in the abeyance of enterprise that one might find, might heed, the primordial address of the place in which the potential of speech may be trued and renewed.

If wilderness may yet speak to us and place us as respondents in the ambience of respect for the wild—for Nature as primordial—it must be liberated from ultimate subsumption to human enterprise. That is, its voice will be heard anew only as we come in decisive forbearance into its presence. Attentive listening, active receptivity, candor of spirit are the mood of the place. Or, as Kant might say: disinterested interest. I suggest wilderness is not to be understood as a place appropriated to human interests or to a special human interest. Its fundamental gift lies in the qualification of disinterestedness with which human interest requires to be informed. But for such qualification we tend to lapse into a wallow of anthropocentricity and suppose ourselves to be titular on the face of the Earth. Such was the supposition our Indian forebears simply could not understand: how could we assume a *proprietary right* over the land? What, indeed, could that mean? How could that which bears sacred power to man be obliterated in that capacity by an absolutized claim to exert a power of disposition over it?

Even for the Indian, when he lived so unobtrusively upon the land which owned him, wilderness seems to have afforded a measure of dialectical interplay with daily life—as an ultimate place of withdrawal, of purification, of fasting, of vigil, and of prayer. There if anywhere he might find himself addressed in a manner decisive at once for his own life and that of his people. His withdrawal, his removal from others in solitude, marked a suspension of normal pursuits and a bringing of the manifold of his cares into closer proximity with that sovereign spirit to which he felt himself to belong: gatherer of the world of fellow creatures and sustainer of the ancestral voices which might speak to him again; source of those promptings from which his whole life might take on direction more appropriate to it and which his own intentions and daily endeavors might have tended to dissipate, to inhibit, or to misconstrue. The dialectical interplay between such wilderness placement and the mainstream placement of everyday life was implicitly appreciated as something fundamental and not to be intruded upon by other members of the community. Correspondingly there was nothing ostentatious about either the withdrawal or the return. Others could understand what such a thing might mean and the discretion it would presuppose. The community carried wilderness in its heart and wilderness spoke to men in their solitude as bearers of the community as well. Even for the Indian, living in the immediacy and constancy of wilderness, it seems to have called for some measure of placement in withdrawal from everyday life. One might speak of this as a kind of sabbatical placement relative to the currency of everyday pursuits. Of course in everyday life, too, and seasonally as well, rituals of mindfulness, of acknowledgement, kept faith with the deliverances of solitude.

In the Indian cultures of former times, most salient of our consideration is the tradition of reverence and respect in which the land was received and acknowledged. Can it be that this is the vein in which wilderness requires of us that it be understood? And may it be that even the wilderness left to us is itself our vestigial hope of being instructed in such a vein? If so, by inverse proportion the need of the instruction increases as the opportunity for it decreases. And the opportunity decreases by reason of the want of instruction. To the extent that we may be far down the road of such a progression, it would follow that the essential significance of wilderness in American life may be as critical as obliviousness to it may be prevalent.

The pervasive culture seems to be in dialectical *contrariety* to a wilderness ethos. Technology may be the mechanical embodiment—the vehicle—of that culture, seemingly endowed with overwhelming autonomy. Yet the language of culture betrays the underlying human stance: the claimant's stance, speaking in terms of want and use, resources at our disposal, the exertion of control, the projection of goals, and the humanly conferred status of "values." The language itself is programmed and consumerized, accomplishing a packaging and marketing of meaning in banalized form. A "processing" of meaning has tended to supplant responsibility for meaning, and human communication has become a problem to which techniques of solution are sought. Feeling, having become subjectivized, is one thing, and thought, having become objectivized, is another—rendering thoughtful commitment an anomaly hardly to be recognized, let alone carried out. Yet everywhere rights are asserted and demands are pressed, and accountability has become a watchword of the day. Responsibility is chiefly what one insists upon from others, and quantitative measurement of how they are measuring up would get us down to the brass tacks. For oneself there is the central possibility of a life of one's own to do with as one pleases, in exchange for an abstract concession that others are like-minded about this and will expect not to be interfered with in the right they likewise claim to jurisdiction over their own lives. And isn't property, too, the embodiment of that claim? Indeed it is a property claim, through and through.

What, then, of lands not owned by private and corporate interests? They come under public ownership and the mediation of government jurisdiction. In the aspect of property, nonetheless, they are subsumed under right of use. One has the right to use public land as he pleases so long as his exercise of that right does not conflict with that of other users. The values for the sake of which a person uses such land remain his own business; let him use it for what he gets out of it. Some get aesthetic values. Some get economic values. Some get recreational values. Some get religious values. Some get wilderness values. That's the package. And the public buys it so long as human uses and value-profits are kept equitably distributed, and the resources made use of are not getting scarce. While the uses and corresponding values remain the business of those concerned in them, the disposition of the public land requires a neutral managerial stance in arbitrating to accommodate competing uses and values. The weighting of uses and values is to be adjudicated according to the numbers of their respective adherents and advocates. And what if a comparatively few were to claim large tracts as appropriate to their peculiar use and values at the expense of excluding a host of others with their uses and values? Where interest confers status on the land, what a high-handed lockout that would be. In such terms the keeping of wilderness would seem tantamount to an arbitrary transferal of public property to the status of the private property of a very few—even if unspecified persons. A selfish self-appointed elite, no doubt who want the land all to themselves. In an age when the very resources on which our way of life depends are in shrinking supply and in increasing demand, is someone going to have the temerity to pose *wilderness* as a scarce resource? Why, the very category of resource commits one by implication to development of it, and to pose wilderness as a resource implying the contrary would carry contradiction to the point of perversity indeed. Such is the embarrassment of the Forest Service when called upon to manage land by leaving it alone, a *reductio ad absurdum* and emasculation, it would seem, of this managerial agency. No, it would be difficult for this agency of ours to represent us in a capacity other than that of handmaiden of development. Even to enforce a measure of restraint in this capacity has often placed it at odds with the thrust of a "culture of values," for which economic development is the underlying and dominant character of our orientation and destiny, setting the very categories of our thought and speech.

Of what significance, then, can wilderness be—in dialectical *contrariety* with such a culture? Well, it can give the lie to it. It can extend, now and then, its elemental emissaries to shores, to suburbs, to the folks downriver, to throngs in airports, to the passengers of balked transports, to the breadbasket of America, to swaying buildings and empty streets. In pelting downpours, the reach of sky, the weathering willy-nilly impartial to all, the crawling of ants, the cry of gulls and the caw of crows, the rankness of weeds, the silence of snow. Perhaps too in occasional revels Dionysus comes, and the wild is revived in the human frame, the fibers of life plucked to the wild strain. The stirring of barnyard fowl to their migrating kin. God save us, then, 'ere there be life in us yet. May we struggle the birth of tongues of our own and derive our words as we use them in from the wild stock. As we may yet believe "that a tide rises and falls behind every man which can float the British Empire like a chip, if he should ever harbor it in his mind." Our very dreams might suggest the hidden bulk of the wild which is immolated by our day. And the culture *contrary* to the wild may prove after all, though cloying, to be made of feeble stuff, able to pass itself off only in our waking sleep; some pantomime of life, a common dream, mumbled in unison by an endless crowd.

Need the awakening be rude? Or might it be graced by some gentleness and simplicity? That would seem to depend on each one, who must determine in his heart whether he will be party to claiming ownership of life, thus to remain the slave of compulsion, rigidified in the conflicts of control, anxiously demanding, stultified in imagination, and ungenerous toward life itself. Not just in getting and spending, but in passing time, too, there is fostered the sense of the world running out, tending into vacuousness, a deathly trend. Apocalyptic visions only dramatize the sense of the affair.

A more radical reckoning and a more thoughtful way seem to be gaining upon us, if even in spite of ourselves. The revulsions of younger people are telling signs. They clearly do not subscribe to the propertied life. They seem prepared to do with less without feeling deprived. The quality of lived relationships concerns them far more than the setting and achieving of goals of accomplishment. And it is above all among the young that a new sense of the land seems to be gathering force. They can understand what it might mean to renounce the titular stance in relation with the land. When they speak at these wilderness hearings, as so many of them have, they speak almost univocally of places and creatures having claim upon us to be recognized in their own right. Their plea is not to appropriate a few pristine places to themselves but, here and there, to acknowledge what is thus given us in a manner appropriate to it, with gratitude, with forbearance, with respect, in a more liberal frame of mind akin to sacrifice. For them wilderness is the stronghold of a new ethos upon the land, working in dialectical *complementarity* with the full range of the relationships and activities in which we may stand.

Yet, how could it be that a place might hold such force? Only, it would seem, in some radical way—positioning us, as it were, with respect to our involvement in reality, as a matter to be resolved. No doubt our situation is always implicitly a metaphysical affair. But wilderness, to the extent that it will not permit one to take one's surroundings for granted, is a place which will not let one off the metaphysical hook. At the same time it establishes us in such decisively lived relationship with our surroundings that it precludes subsumption of the lived relationship to any depictive representation of how we are situated in relation to our surroundings, for example in ecological terms. We are not there as seen by ourselves, as parts within a whole. No, we are there as on the spot with respect to the meaning of what we behold. How does nature speak to our concern? That is the question. And the relationship is one of participation in what occurs, the presencing of heaven-and-earth and all that abounds therein. One is brought to realize that one is held within the embrace of what is proffered in its being proffered. No behind or beyond the things themselves. Therefore no understanding of their presencing in the mode of a comprehension of it. From within the lived relationship in which the presencing occurs must arise the *sense* of the occurrent, if at all. The givens of life are laid down. The foundations of the world are laid. Things are in place and stand firm. Beings stand forth on their own. They do not ask our leave. They invite mutuality. That measure of trust. If one agrees to live with them, rather than summarily to reduce them to the service of intention. In contrast with the subordination of attention to intention, to be intent in attending is to give heed, and therein the perceived may work evocatively, to cumulative effect. Together, the perceived and the perceiver enter into the working of the world: things in their meaning as responded to, taking shape. In wilderness the partnership of man and nature dawns on our surmise—prior to all undertaking and use to which nature may lend. The partnership seems to be a dialogic affair, in which we are charged with responsibility in the way things come to mean, having been placed in that way. Even as the things of the place command attention in the presence of the world they are discovered to us from within the depth of responsiveness in confirmation of our mutuality with them. Reflexively we acknowledge ourselves in promissory relation with the given, even as the given warrants our full attention. A two-fold authorization, or sponsorship, of the pledging of ourselves in the relationship seems to obtain: At once salient in attention, there is the initiative of the reach of nature as given—primordially given—yet given at the same time in a receiving of the given reflexively sponsored from within a depth underlying our own ability to respond. Thus nature jumps with the responsive soul on the strength of a power imparted in unison to both. Its grace is twofold and affords the foundation of respect, which is in turn at once respect for beings as given in attention and—reflexively—self-respect. In this fashion we are ordained in responsible relationship with beings given into our keeping in the very presencing of the world. The mystery of this, it would seem, can only deepen, and with its deepening enhance the sense the world might make. But one is charged to make good on that sense, and in the mainstream of human destiny within which its implications require to be worked out—within the full gamut of ambiguities, of perplexities, and of anguish that prevail in the received world. Primordial placement again and again requires to be worked out in the flux of our historical and communal placement, in our shared participation in the lived world. But what has been found meaningful asks to be shared in the lived world, in a bringing forth of consciousness, in a speaking it both sponsors and calls for, in a finding of embodiment. True solitude is a wellspring of communal life; its return affords measure of what has become of communal life, perhaps most closely in the dissipation of one's own resolutions, the forgetting of one's whence and whitherto. For wilderness puts our standard of living to the test. What can stand to the mutuality of man and nature can be affirmed in the relations between men. What cannot stands to exposure as scurf. And without respect for nature man cannot stand, not even in the mutual regard of men. For it is in coming to know creatures as such that respect for them can obtain as warranted and upheld. One's fellow men as well come to one in solitude, for how else should one come forth to greet them, knowingly, and by way of confirmation of that in which we share?

Neither the proportion of time one may spend there nor the numbers for whom it figures in direct encounter would seem indicative of the potential significance of wilderness for the quality of human life. If its instruction goes deep its implications are lifelong, and only with long discipline, it seems, does one commence to fathom the instruction received. That discipline may well be as intensely an affair of embodiment as it can become one of reflection. The sea and the land we walk are prolongations of the task. Again and again it is as if one first gets the feel of the matter simply in movement and the coursing of breath and blood, the working of a frame of mind, a disposition sent in quest of forms appropriate to its explicitation and the realization of what is asking to be born. Incipient gestures are fledged in fumbling speech, fragile winged and fleeting. But permission is granted to participate in the world, and nature invites it. To breathe, to walk, to sleep, to rise, to eat and to drink; to talk. In all of these, of our daily doing, the style of nature may qualify our life—with some measure of primordial simplicity, so unobtrusively withal as to escape notice quite. That nature is with us more surely than we know seems sure. Out of a very piety of the body some places might be kept sacred to us. They will bless the lands in which we dwell. But nothing can bless us apart from being acknowledged in its own right.

PART

III

Unpublished Writings

The Revolution in Western
Thought: Another Step (1962)

"The Revolution in Western Thought: Another Step" was written in response to Huston Smith's "The Revolution in Western Thought."[1] Smith
argued that the twentieth century must lead to "genuinely new epochs
in human thought . . . and this change, which is still in process, we of the
current generation are playing a crucial but as yet not widely recognizable part."[2] Contemporary theories of science have "crashed through the
cosmology which seventeenth-to-nineteenth-century constructed as if
through a sound barrier, leaving us without replacement."[3] As witnessed
in the wake of the Copernican Revolution, "modern physics shows us a
world at odds with our senses. . . . Instead [contemporary theories of real-
ity] appear to point to a radical disjunction between the way things behave
and every possible way in which we might try to visualize them."[4]

A similar problem exists in philosophy: "The clearest evidence of this
is the collapse of what historically has been philosophy's central discipline: objective metaphysics, the attempt to discover what reality really
consists of and the most general principles which describe the way its
parts are related . . . For 2500 years philosophers have argued over which
metaphysical system is true. For them to agree that none is, *is* a new
departure."[5] The movement broadly associated with the phrase "existential philosophy" grew through increased recognition of the important
insight that:

> [T]o be human precludes in principle the kind of impartial and
> objective overview of things—the view of things as they are in
> themselves, apart from our differing perspectives—that metaphys-
> ics has always sought . . . [T]he existentialist's way toward this goal

97

[of complete metaphysical understanding] does not consist in trying to climb out of his skin in order to arise to Olympian heights from which things can be seen with complete objectivity and detachment. Rather it consists in centering down on [one's] own inwardness until he finds within it what he is compelled to accept and can never get away from. In this way he, too, arrives at what he judges to be necessary and eternal. But necessary and eternal *for him*. What is necessary and eternal for everyone is so impossible for a man to know that he wastes time making the attempt.[6]

For Smith, this change in perspective leads to a historical juncture of reflexive significance:

What it will be like cannot at this juncture be surmised . . . The most that can be ventured is . . . that its order will be recognized as partially imposed by man's mind and not just passively mirrored within it. The order will not describe reality as it exists in itself apart from us. Instead it will describe an ellipse in which man in its entirety—his purposes and feelings as well as his intellect—stands as one focus in balance and tension with its complementing focus: the cosmos in which his life is set and against which his destiny must be enacted.[7]

Bugbee read Smith's essay carefully and his response echoes several perennial themes of his own philosophy: the importance of an experientially based metaphysics, the reflexive (elliptical) nature of experience and reflection, as well as the need to recover the sense of mystery essential to all forms of experience.[8]

∾

It is only because there is an inescapable finality about our lives that we are able to enjoy real joy and real sorrow, of real despair and real hope, of radical loyalty and radical betrayal; that we can be superficial, reckless, or that we can detest ourselves. One cannot avoid living in such a way that his or her life is at stake, in the sense that what that life signifies and how it shapes up, in the end, is what we each come down to. And somehow, what that life signifies—ultimately, is just that which is required of us.

In this sense our lives assume the characteristic of an account we render: To live humanly is to give account of oneself. I do not mean particularly in so far as we set ourselves to take stock of what we stand for or to explain ourselves. I mean now something more primordial and unevadable than this: Our hours, our days, years, our doing and speaking throughout, are rich or poor, faltering or firm, dense or vacuous with respect to the significance to which we actually bear witness—the significance, quite simply, of the things and people and events with which we have to do and their cumulative force within the span of our lives.

Even as we laugh or weep, are bored or buoyant, play or work, stay or resign ourselves, doubt or ponder, make promises, take adversities, and so on—in all these, our ways, we move and are moved in the dimension of the significance of things, of people, of events, of undertakings, of our situation; and so, ineluctably, we commit ourselves to some sense of relevance in whatever we are doing. Always situated in a way potentiating and exacting relevance on our part, some venturing on what may be at stake, we have no recourse but to orient ourselves appreciatively in our situation, however adequately or inadequately that may be.

It is in the mode of appreciation, then, that we are at a loss to find ourselves, that we become concentrated or diffuse, alert or indolent, firm or infirm, flexible or calcified, and that our cumulative sense of reality is formed.

Accordingly, I am going to speak of the person and of reality—correlatively, in advancing on the current situation in Western thought. First, in speaking of appreciation as the quick of the person—as that through which we are founded or failing, located or dislocated, fulfilled or unfulfilled—I mean this quite simply as it is suggested in the Book of Job. Here in this narrative appreciation is reckoned with in a decisive way; as the one and ultimate thing needful, with respect to which our essential transition and transfiguration may take place. With the way things come to Job in the appreciation of them to which he comes—all unexpectedly, he is clarified with respect to himself as having been wanting just with respect to *that*, namely, in appreciation. And manifestly, here, the decisive mode of appreciation is an awakening, a quickening of the person in his relationship with things into a placing of himself with them in reality.

With the everyday availability of things, their accessibility so much as a matter of course, with our deeply grooved and familiar ways with them, how readily—as a matter of course—we take them for reality in themselves. On this persuasion, one can simply take reality for granted, for it will always appear to him as merely

as identical with the things that are patent for him. Such an her-
metically sealed persuasion, however, does not take seriously and
thoughtfully one's own manifold relationship with these very things
in its bearing on how reality might turn out in the fruition of that
relationship, in so far as the potentiality of that relationship were
to deepen and mature, within the span and conditions qualifying a
mortal life.

Let us grant that reality would involve things, yes visible, tangible,
thinkable, describable things, indeed things with which we have to
do in a whole manifold of ways hardly suggested by calling attention
to our seeing, touching, thinking, and describing. Let us suppose, too,
that they enjoy a certain independence of us: that even as they stand
out toward us, offering themselves in and for our appreciation, they
also stand away from us, to the effect that we may appreciate them as
foci of inexhaustible perspectives, and accept the measure of contingency in any actual perspective of them we may take up. Indeed let
us stress this very independence of us on the part of things as likely
to lie at the base of the most profound significance they may hold in
relationship with us and for appreciation. It invites—I would say—it
calls upon us to open ourselves to them in appreciation, and so to assume our place with them in a reality that can be genuinely concrete.
Now that reality, I submit, would necessarily be—and would require
to be thought as—a reality obtaining for things and for us, conjointly,
in and through our relationship with them. It would be that in which
we might come to share with them through the actual relationship
establishing us together—in reality. The concreteness of the real is
the cue to which I suggest we must hold.

What can it mean? The expression itself means literally a growing together, from the Latin *con-crescere*. Now what kind of growing together of things in our relationship with them can occur to
which appreciation would find itself germane in essence? It would
have to occur in the dimension in which we have to do with things,
in which we move and are moved in active relationship with them:
that is the dimension of the significance things may come to assume
for us. Therefore I am suggesting that concrete reality with respect
to things would be a matter of their growing together in significance:
significance which we may *find* appreciatively only in and through
the fullness of relationship with them as that in which we may *be*
concretely. And we also, we would find ourselves, and find ourselves
as founded in that which is coming to pass—in so far as what is
coming to pass is a growing together of things in significance on *the*

strength of which we might decisively orient ourselves as active and responsible beings with respect to them, and with respect to one another. This, indeed, would be world orientation; for it would be the coming to pass of a world inseparable from the enfoldment of things and ourselves in it, and the unfolding of each as each and all as all in it. Perhaps we may say, then, that the ideal limit of concrete reality would be participation in the world as a plenum of significance in the fullness of time.

Could that be now? Was it ever? Will it ever be? Or is it rather an infinite potentiality of reality in which all times and places and things and people are susceptible of realization? "World without end . . . "

What we have to fathom is our being here with things and one another as it may bear on our intent, and as the shaping of our intent may bear on the cumulative character of the way in which we are with them and with one another. Now in what way are we conjoined with things and with one another? Precisely in the manner of a *way*, I think: temporally, dynamically, transitionally, transformably, admitting of concrete realization, always a way in the making. It never lags in what has been made; it never leaves of being in the making. Therefore I suggest that everything we grasp in the mode of fact is only abstractly appreciated—let the facts in question be as specific and as patent as you please—in so far as we miss the sense of fact as that which happens and appears as done, *factum*, in the course of a way that is in the making, in which we too, always here and now, are presently and questionably involved, in which we are caught up, mindfully or not, and must perpetually work out our *way*, with things and with one another.

If we hold by reality as concrete, as coming to pass in a growing together of the things and persons involved in it, then we may enter upon the realization of things and persons prepared to recognize it— through the mask of vaunted fact—as a matter of common destiny, to be lived as such, in the utterly mysterious partnership of fellow creatures. The fulfillment of our part in this could hardly mean a patterning of ourselves on any ideal image or way of life we might strain to appropriate. It must mean rather that we actually take our way upon ourselves, opening ourselves to the things and people we contingently encounter, as they single us out, in the circumstances and events in which we happen to be moving, so that constancy in their cumulative significance may prove the rooting of us in concrete reality and come to prevail even in the events of everyday life.

I would call this, more simply, a matter of being patient of creation, even unto the discovery of our being in the world with things and persons as fellow creatures.

The times of such discovery seem to be those in which we are able to do what we mean and mean what we do, whatever we happen to be going about doing. The imperatives of life do not slacken. They quicken and simplify themselves into the indicative mood. For even so—simply—in being—the dispensation of life with things and one another, is received in appreciation, without distraction.

In nothing short of that participation in concrete reality, that coming into the fullness of the world with things, can decisive reason, sense, or raison d'être be found for things or persons. But the touchstone of such reality is that simple being in and of creation is itself the sense of the matter.

What comes first with respect to temporal existence does not lend itself to thought in the self-confounding formula of an event with which time—once upon a time—began. What comes first, logically, we move toward the discovery of with the deepening of our existence in time and with time; namely the discovery in and of that existence as making sense in the way of creation, in the continuous coming into the world together of things and persons in an ineffably destinate way, gathering all together with ineluctable sureness and constancy, forever and evermore. In so far as we become permeated with the way of the world even to the point where it bursts in on us as in a dawn of fire, touching decisively the things and persons gathered up in it, with that radiance of being in which we truly are, then we instantaneously "begin with time." From that beginning heaven and earth and all that is therein may be recognized as coming into the world with a certain fittingness, simultaneously with the disposition of ourselves. Since that disposition is received in the act of appreciation, however, what is given in and for it, salient in attention, are all the things whose names burst from our lips, given unto our keeping, to be lived with: in the manner of heeding, minding, tending, caring for—giving careful attention to them, even in use; with patience for the issue of our time.

The Revolution: Connecting Analysis

Now, how we are going to connect these suggestions of the possibility of thinking concrete reality as creation with some of the crucial features of our current situation in Western thought?

To begin in positive terms, it seems to me that the epochal promise held out for the shaping of thought in our age is that of subordinating thought to concrete appreciation, so that it may serve and enhance and more nearly interpret such appreciation rather than attempt to dictate to it from one or another of the manifold phases and moments of abstraction, whatever their relative legitimacy.

Now we may say in a general way that to think is to always abstract, in multiple respects, no doubt, and shifting with the mode of thought. To consider at all is to focus on that which is taken under consideration, and by making of it a matter of explicit thought, one cuts it off and demarcates it as explicit from implicit and background elements of the situation in which the thinking is being done. The intentional way in which we situate ourselves in thinking is also a controlling factor making for abstraction in thought. What matters, however, is the sense of what one is doing in one's thinking, by which one places relevance of a mode of thought within the conditions and the intention governing the abstraction. Without such presence of mind concerning the modes of thought in which we engage we tend to be taken in by the abstraction they involve. Therefore the point is not, quixotically, to try to do away with abstraction in thinking, or thoughtlessly to turn against thinking, but to make it serve and enhance appreciation as best it may through exercising a central concern not to be taken in by abstraction. And this means, in part, to effect thoughtfully a recognition of those factors governing the more or less limited relevance of our modes of thought.

Now the thought we take in the interest of such recognition is peculiarly reflective and critical. It must reckon in particular with the liability most constant and least obvious in our thinking—the tendency to arrogate unthinkingly to modes of thought in which we become immersed and habituated a relevance—even an exhaustive relevance—which the factors of abstraction obtaining in the situation cannot bear out.

Most crucially of all, however, critical reflection is called for by what we might call the kind of presumptive—but not necessarily presumptuous attitude tending to consolidate at the core of human undertakings, implicitly qualifying the stance from which we are taking persons and things into some kind of thoughtful account, and qualifying their standing for us in that mode of thought by which we are taking them into account. We come of age philosophically only when we accept this uneasy task as fundamentally a work of self-critical reflection. For no one can escape the pertinence of the question: In what attitude am I taking my stand and orienting my-self in the very act of interpreting and estimating what lies at the bottom of whatever mode of thought I am considering?

The momentousness of ours—the "Atomic Age"—is that we are each and all first-personally haunted with peculiar urgency by the substance of this question. We sense it in the profound irony that with the rapid and immense strides being taken in scientific and technological thought, we are ourselves nonetheless in an extraordinarily uneasy position with respect to ourselves, the significance of our lives, our standing as potential human individuals, in our relations with one another; yes, and in our relationship with the non-human, too—with the very things we treat in terms of unparalleled possibilities of control.

This predicament, upon which I will not dwell, is potentially salutary for Western thought. For it demands reflective interpretation above all, articulated upon a sense of human existence as responsible, first-personally grasped and assumed as such, and only in the way that it is possible, namely—reflexively and in the act in which we actually are. In working out that reflexive grasp of myself as a responsible being, assuming my existence with things and others as such, and in that alone, may it happen that I ground myself for thinking in which I can come to take measure of those modes of thought in which I take up the stance of a knowing subject thinking about objects.

Now that is precisely the stance that has dominated modern Western thought. It is the stance notably developed in the 17th Century, from which the thinking embodied in the modern sciences became possible. But it is also the stance which was concurrently taken up in philosophical thought. Indeed reflective definition of this stance, assuming it as an authoritative point of departure, has been the main generative concern of modern philosophy as an epochal movement of thought. In one way or another the objective standpoint has ruled modern reflective thought, most deeply as the presumptive attitude governing the way issues have been conceived, questions formulated, and priority assigned in dealing with them.

The revolution quietly and unobtrusively taking place in Western thought is not fundamentally of revolutionary development within the range and application of objective thinking—as organized and epitomized in the sciences and in technology. Nor does it consist in the shift and expansion of the focus of objective thinking to include man and his institutions and affairs within its purview—at the other pole of an ellipse with nature, so to speak. It is not a revolution in thought to be differentiated with reference to any field of objects yielding its subject-matter with which it is directly and self-forgetfully occupied, holding out the possibility of manipulation and control which companions objective thinking.

It is, quite simply, a revolution in reflective thought animated in and attuned within the first-personal relationship actually and ultimately obtaining between persons and whatever they may be said to encounter. Now whereas it is a requirement of objective thinking that the thinker subject himself—we might say—discount himself and his concerns in what he makes of the things he is thinking about, the radical task of reflective thought requires the reflexive appreciation of concerned selfhood in the activity of thought brought to bear in situational and relational thinking with respect to things and persons, places and times, with which we have to dwell reflectively. Such a task forces the thinker to realize himself on the spot as human, with all the liabilities he incurs as such, subordinating—though not dismissing as irrelevant—all competencies he may deliberately develop and bring to the task, including what he may objectively know.

Reflection animated on a sense of responsibility on which its peculiar issues hinge is quite a different matter from thought addressing itself to a "field" in a professional way. It cannot settle down into methods and procedures which structure and sustain its relevancy. All the more reason is to be found in this connection for being versed in the history of reflective thought, as a shared enterprise, which it behooves a reflective thinker consciously to inherit. There is no appeal for the emendation of human reflection outside of the encounter of reflective minds—or rather, of reflective men. The more deeply we can understand the reflective thought of other men, as they are historically placed, the more confirmation we earn in our own reflection. Therefore the measure of the revolution in Western thought is likely to be taken in the power of appreciation it brings to bear in dialogue with reflective men of the past; these men, not only of the West, but of the East, require of us to be more deeply understood.

And the thinkers who may most pertinently discipline our ear if we are newly to inherit the reflective task are those who have spoken of men and things out of a strong sense of being called upon as men. For it is only in and through vocational engagement with things and one another that we discover ourselves in reality—*according* to this, our authentic mode of being in it, with things and with one another.

In the end, it is concrete reality we are accountable for in thoughtful speech. In thoughtful speech concrete reality may consent to dwell. Indeed, things themselves may come to rejoice in it as "when the morning stars sang together, and all the sons of God shouted for joy" (Job 38:7).

But we are questioned, and we must declare ourselves. This is the step to be taken, again and again, Beneath and sustaining the radical reflective task into which we may move there is yet a more intimate, silent, communal, and decisive mode of that: That is mediation. Or: That is prayer.

Nature and a True Artist (n.d.)

"Nature and a True Artist" explores the intimate line of continuity between humankind and the world of nature. Bugbee was deeply convinced that nature primordially proffers itself through an experience of resistance, contributing to "an activity but for which [we] would neither realize (nor discover) an essential agreement with nature. 'A true artist' [can] only be forged in and through the activity in which such agreement is brought to pass." In this important sense, one's relationship to nature consists of "reciprocal strengthening" and "mutual support"—a potentiating experience offering the possibility of transfiguration on behalf of both self and world.

According to Bugbee, the primitive character of nature does not exhaust its depth. Purposeful action that is artistic must seek to transmute—instead of transcribe nature:

> [W]e carry nature with us, taken up into a possible world. Through us, too, then, nature comes to participate in historical existence. Reality is the direction in which the work tends, and not its point of departure. Yet nature, as point of departure is not left behind in so far as the work comes off. Rather it seems to be more nearly realized.

As beings rooted in nature, our charge is to "transmute our sustenance at the root upward into the stem, branch, leaf and flower of human existence." Now viewed as the reflexive counterpart of human awareness, our relationship to nature no longer remains "*merely* natural." Anticipating the thesis of Bill McKibben's *The End of Nature*, Bugbee writes: "Reality, for us, cannot be taken in abstraction from what we do with

107

nature."[1] While this is surely a historical process, Bugbee emphasizes that historicity need not imply ethical relativism or the destruction of the environment. Historical existence occurs *in the modality of meaning*: "In so far as concrete reality *is*, the force of this *is* can be at once in the indicative and the imperative mood: it would be a destinate affair." Philosophical reflection must not let "representation of 'things of nature' tyrannize any attempt to interpret 'the nature' of things." Creation is a process of concrete realization in which reality comes to pass. It is "not nature but *creation* [that] makes itself told."

~

I do not stand helpless before nature any longer, as I used to do.

Nature always begins by resisting the artist, but he who really takes it seriously does not allow himself to be led astray by that resistance; on the contrary, it is a stimulus the more to fight for the victory. At bottom nature and a true artist agree. But nature certainly is "intangible"; yet one must seize it, and that with a strong hand. I do not mean to say that I have reached that point already; no one thinks it less than I do, but somehow I get on better. (From a letter written by Vincent van Gogh to his brother, Theo during April, 1881; see *Dear Theo*, p. 63)

The resistance here in question, the overcoming of it, and the realization of "agreement" of man and nature: these seem to be recognizable "moments" or elements of the sublime—that is, of concrete and destinate reality.

Nature is that element to which primitiveness clings. There is a "firstness" about it, the element of initial presentation. One does not go behind it to something more original, and no good trying. In fact "he who really takes it seriously" starts from and with nature. Now in doing so, the suggestion is, he meets with resistance, but also his seriousness is sustained, and may lead him into an activity but for which he would neither realize (nor discover) an essential agreement with nature. "A true artist" could only be forged in and through the activity in which such agreement is brought to pass. If in such activity nature figures in the mode of resistance, surely it must also figure potentiatingly, too, with respect to that activity and man's undertaking of it.

What comes "first," of course, can't be construed as nature-pure-and-simple. For it is a polarity of experience: nature as that which occupies attention, and as presented in attention. If we take nature as that which offers or proffers itself to us, posed with respect to our possible response, perhaps we will be on the right track. Yes, no doubt we are already and necessarily responsive in so far as we receive nature attentively at all. Yet we may distinguish a moment of active responsiveness that has a "secondness" about it relative to the moment of nature-in-attention in its "firstness." The distinction may be somewhat analogous to that between attentive listening and then replying in a conversation. Reverting to the idiom of van Gogh, the activity of the true artist supervenes upon nature-held-in-serious-and-steadfast-attention. The artist must bestir himself to do something about (and on the strength of) that which initially occurs in the appreciation of nature. In someway it would seem that nature requires of him that he do something with it and on the strength of it. And what he has to do is somehow to "take it up" into a work, to put it into a work. The work itself must define and make good the requirement it meets. Perhaps it is only through such responsive works that nature's silence can be understood as calling for anything. True works reveal that they are called for.

Thirdly: through essential activity, as touched upon, I believe, in van Gogh's notion of "a true artist," man and nature receive transfiguration; only *within* such emergent transfiguration could we develop appropriate understanding of the theme van Gogh suggests: "At bottom nature and a true artist agree." Beauty is the intimation of that harmony; the sublime is that veritable harmony itself.

So construed, beauty seems to be our strongest clue to reality.

"To study from nature, to wrestle with reality—I do not want to do away with it for years and years. I should not like to have missed that *error*. One starts with a hopeless struggle to follow nature, and everything goes wrong; one ends by calmly creating from one's palette, and nature agrees with it and follows. But these two contrasts do not exist separately. The drudging, though it may seem in vain, gives an intimacy with nature, a sounder knowledge of things" (*Dear Theo*, pp. 363–64).

"And we are enabled to apprehend at all what is sublime and noble only by perpetual instilling and drenching in the reality that surrounds us." (Thoreau, *Walden*, New York: Modern Library, 1937, p. 87.)

Intimacy with nature, sound knowledge of things—these are ever presupposed and indefinitely susceptible to enrichment. Without profound intimacy with nature we must miss the calling and the impetus which can carry nature into the work she requires of us. Without the firm knowing of things they cannot discipline us to the task, they cannot carry through into that transfiguration which would be the transfiguration of nature herself. That knowing of things is at least part of the strong hand with which van Gogh says nature must be seized.; but one may also say that a sound knowledge of things is a reciprocal strengthening and mutual support in which we and things offering themselves to be known are established in the potentiality for concrete reality.

Nature taken up in intimacy and that knowing of things, however, is primitive. And though we must deepen and extend our rooting, our groundedness in nature, we utterly mistake the situation if we take, or seek to take, the primitive orientation of our existence as exhaustive, as standard of itself. We exist from and out of such innocence, constantly nurtured in it even as a continuing *element* of our existence; but continually life transmutes the innocence which like an atmosphere lies the more densely about the primitive polarity of experience; for example, at the wells of sensibility. Responsibility transmutes innocence; in assuming the former we are tending out of and beyond the latter. And in doing so we carry nature with us, taken up into a possible world. Through us, too, then, nature comes to participate in historical existence.

What might be the *error* of the artist having studied from nature and wrestled with it for years and years? Surely not at all a matter of inaccuracy pertaining to those studies. Faithfulness to nature might appear a matter of transcription, as if nature were reality ready-made. But in the long and arduous experience of the artist's faithfulness to nature, while presupposing precise and ardent attention in the form of studies from nature, turns out to be an accession of nature to metamorphosis in the work of art. Reality is the direction in which that work tends, and not its point of departure. Yet nature, as "point of departure," is not left behind in so far as the work comes off. Rather, it seems to be more nearly realized.

As blood in our veins, as air in our lungs, as ambient atmosphere bathing our skins, as food in our stomachs, as appetition welling up in us, as the exfoliation of sensibility, as the rhythm of exertion and repose, as the capacity of movement through which we come knowingly in touch with things, as rapport with day and night and seasons, as the beating of our hearts, nature enunciates herself in us and lays claim upon our lives. Our bodily being roots us in nature, ensuring the primitive polarity of our experience—though not our degree or quality of alertness or animation at the root.

Optimally, however, nature is music and dance in human life: Our natural powers are plunged in mutual play with all that primitively engages our active attention. We wake and sleep to her rhythms, stir and move to her cycles, heed, acknowledge, relish her offerings and promptings. And if we but trust in her with the fiber and sinew of our being, so much of which is nature herself in us, she does not betray us.

And yet . . . Trust in nature cannot mean leaning on her or merely relinquishing ourselves into the keeping of the natural. Much less can the elemental, the primitive in life come to its own by a turning back on it: a reversion. To trust nature is to live *from* the primitive, to take it up into life; not to fall back upon it. If our confidence in the primitive is justified, we can only discover and confirm it to be so as we transmute our sustenance "at the root" upward into the stem, branch, leaf, and flower of human existence. Since this is a re-sponsible existence, however, the image of natural growth for what may happen in the course of it must be taken guardedly indeed.

Our appreciation of nature and of our participation in nature seems to hold a rather decisive clue for interpreting our position with respect to her. As natural beings we are born and we die. Our status as natural beings in this—as in other respects—is taken up into awareness, so that what is and remains natural about our lives in this respect, their beginning and coming to an end, cannot remain *merely* natural. Perhaps we should say that a *mortal* existence is already a transmutation of nature, and a transmutation of nature which calls for being undertaken as such. Reality, for us, cannot be nature taken in abstraction from what we do with nature. It must be of the order of situational and historical occurrence, in which na-ture is essentially ingredient, and our own action as well necessarily contributory.

If nature admits of being taken up into human life in the course of all we have to do with nature, we may construe what happens as throughout an inflection of her meaning engendered in historical existence. Indeed we may say that her meaning is at stake in and through our existence as something to be worked out, established, resolved. Her meaning happens in the course of our doings; she enters into that meaning and is qualified by it; not in the mode of what we are wont to represent to ourselves as "natural phenomena," but *in the modality of meaning*. Even such representation itself, no less than other inflections of her meaning, *occurs* historically, *in* the modality of meaning. As entering into the modality of meaning nature may grow concrete; that is, "the things of nature" gain possible accession to concrete reality, a growing together in which they become established in a world. Concrete reality, then, is accordingly being conceived as *occurring*, and occurring in the modality of meaning. We may therefore say that in so far as concrete reality *is*, the force of this *is* can be at once in the indicative and the imperative mood: it would be a destinate affair.

We have noted the patent etymological commitment to the effect that reality has to do with things: it conjures with "thinghood." An implication of the line of thought we are following is that we must be on our guard in thinking of "the things of nature." As so thought, the "things" we may have in mind, taken in the way we have them in mind, may be something less than concrete things. Things-in-their-beauty, for example, are nearer concrete thinghood than are things-taken-in-relative-abstraction, i.e. as in their representation merely as "things of nature." It is most important, therefore, not to let representation of "things of nature" tyrannize over our attempt to interpret "the nature" of things. We have to waken and remain alert to the inflections of meaning by virtue of which "things" may become things, as constitutive for what they may become.

At this point we can get a preliminary grip on the theme of creation as it occurs in mythological form. These myths presuppose "nature," including the generation and destruction which are companionate primitive aspects of nature. What these myths conjure with is neither a natural or a supernatural occurrence. It is a spontaneous and cosmic occurrence through which reality comes to pass. Creation is realization, concrete realization. This is the point. Myth, poetry, and narrative are intrinsically germane to the telling of it. Not nature but creation *makes* itself told. Yet creation does not occur apart from nature, or least of all as excluding her. Rather, we and nature in partnership become creaturely, co-creaturely. Together, we "find our place," a place into which we fit. Then nature herself appears as "fitting" in a cosmic order to which we belong. This order is the harmony in which generation and destruction are—not annulled—but transfigured.

Only in so far as we participate in the coming to pass of such an order, in resolute partnership with nature, does our finite existence admit of resolution, and find completion.

Other ways of putting what we are getting at here may come to mind. For the time being I will only set down the barest allusion to a few.

On the matter of the need for us to undertake nature in the mode of resolute partnership—in contrast for example to taking nature as a field for conquest, the Buddhist tradition is extraordinarily strong and clear, marvelously appreciative of our grounding in the impersonal and primitive, acceptingly taken up and lived from in a life that may come to enlightenment. This is *part* of the meaning of that acceptance of karma through which a true and free existence is thought to come to pass, into which things may accede with us, so that our relationship with them may even come in time to assume the character of a mutual acknowledgement.

Again in the vein of the Oriental tradition, more markedly Hindu than otherwise, the theme of reality seems suggested in a way almost exactly parallel with that in which our analysis culminates. The expression signifying reality in this tradition is *sat-chit-ananda*. "*Sat*" or "suchness" I take to mean "thinghood," or things-in-their-true-being; "*chit*": the apprehension inseparable from "suchness"; and "*ananda*": the blessed animate in and as this realization.

For the finest reflective discussions of things in Western literature it seems to me one must turn to Heidegger's essay, *Das Ding*, (and its companion essays), in *Vorträge und Aufsätze*. This essay speaks of what it may mean to dwell in the proximity of things, in contrast with all attitudinal positions which might be adopted in and through representation and objectification. That proximity is itself distinguished from absence of interval, or rather, nearness and farness are distinguished from the bland uniformity of lesser or greater interval. The nearness of things is beholden to the far, and it is a nearing grasped as transpiring, through which heaven and earth, mortals and divine come to belong to one another, gathered in the simplicity of things. The coming to pass of things is in function of what we may call "the play of the world," a theme in Heidegger which seems to me conceived in a way strikingly reminiscent of Tao. The sense of being in their coming to pass is of fluency, resiliency, suppleness, simplicity; so akin is this to the life of mortal men dwelling in the world that there is nothing obtrusive about it. We are bound up in the happening of things, not in the manner of producing them, but through a heeding of vigilant attention. In so far as they occur, they occur in nearing us; and we dwell in their proximity, our concern attuned to their call. We undertake them carefully. Careful speech finds its origin and "standard" in things: in things of the world, in a world of things.

A Way of Reading
the Book of Job (1963)

"A Way of Reading the Book of Job" is Bugbee's reflection on the story of
Job from the point of view of Job. The story of Job has become somewhat
commonplace in the Western canon. Job's mettle is tested in order to
prove his faith. The scales of justice are tipped for no apparent reason. The
significance of Job's response is that despite the complete absence of *material* evidence to the contrary, he remains steadfast to an understanding of
cosmic justice mysterious and resistant to the coordinates of any anthropocentric judicial compass. Job must make sense of *being God-forsaken* in
a most personal way: "It is through their interpretation, and only through
the bearing they thus implicitly or explicitly exert upon significance, that
they acquire the force of *affliction.*"

Job's condition forces him to pose the most urgent of ethical questions: "God, why hast Thou forsaken me?" The turning point in Job's
life occurs while encountering the presence of God disclosed through the
tempest. Job experiences a revelation in the form of an ecstatic vision.
The space of readiness for this revelation has been prepared not through
any sense of feeling downtrodden, resentful, or being-without-faith.
According to Bugbee, Job is "given over"—*opened* to the experience
of revelation through his capacity to engage in a fundamental mode of
mutual address:

> Simply it is the vision of things: the things of heaven-and-earth,
> dramatized in their emergent majesty, wonder, and inviolable re-
> serve. But seen in the mode of this, their being. And seen as if, for
> the first time, yet as belonging to a domain, in which dominion (not
> domination) reigns, forever and ever; the dominion of being itself.[1]

The lesson to be learned from the story of Job is the need to step outside quotidian understanding, remaining open to the absolute source of things. The openness embraced by Job leads to a sense of grace, *recalling us to our senses*: "Thinking dedicated to essential truth seems consummated only as it is graced . . . [by] an unanticipated precipitation of meaning." Job is able to effectively achieve some type of stasis within the life of spirit by re-inscribing the sheer immediacy of the present, *which was there all along*, within a sense of greater unity achieved through "secondary reflection"—a notion Bugbee appropriated from Gabriel Marcel. As Job realized at the end of his ordeal in Chapter 42, verses 3–6: "I have spoken about great things which I have not understood . . . . I knew of thee only by report, but now I see with my own eyes. Therefore . . . I repent in dust and ashes"[2] Abstract reasoning is a foreign medium here. What is perceived at first *per speculum et in aenigmate* is now seen "face-to-face." Regaining a sense of the sacred dimension of experience is, for Bugbee, essential because oftentimes day-to-day living renders us deaf and mute—unable to hear and to speak about the world of which we are a part:

> Yet—perhaps even when so situated, some things need to be said, await being discovered in a way of saying them . . . . [I]t might even be as well to set out from a sustained reticence to speak . . . . [R]eticence also seems attuned to the quiet of heaven-and-earth, the unprejudiced silence of things . . . . [I]t is a measure that makes for reflection, and finding out what we make of things, in the course of having to do with them. In a mortal life.

"A Way of Reading the Book of Job," written in 1963, was never intended to be a full-fledged study of Job. Bugbee's "subsequent reckoning" with the story of Job led him to view his effort as an attempt "to fledge something central in his own thinking, rather than an interpretation directly deriving from his absorption in the text."

～

Prefatory Note: The ensuing reflection was written in January and February of 1963. The Book of Job was certainly of central importance at the time in eliciting the thought engaged upon. Yet it will be observed that the basic drift of what is said does not derive from a full-fledged and detailed study of Job. Subsequent reckoning with that book, and in particular, study of it with the great help of my colleague, Professor John Lawry, have led me to regard what I wrote back there in '63 more as an event in attempting to fledge something central in my own thinking, rather than as an interpretation directly deriving from absorption in the text. (HGB)

It came to me as in a dream, and it has that kind of logic, you know. Something about God and Satan and a man named Job.

Here were God and Satan getting into a bit of a dispute about this man, God contending that Job was a pretty staunch follower in the ways of righteousness, the ways laid down by God for men to follow, and Satan maintaining this man could be corrupted and pried loose from the fold of the faithful. So God says to Satan to go ahead and do his darnedest, short of taking the man's life, and let's just see how it turns out. And maybe God harbors a little additional reservation to make amends for Job for the hardship this experiment is going to mean for Job if Job comes through and stands up under it. After all, a man who proves himself a staunch follower and retainer under se- vere trial really deserves to be rewarded by his Lord, and the Lord's good intention to follow through and make things right for Job in the end may ease strain in the Lord's conscience of being a party to the plot.

Sounds like a rather rough deal, doesn't it? Never mind; this wouldn't be the first time a man had a rough deal. Let's get on with how the righteousness and suffering pan out. After all, the Lord isn't letting Job in on any secrets, so now we have to take it from Job's point of view.

Satan lays it on pretty hard, to be sure. He piles calamity on ca- lamity on Job, and just to give Job's fellow-men the cue to carry on where Satan is going to leave off, Satan so afflicts Job—as with scabs and boils—that he becomes repulsive, despicable, even a touch ri- diculous, in human eyes, yes, even in his own. So here sits Job, as the story really begins to get underway, a sitting duck. And you can't say Satan didn't do his work in consummate fashion. He knew just what he needed to do, and where to leave off and let men take over. You might say he gave them the material they needed to work on and a clear hint on how to use it in carrying on Satan's purpose where Satan himself couldn't turn the trick.

You see the plot thickens only with human interpretation of what has befallen Job. The question is, what do these catastrophes mean? And it's *that question* that really plagues Job. The question intro- duces a suffering, an anguish suffusing but not going quite beyond all that has befallen him. No telling what a man can or can't bear, but everything seems to depend on how profoundly *he* is shaken, uprooted, or undermined in the course of events. And with Job the drama is a drama of belief, of belief *in* . . . of what he stakes himself on.

Well, here comes his wife, the first to hit him where it really hurts. "Curse God and die!" she screams at him. What is the bitch saying? How does she mock and taunt him?

"You wretched, you miserable, you pitiful fool! So you persist in your old 'do what is right and trust in the Lord.' Look where it got you. Look what's become of all of us. Why if there's any man left in you, go ahead. Stick by your position. Admit you have to see yourself betrayed. Then go ahead and say it: to hell with the pious cant! And to hell with God! And let this be your last breadth! What else is left for you to say?"

She knows he won't do it, and heaps him with her shrill vexation, with maddened contempt: this caricature of a man.

And now come the friends of Job, ready to sit with him in his travail. Initially they seem respectful of his suffering and keep silent. Perhaps his suffering makes them uncomfortable. One can feel their relief as they begin to find their tongues. They will console him, patiently reason with him, help him to a proper perspective on what has befallen him:

Divine Providence, Divine Justice is at work in all events, in all that touches a human life. There is the basis of man's acceptance of whatever befalls him.

A pretty touchy theme, since they can hardly voice it for Job's benefit without making explicit the tough implications for his case which they want him to swallow:

You see, Job, it's this way; a man gets what he has coming to him. (Right now the friends are feeling no pain.) And so, Job, it is no accident you have been brought to suffer like this. If you hadn't put yourself in wrong . . . You see? Accept, then, the stern hand of Divine Punishment upon you. Repent, and be reconciled to your sufferings.

It is hard for them to be as tactful about this as they might have wished, but Job soon relieves them of any anxiety on that score by protesting his own innocence, nay, his integrity in his own eyes. Accordingly, it becomes the duty to remonstrate with him, and then as he persists, to rise up in righteous indignation and rebuke him.

Well, they have a field day at his expense, going one another better in justifying the ways of God to man, and to Job in particular.

Small wonder they get him riled up and side-tracked into a defense of himself. But also they goad him to the point, and bring him to the abyss of his own despair. For if their version of Divine Justice does not hold, what is it that Job can believe in, and what is left for him to believe in still? What can sustain him—not in a belief in his own righteousness, but in keeping faith?

In the idiom of his faith Job calls upon God for understanding. With utter singleness of heart and will and mind, his whole soul, his whole life issues under the pressure of his suffering into that cry. A cry for understanding of man's predicament—and not a curse; this is the last breadth of the man left in him, feeling himself utterly forsaken.

Tuesday, January 15, 1963

No wind stirs. At Zero Fahrenheit the flakes of snow are not all large. Incredibly lightly and unwaveringly they fall. A myriad of them fills our meadow round the house. One sees them best looking at the trees beyond. Their falling accentuates the still-standing trees, the dark trunks. And the still of the trees is the nearness of the falling snow.

Occasionally, in the meadow, a weed nods and lifts again.

The low fire of the hearth is even more discreet.

Tuesday, February 12, 1963

No great pressure of anything to say. No salient point to be made. No sureness about what might need to be done. Doubt with respect to so much of past thought. A sense of turning away from overstatement, a reticence almost to speak at all.

Yet—perhaps when so situated, some things need to be said, await being discovered in a way of saying them, if one were only to try it patiently and unassumingly enough, beginning over and again just with what offers itself.

Perhaps some things need to be said; and it might even be as well to set out from a sustained reticence to speak. For whatever there may be amiss in it, that reticence also seems attuned to the quiet of heaven-and-earth, the unprejudiced silence of things that are, companioning an unlonely solitude. Not a life apart or solitary, but such solitude as heaven-and-earth dispense, to which one may give himself. Surely silence and solitude may be the measure for our thought and speech. And since by this measure we are simply placed on our own as well, it is a measure that also makes for reflection, and a finding out of what we make of things, in the course of having to do with them.

In a mortal life.

Thursday, February 14

Three elements are bound to be powerfully related to what may need to be said here: a certain style of life, closely related to the second—a certain region, a place, in which that style of life is nurtured; and a certain company of thinkers and friends.

Among the thinkers are some who provide comments helpful in fixing the character of the style of life in question, and the importance in it of the place to which it belongs.

First, as to the undertaking of what may need to be said, in its kinship with the style of life, there is something Vincent van Gogh says in a letter to his brother that comes very near to the matter:

"... the figure of a laborer—some furrows in a ploughed field— a bit of sand, sea, and sky—are serious subjects, very difficult, but at the same time so beautiful that it is indeed worth while to devote one's life to the task of expressing the poetry hidden in them." (*Dear Theo*, New York: Doubleday, 1957, p. 173).

And again:

"I believe one gets more sound ideas when thoughts arise from direct contact with things than when one looks at them with the set purpose of finding certain facts in them." (Ibid., p. 183).

This also:

"Yes, lad, if one perseveres and works on without minding the rest, if one tries honestly and freely to fathom nature, and does not lose hold of what one has in mind, whatever people may say, one feels calm and firm, and faces the future quietly." (Ibid., p. 244).

But this also:

"To study from nature, to wrestle with reality—I don't want to do away with it for years and years. I should not like to have missed that *error*. One starts with a hopeless struggle to follow nature, and everything goes wrong; one ends by calmly creating from one's palette, and nature agrees with it, and follows. But these two contrasts do not exist separately. The drudging though it may seem in vain, gives an intimacy with nature, a sounder knowledge of things." (Ibid., pp. 363-64).
    "It is looking at things for a long time that ripens you and gives you a deeper understanding." (Ibid., p. 462).

Looking at things for a long time . . . , or as Thoreau says, with his touch of hyperbole: "And we are enabled to apprehend at all what is sublime and noble only by the perpetual instilling and drenching of the reality that surrounds us." (*Walden*, New York: Modern Library, 1937, p. 87).

"And to be among conditions that work at us, that set us before big natural things from time to time, that is all we need." (Rainer Maria Rilke, *Letters to a Young Poet*, trans. M. D. Mercer, New York: W.W. Norton, 1937, p. 78).

Monday, February 18

"You can't idealize brute labor. That is to say, you can't idealized brute labor, without coming undone as an idealist." (D. H. Lawrence, *Studies In Classic American Literature*, New York: Doubleday Anchor Books, 1955, p. 121).
    "You can't idealize mother earth. She will have no pure idealist sons. None.
    "If you are a child of mother earth, you must learn to discard your ideal self, in season, as you discard your clothes at night." (Ibid., p. 122).

It is not in the direction of idealizing heaven-and-earth, and the things therein, that one is sustained by them. In this sense, *making something of them is making nothing of them.* As Gertrude Stein says, a rose is a rose.

However. Let us consider what is said of the rose by Angelus Sile-sius in the sentence taken by Martin Heidegger as the text for so much of his work, *Satz Vom Grund*:

> "La rose est sans pourquoi, fleurit parce qu'elle fleurit,
>   N'a souci d'elle-même, ne désire être vue." (Quoted from the French translation of Martin Heidegger, *Satz Vom Grund* by André Préau, *Le principe de raison*, Paris: Gallimard, 1957, p. 103 ff)

Something may happen in relation with things themselves, in mutual address, that is the mode of sense they make, and it has nothing to do with explaining them. The mode of sense in question imparts to life a purposiveness without purpose. Purposes exfoliat-ing and sustained out of that purposiveness, as they may well be, cannot explain it, nor do they explain things. A purposiveness prior to purposes, to which they remain subordinate, precludes reading the sense things make in terms of purposes.

Thus it may well be in a style of life governed by mutual address with things, one may stand to attune hearing to that language which things and events speak without metaphor, "which alone is copious and standard" (Thoreau, op. cit., p. 101). Perhaps that, precisely, is their beauty. As, for example, it concerned van Gogh.

Tuesday, February 19

> "Bien courte, à vrai dire, serait notre pensée, si nous admettions que la sentence d'Angelus Silesius n'a d'autre sens que d'indi-quer la différence des manières dont la rose, dont l'homme, sont ce qu'ils sont. Ce que la sentence ne dit pas—et qui est tout l'essentiel—, c'est bien plutôt ceci qu'au fond le plus se-cret de son être l'homme n'est véritablement que s'il est à sa manière comme la rose—sans pourquoi." (*Le principe de rai-son*, p. 108)

At the core of the personal life there seems to be something in-violately impersonal, akin in our fashion to the mode of being as a rose, or rock—known and owned by all weather. It is through this in us that the elements seem to most deeply befriend us—sun and rain, earth and seasons, the constant rivers and the starry night. It is through this that one may "go and come with a strange liberty in

Nature, a part of herself." (Thoreau, op. cit., p. 117). And it is this as well which may ground and fortify both critical reserve and human warmth: something inviolately impersonal.

Perhaps it was to this that Job was led; and one may discern it through the lifeand thought of that man of our times, Albert Camus. (See especially the essay, "Retour à Tipasa," *L'été*, Paris: Gallimard, 1954, pp. 141-63.)

Thursday, February 21

Justice: In a way, that is the great issue. If one can believe in it, and willingly align himself in what he feels as accords with it, then to that extent he is not undermined, dissipated and adrift. In the broadest terms this would mean participating in a situation that makes sense, and in such a way that it makes sense. In those terms justice appears to be the issue defined by the Book of Job.

And here the situation must be construed as both cosmic and that of a man. The meaning of his situation is what is at issue. Job *as a man* stands revealed as dependent on what his situation means to him; it is through their bearing on that meaning—or as they seem to consolidate that meaning, that things, people, events prove telling. It is not sufficient to think of him as having been the victim of a succession of catastrophes, to the point where his sufferings become virtually unbearable. The caustic bite of these catastrophes is their inducing the definingly human anguish of doubt to the verge of unbelief in human existence and the significance of everything entering into it. The raw catastrophes themselves occupy little space in the story. Their afflicting power and threat to Job *as a man* is dramatized at length, and is to be seen as the drama of their interpretation. It is through their interpretation, and only through the bearing they thus implicitly or explicitly exert upon significance, that they acquire the force of *affliction*.

Justice is in question. Justice pertaining to man's situation as a cosmic one, and as a situation which cannot be lived except interpretively—however implicitly so.

Now Job is presented as having believed in cosmic justice. And it is through that very belief that the sufferings befalling him acquire the force of affliction. His "friends," and perhaps his wife as well, appeal to that very belief: in terms of it, why should he not feel himself *in contempt*? How can he reject the implication of being *stigmatized* by the holocaust of adversities besetting him?

Cosmic, or if you will—divine—justice: Very well. How can you believe in it without giving unlimited range to your moral persuasions, and to accept it that a man gets what he has coming to him, from whatever quarter it comes? How can you believe in it without reading all events as the expression of a cosmic agency whose intentions and purpose are everywhere at work, seeing to it that only justice comes to pass?

What is this belief, then, on which Job stakes himself, if it does not entail either holding sufferers as such in contempt; or rejection, resentment, defiance with regard to the agency of cosmic "justice" seemingly revoked? Shouldn't Job knuckle under to the verdict of events, and acquiesce in the stigma which his "friends" have it that these events brand him; or shouldn't he, as his wife taunts him to do, curse God and die?

The tone of Job's protests suggests that he has become vulnerable to these hateful alternatives in terms of his own belief, for only in such terms can a man come near to despairing.

Yet, uncomprehending, profoundly confused, with the bitterest of irony both foisted upon him and gaining hold in the ambiguity of his belief—and in the temptation to turn the issue into one of self-justification, at the point of utter desperation. Job holds open to a possibility of cosmic justice which nothing seems to sustain. Yet no way seems left even to grasp what it might mean.

What happens now in the story is naturally crucial: a verdict on the issue and a version on the theme, touching on what Job is able to believe in. For his reconciliation and renewal depend on the possibility of *believing in*. In what? Plainly, in the significance of things and events entering into human life, and as decisive for man's cosmic situation.

Perhaps it will seem, since what happens now transpires in the idiom of speech—the utterance of the voice from the whirlwind—that what the story offers is in the vein of emphasis on a super-human, a cosmic agent calling attention to evidences of himself, his power, and in a way sufficient to still any human doubt or challenge to his authority. "Job, when you consider my handiwork, even a little of what I can do, and then consider by comparison how puny a man is, what right have you to insist upon accounting for what befalls you, or to presume that you could understand what I may be up to? Now aren't you ashamed?" Job covers himself with contrition and his fortunes improve! And how consistently arbitrary this divine agent would be, turning on Job's friends, at the end. For haven't they them-selves been holding for that length to precisely the same effect?

Friday, February 22

Indeed, the explicit thread of argument running through the utter-ance of the voice from the whirlwind seems to be some such disap-pointing effect. And after what has been revealed to him, does not Job himself say that he has seen God, and to such effect that he despises himself and repents?

So Job turns out to be guilty of insisting on his integrity? Per-haps. So, though he had freely emphasized the possibility himself, his questioning and tormented speculation had gotten him in way over his head. Guilty then too of a certain presumption in having uttered what he did not understand, even in crying out, above all, for understanding. Still, what is there interesting in this? Suppose Job stands convicted "before God." Suppose no mortal man is ever sustained of "righteousness." What has this to do with the issue of cosmic justice, touching Job? That is, what is there in the vision, the revelation that comes in him, not merely confounding him and casting him down, but actually making sense of his situation and speaking to its condition?

If we turn to the vision actually set forth in the utterance of the voice from the whirlwind, perhaps we must distinguish between the thread of argument intertwined with it and what actually emerges as to be seen, co-articulate with the *mode* of vision enacted. Simply it is a vision of things: the things of heaven-and-earth, dramatized in their emergent majesty, wonder, and inviolable *reserve*. But *seen* in the mode of this, their being. And seen as if for the first time, yet as belonging to a domain, in which dominion (not domination) reigns, forever and ever: the domain of being itself.

Job's questioning has presupposed an explanation of things and events; he has believed in a justice embodied in them, but in a way suggesting the possibility of a raison d'être through which compre-hensions of them would be the appropriate mode of understanding with regard to them. But his presupposition does not seem to be sus-tained; rather, it is shown to be irrelevant. No explanation of what has befallen him is forthcoming; certainly not any "justification of human suffering." In fact nothing by way of justification conceived on the model of moral persuasions occurs. No hidden purposes are revealed, to disclose that these, then, explain, or exemplify how explanation might be forthcoming, to whatever extent withheld.

Instead, wanting to understand as he does—with his whole heart—and at his wits' end, prepared to risk whatever in his belief he may have clung to, Job is opened in mutual address with things. And the vision enacted speaks, not according to his presuppositions, nevertheless in accord with his situation and condition. His belief in raison d'être is strangely and wonderfully controverted and confirmed:

L'être-même, c'est 'la raison.' But therefore: no raison d'être.

Thus it is a certain appreciation of things, in a relation of mutual address with them, and not in any comprehension of them, that a basic mode of understanding comes to pass.

Notes on Objectivity
and Reality (n.d.)

"Notes on Objectivity and Reality" explores further the importance of aesthetic appreciation during the course of philosophical understanding. Unlike Descartes's characterization of objectivity as the condition that allows us to "make ourselves, as it were, 'masters and possessors' of nature," Bugbee claims, "we are objective when we submit to the control of what presents itself." In a most important sense, the experience of appreciation is not something instituted by the subject. Appreciation *measures* "the manifold of activities in terms of which we measure ourselves . . . within the span of our lives. It is only in terms of [appreciation] that reality can obtain." Appreciation must seek to be responsible in the very sense embodied by Job—radically responsive to a revelation of reality that remains "patient of creation."

Reality comes to pass through meditation— according to Bugbee, "a non-pictorial and non-pictorializable style of thinking."[1]Meditative thinking involves an act of suspension while attempting to access the "ultimate givens" of our situation. Philosophy's goal is to be revolutionary, "deepening understanding and giving added significance to what it interprets." A mortal life is ramified, strengthened to the extent that it is reflexively engaged, bearing witness to the process through which "existence assumes a decided character [as] we become decided in it." The task of philosophy is to participate "thoughtfully and appropriately" in the activity of rendering meaning and significance experientially concrete.

∾

The word literally conjures up a throwing—or placing—before or against, an op-posing. Thus we throw or place before either by way of objection or by way of objective, now in opposing, now in aiming at.

What, then, is an "object": whatever is attended to in being cognizant of it or being interested in it? In medieval thought "objective" signified the status of being entertained, posed in thought . . .

But in modern thought "objective" more exactly signifies conditions to which we have to adjust, imposed on us, independently of our wish or will in the situation. The objective is that which we find we must adjust ourselves to . . . An experimental attitude is required in finding out these conditions and in adjusting to them. Subjective selection will not disclose what may prove yielding or unyielding in what we have to do with; in this sense objective conditions are determinative in op-position to subjective selection, they stand opposed to subjective interest; the latter must be adjusted to them. We are objective then when we submit to the control of what presents itself. We let our thinking be determined by the nature of what presents itself, as opposed to . . . what we might merely wish, or will, or fancy . . . .

I mean this as Job saw it to be so, and in the only way it can be discovered for what it is, namely through what happens to oneself, with the willingness to acknowledge it.

The measure of appreciation does not seem to me something we institute. It is taken simply in the events and situations of our lives, in the course of our encounter with things and persons, out of which and in league with which our appreciation is formed, inflected in the manifold of activities in terms of which we orient ourselves in these events and situations with respect to things and persons, placed and timed and circumstanced as we may be, within the span of our lives. Significance is of the essence of what we do and of what happens to us: we reckon in terms of it, participate in its formation, are found or lost with respect to it, ineluctably act upon it and interpret it, speak from it; it is only in terms of it that reality can obtain.

I am suggesting, you see, a way—a direction we might take, in assuming reflective responsibility for a traditional and fundamental theme in the presence of which many contemporary Western philosophers have grown if not shy then somewhat mute or disdainful: the theme of reality. I mean this in the way Job comes to experience it, when with that radical access of appreciation which occurred to him he found that it was simply with respect to this that he had been wanting. Somehow the story of his situation quite undercut the presumptive alternatives—either a reality ultimately devoid of significance or a reality working in terms of reward and punishment, such as persons might institute. Let us make no mistake about it: It is a revelation of reality with which the book of Job deals, and of reality as basically just that which requires appreciation of us—an appreciation in which we may come to ourselves, find our place, and orient ourselves in patience, neither listlessly, resignedly, nor in abortive decision. To become similarly patient of creation, to learn to wait upon reality in thoughtful appreciation, but in our own way as befits our own time and occasion, that seems to me pretty much the unheralded and unsanctioned task now lying in wait for Western thought, for each of us, that is, in so far as we may be prepared to heed it.

I can put what I have been driving at in the form of a very simple question: What does responsibility have to do with reality? Is reality a sort of ready-made affair in relation to which a responsible being could be merely one of adjustment? Or is reality such as to be at issue in responsibility?

The step I want to sketch might be put this way: that reality is more fundamentally a theme of meditation than it is an affair of observation and description. Of course what we glean by observation and description would have to be ruminated upon and digested in meditation. Meditation would be vacuous indeed if it did not grow out of all that our manifold experience and non-meditative thought might yield to be meditated upon. But there is essentially a non-pictorial and non-pictorializable style of thinking which we carry out in being meditative that seems to me both to partake of the basic motives which lead us to reflect on reality and to be nearer to what we might come to understand by reality.

When we are lost and exercise presence of mind it seems sensible to get our bearings, take stock of our resources, scrutinize our circumstances more closely, define the alternatives open to us, and then decide what to do. First we institute an inquiry, then we act in the light of its results. Now I find myself wondering to what extent this sensible course may have governed an attitude in which men of the Western world have tended to address themselves to the theme of reality: reality would be that which we try to make out and get a grip on in phases of inquiry during which we suspend the attitude in which we mobilize ourselves to act and decide; accordingly, to ascertain the real would be analogous to determining without distortion the ultimate givens of our situation, perhaps so that having located ourselves with respect to them, we may then be enlightened on what it makes sense to do in a given situation—and get on with it. To orient ourselves with respect to reality, then figure out what to do: to take thought, and then to act. Or by extension, first the theoretical vision, then its practical application. From philosophers, then, may we not expect some general orientation with respect to reality, some general outlook or world view, so that at least we may take undistorted account of the overall givens of our situation, whatever their bearing may be on what is practically at issue for us?

You know, I believe dyed-in-the-wool and inveterate philosophers are, and have always been, most in their element when they are venturing a fresh start in their reflections: when some line of thought is just occurring to them, just opening up, inspiring them with the promise of doing fuller justice to that heritage of considerations, ever accumulating, shifting, but bearing on the responsibility they assume as reflective men. The very spirit of philosophy is revolutionary in this sense, as we grasp in the appreciation of Socrates that Plato makes possible. At the same time revolution in philosophical thinking is necessarily always reinterpretation of a complex heritage; it can only succeed in the measure in which it deepens understanding and gives added significance to what it reinterprets. Thus the authentic revolutionary in philosophy is the man who by reflection gets nearer to the point with his predecessors, and earns their backing in what he is about. A genuine philosophical revolution, then, can never be at bottom simply iconoclastic in its treatment of antecedent thought. Why it is positively charming in those seventeenth century revolutionaries, Descartes and Francis Bacon, in how much they exaggerated their break with the Aristotelian tradition in their programmatic departures from it.

Over a hundred years ago, in explaining where he lived and what he lived for, Thoreau thought his way to the point of explaining: "Be it life or death, we crave only reality." Either, in the end, reality is our undoing, or, since we do die, in some strange way, it is not. To live as a mortal is to be subject to the questionability of reality in this sense. Reality is just that which is ultimately questionable and at issue for us. Existence as we live in it and encounter one another and all manner of things is permeated with the question of the ultimate bearing and portent of what occurs along our way on reality. The question is: how does reality shape up, what mode of sense might it make—or even, in what mode of sense might it occur?

Now it is *for us* that the question arises, as *the* question pressed home in and by mortal life, whether we take it up and permit it to proceed in a reflective way or not. And nothing in the end could suffice us and satisfy the conditions of our participation in existence save some taking for real on which we could stake ourselves. We *need*, if not to know, then in some way to *realize*, or to come to a realization which occurs to us—and in such a way that a fundamental unity of meaning gathers up existence, with all that is therein, and resolves us.

What Thoreau hits upon is just this: reality is precisely what is in question and at stake for us as beings who are essentially defined in the capacity and the need for resolution. Thus the mode, intensity and integrality of meaning with which reality may occur to us is far more crucially and ineluctably manifest in our *style* of life, of decision, and of thinking, than in our deliberate effort to give an account of what we understand by reality; yes, perhaps even if we are versed in the literature of human thought dealing explicitly and thematically with what is in question. We bear witness to the way reality occurs to us—whether more or less privatively or in the mode of fulfillment, more fundamentally than when we make it a matter of explicit and reasoned reckoning. Yet to bear witness in the fullest sense is to take a conscious stand; it involves an act of testifying. Therefore, in that curiously chiding, jocular-serious tone of his, Thoreau immediately adds to the exclamation I have quoted: "If we are really dying, let us hear the rattle in our throats and feel cold in the extremities; if we are alive, let us go about our business."

Is the import of reality to the effect that we are, so to speak, tolerated in existence—for a time? Or is it such as to hold for us and even to claim us to the possibility of a life which we can really mean, strengthening and fulfilling our intent, carrying it beyond and supporting it, even as we may fail, and eventually will? All interim, conditional and tentative undertakings await the possibility of what we can really mean—of reality, that is, as resolving our intent.

What if existence were in its essence both situational and transitional? Why, then something like concrete reality might occur, and we participating in it—as the very meaning of situation and the point of transition. Since reality then would be akin to the sense of things come to make, it would, on such a conception of reality, be absurd to ask for an explanation of reality. Reality would be existence insofar as existence assumes a decided character, we becoming decided in it. And if, as Western people, we were to participate thoughtfully and appropriately in such an occurrence, in some measure, that would indeed mark a revolution in Western thought.

But I should think it would be a revolution that would lead us to a much better understanding of the thinking of our predecessors—indeed of *them*, for would not reality involve them, the whole human community including them, even in the embrace of what we would mean by ourselves? Robert Frost, for example, seems to have had a sense of this. Common venturers in existence, with ourselves and the world at stake—and therefore in question; thus situated, we are, along with those who have gone before, and those to come, in the thrust and flow of existence.

Transition is the mystery of existence in that we are inalienably bound up in it, quite unable to dissociate ourselves from it, incontrovertibly placed in question by it, and no one can hold in arrest what it may bring forth. How can we entrust ourselves to it—in it—as mortals.

Transitional existence—existence as transitional—is radicaled in mortality. Whatever can be ultimate for us—and it must be for someone that anything can be ultimate, must emerge in existence, embrace it, engold it, characterize it, reflect upon it, transform it or transfigure it, in such a way as to speak decisively to that condition. It is in this sense, I believe, that existence sets the question of reality. When we ask after reality—which is very different from taking for granted that existence raises no question as to reality, we ask after the resolution of existence—in some way, we know not what. That is enough not only to make us reflect and keep us reflective, but also to rouse us to alertness and consideration in whatever is coming to pass. Existence calls for reflective presence of mind. And reflective presence of mind is alert for the suggestions and intimations of reality which existence might yield—like the kind of music things might make, such as a musician might act upon, if he were quick enough—lively, not impetuous.

1. Reality is a matter of reflective concern in so far as we assume responsibility for reality in thought. The *reflective* character of such thought encompasses interpretation as a rendering of meaning and significance, and reflexivity in the working out of one's stand or orientation in what is at issue in the act of thought. One's own stand or orientation, indeed one's selfhood, are implicitly in question, along with the way reality is thoughtfully interpreted. One's own mode of involvement in reality, as reality is to be conceived, is integral to the conception of reality.

2. One's stand or orientation—under definition in reflection on reality—imparts to the rendering of reality in thought the character of bearing witness—a matter of testimony, a rendering of meaning and significance integrally connected with the stance and orientation in which meaning and significance are to be *found*.

3. The orientation and stance under "definition," thoughtfully rendered in reflection on reality, are answerable to the principle of concreteness—as a principle of meaning and significance. The criterion of reflective thought is necessarily internal to it: that of "growing together" in meaning and significance, as discoverable to us in relation to the activity of reflective interpretation. (Complementarity and dialectical tension may be essential to concreteness.)

4. I believe we come the nearer to appropriate interpretation of reality the more transparently our thought is grounded in meaning and significance which can be decisive for our whole style of life: decisive in point of what is at stake in our lives—in our relationships with one another and with things, and in point of our ability to fulfill what is at stake through the style of life we live.

5. Perhaps reality, then, is a matter of *realization*: potentiality for which obtains in the relationships in which we have to do with things and with one another. Reality, then, would be the way in which appearance could make sense, relative to the mode of participation in it through which appearance occurs and the possibility of making sense obtains.

6. The mode of participation on our part correlative with which realization can occur seems to be essentially vocational: we are called into, and upon, and by, and it is ours to enter into effecting what is called for.

7. Realization is creation.

Experience, Memory, Reflection: An Interview with Henry Bugbee

This interview was recorded in the early 1990s. Bugbee's memory was starting to fade and, according to close friend and colleague Ray Lanfear, "Henry was no longer writing and beginning to get a little mixed up." The purpose of the interview was to retrieve important memories from Bugbee's past by capturing them in narrative form. For the most part, Bugbee's recall is quite good and the audio-recording reflects that indefinable, unique, and utterly captivating diction and speech for which he was so known.

The reader is able to retrospectively follow Bugbee from his childhood in New York City, to his early education at the Browning and Hotchkiss schools as he developed a passion for fishing, the outdoors, and a zest for adventure. His philosophical interests began to take hold at Princeton, continuing throughout his time at Berkeley while undertaking graduate study. His passion for fishing, the outdoors, and adventure never waned. We are given a firsthand look at his experiences while at sea aboard a minesweeper in the South Pacific, as well as his transition back to Berkeley, where the feeling of "writers block" that had plagued him before the war disappeared. We are treated to an inside look at his experiences at Harvard and other institutions—including the story of the "Thanksgiving goose" at the University of Nevada at Reno—and his subsequent migration to Montana, Penn State, and then again back home to Montana. The interview concludes with an account of the Intensive Humanities Program at the University of Montana that Bugbee was instrumental in creating.

Experience, Memory, Reflection: An Interview with Henry Bugbee

Henry Bugbee: HB
Sally Moore, Henry's wife: SM
Ray Lanfear, friend and philosophy department colleague: RL

Recollections of Youth

SM: Do you have a particular occasion in your time in that school of Browning that you remember?

HB: I remember playing soccer on the roof, on the cement in New York City. There was a network of wire mesh around, to keep the ball from going over and down into the street. I never lost the ball.

RL: Was the roof large enough for it to be something close to an official soccer field?

HB: No.

RL: You played soccer?

HB: Yes.

SM: How old were you when you graduated from that school?

HB: Well, I certainly don't remember, but I can reconstruct it.

SM: Were you twelve or thirteen? You went away to school at Hotchkiss at age fourteen, right?

HB: Yes. So this was from six through thirteen.

SM: Do you remember any particular book, any kind of reading that made an impression on you?

RL: Did you study Latin at Browning?

HB: A little bit

SM: Did you live with your family?

HB: Yes.

SM: Do you have brothers and sisters?

HB: Two sisters.

SM: Where they in the same school?

HB: No. They went to Brilley. That's a girl's school.

SM: Were you in a boy's school?

HB: Yes.

SM: You mentioned on many occasions a particular history book that meant so much to you as a child. Was that at Hotchkiss?

HB: That was not an assigned reading. That was something I read *A Hundred Years of American Independence* by a man named Barnes.

SM: Were you at Browning when you discovered this book?
HB: Yes. I remember hiding under to covers with a flashlight and read that book when I was supposed to be asleep. I really liked it. And one reason I really detested my first history teacher was that he had one thing in mind. That was to teach me what I needed to satisfy the examiners and the college board examinations. And it nearly killed my zest for historical narrative.
SM: What was it about this particular book that you liked?
HB: It was a history of the American people through the first hundred years—through the Civil War. I don't remember that it went to the Spanish-American War. In fact I don't think I really read about Theodore Roosevelt.
RL: Did that book give you a sense of how important history is?
HB: Yes, without my realizing it. I just had a real zest for it.
    Memorizing what were the dates of the presidency of John Quincy Adams, I couldn't tell you what they were now.
SM: Could you describe a little of the format of this book that made it so appealing to you?
HB: Well, it was filled with excerpts from soldiers from the Civil War, especially that had been preserved by their families from their letters. They were very interesting. They made you feel what it was like to be involved in that situation as a soldier.
SM: How did you get your hands on that book?
HB: An uncle of mine, he gave it to me. I still have it. I had it rebound. It was nearly falling apart.
RL: How old were you when you read this book?
HB: When I was sleeping under the covers in the nighttime, when I would be put to bed? It was before I went to Hotchkiss —pre-fourteen.
RL: Henry, it's unusual for a young man to read a book like that at such an early age. What do you suppose disposed you to have an interest in such a thing? Did your parents encourage you to read these sorts of things?
HB: No. They tried to discourage me from reading that book when they found that I was reading it under the covers.
RL: Did your parents supply you with any books to read?
HB: Thorton Burgess, *Old Mother West Wind* and *The Book of Wild Animals*.

RL: You must have taken to that pretty well?

HB: Yes.

SM: Except he wasn't too happy. His father was a hunter and he had this huge moose head mounted above his bed as little boy.

RL: Above your bed, Henry?

HB: That's right. They didn't know where to put it; they had so many heads around the house.

SM: We have a picture of their dining room and it is lined with animal heads.

HB: They were all shot by my parents. They'd hunted in Wyoming and more so still, they hunted in Canada.[1]

SM: They'd go out with these pack horses and a guide for quite a long time. Did they take you with them on any of these trips?

HB: No, not really. I think about 1929 was my earliest pack trip. That was the year my father discovered that he'd had poor advice by some of the patients who cajoled him into borrowing money in order to buy stocks or bonds. Because then he could make more money that way. And you know, people who'd overextended their purchases of that sort, lived to regret it.

SM: How did this fit in to the pack trip?

HB: I remember coming back from a pack trip of thirty-five days—the Sierra Nevada. Because I remember we went to Visalia, the Giant Forest in California. We packed out of the Giant Forest and it was good rugged country.

SM: Well, was it upon the return from that trip that the stock market crashed?

HB: Yes, that's right. When we got out of the trip in August sometime. I remember my father's face when he was reading the first paper he got his hands on. He thought he was in tough shape. He had to work himself to the bone and with much anxiety in order to try and recuperate. I think that was one factor that contributed to his relatively short life. He was in his early sixties when he died.

RL: How were you impressed by the animals you talked about earlier?

HB: They were stuffed—mounted. I didn't know those animals first hand, yet. When I got to know them first hand, it was not a question of my going hunting. So I didn't have to face up to that.

RL: That is to say that you sort of refused to hunt, is that right?

HB: No, I would have, I think. I never did hunt with my father. I'd go with him but I wouldn't hunt.

RL: But that wasn't your choice?

HB: I liked to go with him but I didn't want to hunt. I didn't shoot. But it wasn't a serious thing for me until I came back from the Second World War. I didn't want to hear the percussion of the fire arms.

RL: But you did go on these wonderful outdoor outings with your father?

HB: Yes, but most of the time they were outings in which he would fish, as well as I. It was too early for hunting season. Hunting season then was school days.

RL: But you would say that this introduced you to the wilderness?

HB: It got me to get the feel of the country. And to be especially cleansed by it. Like at a time when I was at school in a situation out in the country, like when I was at Hotchkiss School. I was out in the country most every day, somehow.

RL: On your own initiative?

HB: Yes. Also, a fellow student and I picked up a canoe that had belonged to a previous classmate and a slightly older boy. We bought it up between us and we paid five dollars a piece for this canoe and the paddles. We began to run, especially the Housatonic River in Connecticut. I remember fishing the fundamental tributaries of the water system.

RL: Henry, what is your earliest memory of fishing?

HB: My earliest clear memory of fishing was at Hotchkiss. I met a man fishing where I tried to go. He invited me to come and fish with him. He had been through the infantry in the First World War. When I knew him, he had mustered out and was working and selling securities. And he hated it. But I discovered, subsequently, the he had used some clients' funds to buy securities for himself. We were very close friends. He was always so nice

and thoughtful and apt in his ways his mind would work
and what he said to me.

RL: What were you fishing with in those days?

HB: A fly rod.

RL: Really! Can you put a date on that?

HB: I started fishing with a fly rod in Wyoming with my
father. He would pack me across certain rapids or riffles
that weren't too challenging. I think I started fishing with
him when I was six years old—1921.

SL: How would you characterize your experience at
Hotchkiss as a whole?

HB: Oh, I had good teachers. I had a geometry teacher, who
was the brother-in-law of that Latin teacher, the ancient
history teacher. I became close friends with the whole
family milieu. But Emerson Quail was the name of the
Latin teacher.

SM: I know you have enormous respect for Hotchkiss.

HB: Yes, I did. But my Greek teacher, I never really resented
him though. I was afraid of him because I was never
really well prepared. I was sensing how near we were
getting to my being called upon to stand up and translate
from Homer.

SM: Why weren't you prepared?

HB: I just didn't do the preparation properly.

SM: I've always had the impression that you were such a
conscientious student there. About how you would study
into the night, when the lights went out.

HB: Oh, that's when I was reading novels in an English
course.

SM: He would sit in the bathroom on the toilet to read. He
was so diligent that he achieved a permanent imprint
from the toilet on his buttocks.

HB: It was sort of like that anyway. It was with Dickens that
I read with particular interest. One of the earliest books
that I remember taking to was *Pickwick Papers*.

SM: Did you read Conrad then?

HB: No, a little later.

RL: Hotchkiss is the equivalent to high school?

HB: Secondary school.

RL: You were there for three or four years.

HB: Four years. I went right from there to Princeton.

RL: When did you first become interested in philosophy and how did that come about? Was it at Hotchkiss or Princeton?

HB: I'd say studying Greek is an introduction to philosophy, in which you don't know you are being introduced to philosophy.

RL: Sure. Homer primarily.

HB: Well no. In the *Iliad* more than the *Odyssey*. I at least had a sense from the language, and the sound of it when anyone would pronounce it.

RL: So this would have been at Hotchkiss?

HB: I had a sort of induction into the tongue that was native to the birth of philosophy. My studies in Greek, from the standpoint of the teacher and I, they were poor too. But I came to like the guy enormously. I used to be afraid of what he would say to me when he would discover that I didn't have, wasn't prepared for the translation. Passages that I could expect him to travel right through the class on. He was an older man at the time when I was his student. He was near to the age of retiring from the faculty there. I remember what a surprise I had when I was about to leave the school. I never thought about going back there after I had graduated. I went to his house and rang the bell, and he came to the door. He was surprised. He didn't expect any student to come to see him and say good-bye to him I am pretty sure of that. I don't know any of my classmates who did that. Maybe one who was really a bookworm. In any case, I didn't appreciate him at the time but I could have, if I'd known enough. But I went to see Dr. Brown; he was a PhD. He taught there something like twenty-five or thirty years. He just taught Greek. When I went to see him, he had me sit down near his desk. He sat in the chair behind his desk but he didn't just look at me over the desk. He came to one side and looked over at me. When I said good-by to him, I started to cry. That disclosed to me how much he meant to me. I wondered about that.

SM: What did he do?

HB: I don't remember what he did about that.

RL: You wondered about that. Did you ever come to reconcile that?

HB: I knew the roots for it were in my respect for him and his capacity as a teacher to do one hell of a thorough job.

SM: When you said you think that your path to the study of philosophy perhaps started with the study of Greek, the language and/or what you read?

HB: What we worked on was in the language. I still have my Liddell and Scott's Greek dictionary. I had a feel for what was going on in that language. I didn't realize it. I wasn't conscious of that but I did try. I got some of the discipline of Greek grammar and construction. There's a great logic to the development of the language in terms of the words and complexes of words. I knew you really couldn't fool around with it.

Princeton: The Underdraduate Years

RL: When you left Hotchkiss and went to Princeton, did you go there majoring in philosophy?

HB: No.

RL: When did you major in anything?

HB: I got appendicitis and had an appendectomy. My appendix broke while rowing crew as a freshman, probably in the second or third freshman eight-oared shell. I was just getting started rowing and I was still pretty small. Most of the time we rowed six miles for a workout, which eventually in your second or third year of rowing you'd knock off in less than an hour. But I started to row in a single and I was very much impressed to do that by the rigger at the boathouse who was also a sculling coach and hailed from the east side of Brooklyn and murdered the language. But he had the most decisive and intriguing expressions. And I loved the way he talked.[2]

SM: Can you give us an example?

HB: I can remember the first time I went out in what I thought of as a shell but it wasn't. It's not a shell, it's more like a dingy. I managed to knife in with one oar and wash out with the other and over I went. John came out on the float with his big megaphone and he'd roar at you. "Hey, you! Hey, you!" Finally, I looked over there, trying to keep afloat, trying to keep my hand on the dingy. He saw I was looking at him for some kind of explanation for why he was hollering at me that way. He let out this fiendish cackle of a laugh. "See," when I swam around the boat, "the water's warmer on that side."

RL: Is this the same fellow you recount in *Inward Morning* racing in an automobile along side the regatta that was going on?

HB: Yes. He wouldn't let you dope off out there. Or become a victim of an accident, which you were quite capable of.

SM: Are you implying at Princeton, as far as our question about what led you into your work, that rowing was an important part?

HB: Oh, my God, yes. I was as openly attentive with respect to everything that went on with rowing, as I should have been with lessons that I ill prepared.

SM: What was it about rowing?

HB: I can certainly say that I developed the disposition to see things through. I loved the feeling of developing a capacity to handle a racing shell properly. To get the rhythm and the spacing of the strokes in a single flow.

RL: All your experience was with a scull, right?

HB: No. I rowed an eight too. And I soon rowed in a double scull with a classmate of mine there.

RL: About your academic life there, what was it like the first year?

HB: Mischievous, as the saying goes.

RL: Did you make your grades?

HB: I got through. At Princeton I graduated with high honors. They didn't give many of those around. I became so wholeheartedly involved in rowing that it carried over into my study habits to a certain measure. I became enamored of rowing, really. When I had this appendicitis and got periadenitis, they didn't have antibiotics in those days, so I nearly died. My father would come to the hospital, where he had his patients in the main, and sit on my bed by the hour. He'd just sit there. He would never reveal by actually making it an expressed thing, in that he never alluded to my condition, just how serious it was at the time. But finally, he was sitting one afternoon on the edge of my bed. All of sudden I let out a tremendous fart. He looked as if somebody had made him a tremendous present. I said, "Yes, Dad, that must be that obstruction in my intestine has passed, or at least been relieved of obstruction." And he just went wild. He was just so happy about that. Eventually, in study hall, which I didn't escape very consistently, when it came to the end of the day, after supper time—this was at Hotchkiss—I had a certain following of those who had desks at study hall that we made a little group. Some of them were my "clacks." I would break wind every so often, you know. They would just smother themselves with amusement over that. It would begin to show up from the standpoint of the master of the study hall, who sat on an upraised dais, a desk up there, surveying all the students out there—all of us who were either too dumb or not con-scientious enough to work properly in study hall. So, I became censured. Three censures and you would become sequestered and you wouldn't have any time off. You couldn't go to movies once a week when they were held at school and that sort of thing. It was really hard when you were that age. I got sequestered for breaking wind in study hall. And they sent a notice about this that was perfectly straight-faced to my parents. That was very embarrassing. My mother was particularly shocked.

RL: No, you were still at Hotchkiss. The appendectomy occurred at Hotchkiss?

HB: No, it was at Princeton. I never rowed a boat down at Hotchkiss but we did use the canoe to run some of the rivers, especially the Housatonic. A bunch of us, when we'd have a holiday, which we did once in a great while. Classes were suspended for the day. We'd put in up near the mouth of the stream I used to fish, which was a tributary of the Housatonic. There were some really nice brown trout in there, up to two, even two-and-a-half, pounds. The head master of the school used to like to fish there. I'd run into him over there once or twice. He taught me a class of English for a whole year, one year. Whenever we had a theme to write, I would always write about fishing. He would write a very careful criticism of what I'd written. Then he'd get around to making gen-eral comments that had a considerable coverage of what I would have handed into him week after week in that class. He would say, "For heaven sake Henry, can't you write about anything other than fishing?"

On the Road: *Placet Experiri*

RL: Henry, your excursions down to Florida, did they occur during classes?

HB: I didn't make overnight journeys to speak of.

SM: The long trips were when school was out?

HB: Vacation time. We would take advantage of vacation time now and then.

RL: You got into some kind of trouble, didn't you??

HB: Oh, my parents were pretty disgusted with me but they were so worried that I'd become a "cropper." I was out there shifting for myself amongst, God knows whom or what. I didn't tell them one of the first things I learned about riding the "Yellow bellies," as we called them—the freight cars in those days. You don't try to board an open box car by taking a run at the open door and then trying to jump up and muscle yourself up into the floor of the box car because if you miss, there's a liability that you get under the wheels of the car and you can loose one or both legs that way. But one hears about that sort of thing right away, when you're on the road. There's just no doubt about it.

RL: When you were riding these cars, you would be in company with others that were riding?

HB: I had a roommate, a dear friend of mine from Princeton. He and I bummed all the way out to Cody, Wyoming; worked in the hay fields there for friends who were ranchers.

RL: When you and your roommate would take these rides on these trains, would you run across genuine hobos in riding the rails?

HB: Would we ever! I remember we were looking over a train that was made up and ready to take off but hadn't started. We looked in one of the open box cars and here was one of toughest looking women I'd ever seen. I practically ran for my life! I was so frightened. Most of the people who were on the road we really having a hard time making ends meet. One way was to go where the work might be available, but that chiefly applied to something like the jobs with the crops.

RL: So when you went to Wyoming to work in the hay fields, there were others on board the train to do the same thing?

HB: Yes, only they weren't near the place we went to. We managed to get off the beaten track of hobos. Because we got to know the people who owned the ranch and they'd give us a job. But I didn't think to write them in advance but that's the way it ended up and they were very nice.

RL: This would be when you were about twenty or twenty-two?

HB: About twenty or twenty-one.

∼

SM: You became interested in philosophy at Princeton from this course that you took on the mind–body problem.

HB: Which was not a very typical sort of thing for me to worry about at that stage, or at any stage.

RL: But it seems to me that you became more interested in philosophy more out of opposition to that.

HB: Yes, sure. It nagged me. There had to be some way of speaking to the question. Of course, I didn't yet think much about when you want to tangle with a question, consider analyzing the question to see what it's supposing.

RL: You have a unique way of doing philosophy. How did you come to that?

HB: That's the sort of thing one doesn't know. I remember being very much absorbed in classes that I took with a senior member of the philosophy department at Princeton, named Warner Fite. He was a great reader of [Miguel de] Unamuno. I began to read Unamuno. I had already been interested in the life of Don Quixote and Sancho Panza. Unamuno was very much captivated by those stories. I absorbed a lot of that at Princeton.

RL: Do you think those where the most impressionable courses you took at Princeton?

HB: Not necessarily. I took some courses in which I read

novels, for example, such as—Dostoyevsky, I read on my own, about four books of Dostoyevsky's anyway.

RL: Do you recall what they were besides *Brothers K?*

HB: Well, let's see. *Poor People, The Idiot, Crime and Punishment, Brothers Karamazov, Notes from the Underground.* That's five!

RL: You graduated from Princeton, when?

HB: '36.

SM: I know you had some reservations about Princeton.

HB: I disliked it socially. They had a system of eating clubs there. They were run and managed by students. I don't know how much work was done there by hired help or how much was done by students who needed the money but there was a mixture there.

RL: You didn't take part in these clubs?

HB: I took part long enough to receive certain committees from these clubs. They went around looking into people to see where they were in their career. They would be solicited to join eating clubs. And I joined one but then I never really went to it except that one evening the people there if they were interested you were invited there to supper. I practiced a certain deception because Jake, my roommate, his family didn't have the money to pay his tuition, but they invited him to come to the same eating club that they had signed me on for. But, about ten days or two weeks later, I resigned from the club.

RL: What did you find offensive about these clubs?

HB: Their lives with one another were stereotyped, I thought.

RL: What did that represent?

HB: It represented to my ear, the sound of nothing really being said by anybody that amounted to much.

SM: What was your thesis about that you wrote at Princeton?

HB: It was very narrow and mostly out of concerns of becoming fundamental in the writings of St. Paul.

SM: What was it called, your thesis?

HB: It was a very modest title, "In Demonstration of the Spirit."

RL: It sounds like a pretty prodigious title.

HB: Yes, it was comic enough to mention it.

RL: It was largely about St. Paul.

HB: No. It came out of meditating upon the thought of St. Paul.

Westward to Berkeley

RL: Where did you go after Princeton?

HB: I went to Berkeley, as a graduate student in philosophy. When I went there as a graduate student, what really bothered the Dean was that a man should receive recognition as a very promising student at Princeton, come to the University of California, sign up for four courses and get four F's in them. I did that at Berkeley. The dean of the graduate school pulled me in to talk this over with me and assess whether he could tolerate seconding my continuing to be a normal member of the university student body, the graduate school particularly.

SM: You rediscovered Dostoyevsky in graduate school?

HB: Right.

SM: You were are Berkeley, but your studies there, as I understand it, were interrupted by the war?

HB: No. Strictly speaking, my studies were accomplished. I finished all of my course work from 1937 to 1941. Then I was in the Navy.

RL: What about your course work at Berkeley? Was it significant to you?

HB: While, some of it was, and some of it wasn't. There was a sort of positivist named Will Dennes. That kind of strain of thought, as you can imagine, hardly appealed to me or involved me as significant. He was positivistic in his approach, in the sense of the early part of this century. He knew [Moritz] Schlick's work especially. He dealt with the work of [Rudolf] Carnap some. [Willard Van Orman] Quine's stuff wasn't much published yet. Quine was a colleague of mine at Harvard later on.

RL: Where there any faculty there you liked?

HB: Yes. Donald McKay, I liked. He was interested in [Baruch] Spinoza. He was interested in what I was trying to do with Spinoza.

RL: You were working with Spinoza in those years.

HB: On my own, not a course

RL: Were you at Berkeley when the war broke out?

HB: I was in Berkeley. I'd finished my course work and I'd finished my teaching fellowship for that year, third semester of it. Than I began digging ditches for half a year before I was actually inducted into the Navy. I volunteered to get in and I presented my application to be considered for a commission outright. The Navy was doing that at the beginning of the war for people who had had a lot of education. They weren't too choosey for what that amounted to.

RL: Who were you digging ditches for at this time?

HB: A construction outfit over in Alameda.

RL: Was this just to make money to live on?

HB: Yes, but I liked it. Up at five in the morning and back for supper about 6:30 or 6:45, five days a week—six days a week. Only Sunday off. I was on one of the special details for digging ditches for laying pipe and so on. These two guys, older men, who were both Italian, were old hands at digging that sort of thing. I sure learned a lot from them. And they were the nicest people you'd want to know. I really liked them. I guess it was mutual because they wanted to share their lunches with me, as well as I wanted them to try some of mine, which were plebeian compared to those that they had. They gave me a lot of seed to raise horse beans. They're about the size of lima beans—big limas. They come in pods. You suck the beans out of the pods and then you cook them like they were just beans. Fresh beans. I would cook some and plant some.

RL: While you were digging these ditches, you weren't taking courses; you were done at Berkeley?

HB: Except for the thesis.

RL: Were you working on it?

HB: I tried hard, and I just couldn't get into it. I was sure I was somewhat impressionable with regard to the tumult of Pearl Harbor, and its consequences for the reading public.

RL: Pearl Harbor had occurred while you were digging ditches?

HB: Yes.

RL: Were you fishing during that time, Henry?

HB: Not much. I just used to go up to Fish Rising River in northern California within view of Mounts Shasta and Lassen, two magnificent mountains. Where I used to fish for rainbow and brown trout was in between those two mountains. They're really impressive. There's snow the year round on Shasta. It's about a 14,000 foot mountain. Lassen isn't that high—not that much altitude. It's a rugged mountain. It is more obviously a more recent volcano than Shasta was and more unmistakably a volcanic formation. And I was fishing waters where lava flow from Lassen had supervened over the land as it graduated toward the north. If would freeze there into rock—lava rock. You could wear out a pair of tennis shoes if you wore them for one day. That was great country. I would fish for steel head in the winter. The steel head would run in on the coastal rivers.

SM: Were you still rowing?

HB: No. I was rowing in Berkeley in those years, but by the time I went to the manual labor I didn't have the energy or the time, to do anything but that and a little cooking. Along with working as a teaching fellow and a full schedule of courses, I took usually two or three seminars as a graduate student. I took all my written examinations for my doctorate. I boned up on French and German, enough to be able to pass.

SM: You were pretty good with French.

HB: But that was after I went abroad for a year and I spent it working with Marcel and reading Heidegger in French. My German was terrible. I really didn't work on it.

Naval Service

RL: How did you start off to go into the Navy? You volunteered to go into the military and you went into the Navy?

HB: They had an officer's training program for civilians who came into the service. It took me about a month to go through that. I lived it day and night. I had some good courses in preparations for sea duty which I asked for. When it came for a preference for the type of service I wanted. I specified the type of duty consistent with my training, which was in small ships, in which I really wanted to get into. Get into everything from ship handling and all the rest.

RL: When did you first ship out?

HB: I was shipped out when I was assigned to the mine force out of San Francisco to sweep the main ship chan-

nel between the Farallon Islands and the harbor of San
Francisco.

RL: What was your status on that ship?

HB: I was just an officer on it for the first one I was in. On
the second one I was appointed in charge of a small fleet
of purse seiners—commercial fishing boats. I really liked
that. I had wonderful benefit from the instruction of two
senior petty officers I had in that ship's company. They
were both ex-purse seiners working out of Monterey,
California. My next assignment was to assume command of this new fleet built mine sweeper. A brand new
vessel—to take it on as my first ships assignment—as
captain of it in its shake down. So I joined that crew as
a really much less experienced officer than I became. I
was commander of the commissioned mine sweeper but
they wouldn't call a reserve officer in charge of it a commander. The crew would call you captain but they didn't
respect you entirely.

SM: How old were you, twenty-eight?

HB: I was younger. I was in the service four or five years in
the service, while I was working out of the states. I was
at sea for three-and-a-half years.

SM: So how did it feel at that tender age to be in command of
people who were veterans?

HB: It was anxiety causing but I learned how to handle myself
under such circumstances. Almost from the start when
I joined that first converted purse seiner, I talked to the
crew, I said, "Now look, there's not a guy on this crew
that doesn't know more than I do about what I need
to know. I want you guys to tell me when you observe
what I try to do when I'm trying to assume responsibility for the ship and give me a criticism and don't pull any
punches. Let's just sit down in the galley together with
nobody else present and I'll try to absorb what you tell
me and question what I don't understand." And they did
it pretty well. They took me up on that. For a while they
were nervous. They didn't know what to make of it.

SM: Wasn't that precipitated by them observing something
you were doing that wasn't quite kosher, indicating . . .?

HB: It was poor judgement in handling the currents that
ebbed and flowed through the Golden Gate essentially,

which had to handle the heavy seas over the sandbars out from the harbor. It's much rougher when it's shallow, you know. I was seasick for six months.

SM: In your training where were you taken out?

HB: We had a ship that we used, a purse seiner, to practice with. We had officers from the group of instructors who were responsible for teaching us what they could get through our skulls.

RL: You set things up where the men under your command could come and complain to you about things that they were dissatisfied with.

HB: I didn't want them to take their dissatisfaction or satisfaction as the criterion for what they selected to talk with me about. I wanted them to criticize the way I went about some things, that they noticed what they thought was a correctable error. I wanted them to make it explicit to me what it was they had observed and what to do in that kind of situation to which was difficult.

RL: Do you recall what they said to you?

HB: They talked to me about how to take the ship along side of a pier, where there's some surf running through the harbor and strong currents and particularly when you were trying to cope with a tidal current that was sweeping into the harbor and again ebbing out away from it. If you had to come along side the pier that you were going to tie up to, you couldn't be either set off so much so that you'd probably go up and hit the pier on the off side from the pier you're trying to get moored to. You also had to put a couple or three members of the crew over on the dock in order to tie up to the pier properly. Of course the worst danger is if you start coming around and you're being swept out against the pier—wham! You can stove in your ship.

RL: So they were concerned about the handling of the ship?

HB: Yes, ship handling was the main thing.

RL: They didn't seem concerned about how you were handling the men?

HB: Oh, I talked with them about any problem I had with men. They were sympathetic to that because they had their own opinion about the crew in that type of little ship.

RL: How many people were under your command when you were on that ship?

HB: A total of about thirty-six, including myself.

RL: What was the length of that vessel?

HB: One-hundred-thirty-seven-foot vessel, it was a small ship. I was very fond of that first crew but not as deeply so as the ones I would take command of the ship with for the rest of my time in the Navy.

RL: You left California with that vessel and you went out to sea.

HB: I went out with eight ships and all the personnel. I used to believe that no one would ever bother to expend themselves as a kamikaze in which the order of the day was to expend yourself. You don't come back alive. Their suicide planes were committed to expend themselves doing as much damage to ships of ours as they could, up to and including the complete devastation of all hands aboard that ship and the ship itself. It was an honorable death, from their point of view—it was absolutely their ultimate commitment from everyone that went into sea duty in the Japanese navy. There were no pensions for kamikaze pilots. To answer your question more specifically, we were cruising back from the gulf. We were traveling in a big formation, mine sweeping and hydrographicing ships. Of course everything was blacked out, no running lights, no lights showing from the ships. You could see the wake of the ship in front of you as you traveled in a column and even in foul weather you can keep your position but sometimes get thrown around a good deal if it's rough. Several suicide planes intercepted our task group as we were coming back down along the west coast to Leyte Gulf, which is an island, a big island in the Philippines. A Japanese two-engine bomber, one of their best planes, intercepted our column as we were steaming in formation, staggered about 180 yards apart. This proved to be a determined suicide plane. It was the first big bombing runs against the ships in our column, which was the leading column in the formation. They dropped their bombs so that they just missed one side or the other side of the ships in our column. We were the second or third ship in that column. They didn't do any good with their bombs from their point of view. That must of gotten them mad because then they started in with their automatic weapons, mostly 20mm guns that the planes were firing. They would come down, and come along, the column with more ships there to give the more reference points to keep them in position to hit one of the ships. They emptied all their automatic weapons down the starboard side when they were going that way. Then they came back up the other side coming up the port side. They missed on both those strafing runs. And they expended all their automatic weapons ammunition. So then we thought, well by God we've been missed. I was up on the flying bridge with our lookouts, signalmen, one petty officer and other added help. We thought, well, we were out of it. We didn't see any other planes. And just about that time I picked up a plane coming in off the starboard side as we're headed back down south, parallel to the coast. Here it was coming in louder and louder in on us. It seemed to be headed right for us, as indeed it was. It was zeroing in on us but there was quite a sea running so that when we in the trough of the wave, he couldn't be sure he wouldn't stumble on the wave at its zenith before he made his target. Well, he really did his best. I thought he was sure as hell gonna hit us. One of the lookouts on the flying bridge said, "Captain, he's gonna hit us!" I said let's see. "We can't take that as a for gone conclusion." The engines were just deafeningly loud as he came on and on. I could even catch the silhouette of the plane when we were up high enough to be able to see it well from its distinction from all the sea in between. All of a sudden I realized he is gonna hit us if he doesn't get lower. And hit us broadside too. I told the boys to hit the deck and we all flopped down on the deck and flying bridge which had a sort of pipe rail around it and a laced canvas spray shield for the volumes of water. We were about 23 feet above the flat calm of water. That gives you an idea of how much we were projecting at the high point at the trough of the wave. As the roar became deafening, I laid down with other guys up there and he came over so that it was deafening. I glanced at him as he passed over. I looked back, we had a mast behind the flying bridge

that stuck up about twenty more feet. We felt sure that
he couldn't miss that. But he was about a foot and a half
forward of the mast. His starboard wing passed over the
rail of the flying bridge and the spray shield. And by God,
he never hit a thing. He never hit the mast. He never
touched what was stuck up of the superstructure of the
ship up there. There was a mast and also a cross-tree of it
with halyards we'd hoist the signals on. He never caught
any of that. Like I say, he missed it all by a foot and a half
or two feet, let's say. He never touched this and he was
trying to deflect downward but he was too late. We were
in the bottom of the trough. He went on beyond and hit
the sea and blew up. He was about 100 feet away when
he hit the sea. He was doing his best to hit us. If he'd
compensated unduly, he was bound to pile up in the sea.
He'd over shoot.

RL: Were your gunners firing at him?

HB: I hollered at them, "Not a round is to be fired." Because
what they'll do is simply use that cone of fire to fly right
in to us. A sort of trail finder for us. So you don't react
at all and you're safer then. Cause you have to shoot the
plane down or blow it up or something before you will
be effective with your guns. If we'd had a good enough
crew on our three-inch gun, which was on the forward
deck, that could knock a plane out of the sky with more
that just a slight chance of missing. But we didn't fire the
three-inch gun. It's too slow anyway. It's manually oper-
ated. So we didn't fire anything. He just finished himself
off by being a little bit off. After he blew up over there,
we jumped up. We knew he was gone and we were feeling
exhilarated about being alive. All of a sudden, oh maybe
in about five minutes, we were all just shaking. It was so
close. Just absolutely the luck of the game.

SM: Do you ever think about that pilot and who he was?

HB: Yes, sure.

SM: It's an intense relationship, even though adversarial.

HB: I think you'll find if you read over the passages that touch
on that, you'll see that your concern to ask that question,
was one that we shared at the time. I even recall thinking, "We might as well have been that pilot in that plane.
And he might as well have been one of us aboard the ship,

his target." It cost him his life but it didn't cost any of us ours. We only had one man who was, as it happened, seriously wounded. He took a party from the ship's company, a couple of the sailors over in a small motor-driven landing craft to one of the smaller islands where ship's stores were being landed. You could go to that island and pick them up. We went nearly four months at sea without ever setting foot on land. On a 137-foot ship with thirty-four or thirty-five people aboard, that's rather close quarters. It's almost comparable to a submarine crew.

SM: I remember there was a man who sent you a tape that he made when he was dying. He wanted you to have it. You've never been able to play that again.

HB: No, I haven't, but I still have it.

SM: Could you talk about the circumstances?

HB: He was one of the best hands we had aboard ship. He was an indefatigable worker in everything. When he had the wheel, the wheel watch, among other people that circulated that job when we were underway, I'd look at the compass repeater on the flying bridge and if it varied less than two degrees off the given course, in spite of how rough the sea was, then that must be Elliott on the wheel down there. I said, "Elliott, what are you doing on watch right now?" He said, "Well it was just my turn, captain," up through the voice tube. I said, "Well, I knew it had to be you. You don't seem to know when it is rough out here." He was seasick all the time when he was aboard. That meant most of the time, since we were underway out in the far Pacific in fairly calm water, except when typhoons would come and lesser storms. He had somehow managed to suppress his sea sickness so that nobody noticed it. It turned out that he ruined his stomach.

SM: Where was he when he made this tape?

HB: Back home in Texas. Well after the war, within five or six weeks after the capitulation of the Japanese.

SM: So this tape just arrived in the mail? It must have been quite an experience.

HB: Yes.

RL: You told me one time, Henry, a story of a kamikaze pilot coming at you and everybody was firing except this one guy.

HB: Yes, it was the same guy. He battle station was on the twin fifty-caliber machine guns mounted on the aft rail of the starboard quarter. So that he swung out near the targets out there.

RL: So you asked him how come he didn't fire and he said?

HB: "Just waitin', just waitin', Captain." And he said it that wry Texas voice. We were underway twenty-four hours a day in those days. I was not always on the same watch that he was. I would be up taking star sightings at dawn, for navigation. I knew when he would be on watch as I was and when he wouldn't be. If he wasn't already where I would know he was on watch, I'd seen him there when I came off watch, myself, on the flying bridge. I assumed he was on the wheel or the voice radio or taking messages on the voice radio—receiving changes of orders and so on. If I would go up there and I knew he was on watch, and if I didn't have to be on the bridge for the next thirty seconds, I would whip down the ladder and get down to where the coffee was in the galley and pour two cups of coffee and try without spilling very much of it to get them up there and give him one and I would have one. He would do the same when he was the one to cascade down the ladder and pick us up our eye-opener. I can still feel what it was to be that tired. Because we could never be sure to get to sleep in a bunk for twenty-four hours, forty-eight hours, and as much as seventy-two hours because we were on watch.

RL: I can remember times you said it wasn't all this bad.

HB: Right. What we did, actually, was if there was an opportunity to get fish from the sea, we would. We'd do them by getting our quarry already to launch with an outboard motor already warmed up. So that we could get underway as soon as we got it on the water and got in it. We could head for the target area, where the fish might be expected or surfaced by reason of the explosion of mines. We tried to get rid of any mine that would be in proximity that was dangerous by disposing of it by gunfire. But mostly it was the possibility of aerial bombs that had failed to go off. You could hit one of them and there might be mines that had been cut, that had drifted a way out of the minefield, and you could hit them. So we picked up our share of mines that we dispatched and got rid of by gun fire. Every one of them. Then we'd get the fish that would come to the surface after a while, after the explosion. We'd take aboard enough for us to take a good supply of fish to our Marine friends who where over on the beach, working to catch Japanese who were still on the land over there. They used to invite—they always invited me, a couple of the officers and a petty officer or two to go over and swim at their beach when there didn't seem to be any planes around. Activity had to be monitored. Tended to. We would go to the supply ship for our own provisions. We'd pick up another ship's company supply of provisions to give to the detachment of Marines nearest us over on the beach. We were great friends. Whenever we had a chance to go and swim with them in the afternoon, and we never once got caught with our pants down. We went over there and swam and then they would always serve us a couple of these really explosive drinks that they put together out of medical alcohol.

SM: Do you remember what they were called?

HB: Torpedoes. Terrible, terrible, probably ninety-eight proof. We put some grapefruit juice in it. It was all for our health's sake. You couldn't drink much of that or you'd be looped. We had a cook on the ship. We'd cook up the fish. The food was edible. He wasn't a very good cook. He was a nice guy and he tried hard but he didn't do too well. Under stringent circumstances we welcomed having food. He had a cast iron skillet that would hold almost enough pork chops to fry up for one of the crews and their mess. Then there would be two or three sections to be fed. When we'd look in and see that huge skillet on the stove, these pork chops rolling in the grease, as the ship rolled. It was really something.

SM: So where were you toward the end of the Second World War?

HB: Waiting to be relieved of command.

SM: And where was that?

HB: Okinawa.

SM: Then what did you do?

HB: I didn't take very long in getting a flight back!

SM: Where?

HB: To Pearl Harbor and then to . . . .

SM: Where was your family . . . your wife and children? Were they on the West Coast?

HB: Yes.

SM: Were they in the San Francisco Bay area?

HB: Yes.

SM: What did you do when you got to the states? I assumed you went to see your family and where were they living at that time?

HB: Yes, they were living about five minutes from where I lived before deploying.

SM: Was that Berkeley?

HB: Um-hum [yes].

SM: So they were living in Berkeley? And were you discharged then from the service? And what did you do as far as work then?

HB: I didn't do very much, that I can recall.

RL: You hadn't finished your PhD, had you, Henry?

SM: No, he hadn't.

RL: Didn't you work on your dissertation?

HB: Um-hum; I finished it up that year.

Completion of Dissertation and Fishing

SM: Correct me if I'm wrong but, my memory is that you were struggling with writing your dissertation.

HB: That was earlier.

SM: But then when you came back after the war you found at some point that you could sit down and do that work that you had difficulty doing before?

HB: Yes, that's right.

SM: Was it as if those issues that, perhaps, were composting during the time of the war?

HB: You could put it that way maybe, I don't know.

SM: But by the time the war was over you had experienced some kind of fruition on those issues and were able to put them down.

RL: All then you needed to do is write your dissertation. And I take it that you had attempted to begin that before you went.

HB: And I couldn't manage it.

RL: But after the war . . . What did you write your dissertation about, Henry?

HB: On the sense and conception of being. [laughter] It is just a minor responsibility.

RL: A simple little topic. [laughter]

SM: Narrowly focused.

RL: What authors did you work with most prominently in that?

HB: Well, let's see. [pause] Well, I worked with Charles M. Doughty who was a most remarkable man.

RL: You mean that this was a faculty member at the University at Berkeley?

HB: No.

RL: This was an author you worked with?

SM: What was his orientation?

HB: He wrote a book on essentially the relation between himself and people who would have been involved in the kind of relation in the Bali members of a nomadic Arabian tribe?

HB: He was, I wonder . . . I have the book there. And we can look it up and see what its publication date was.

SM: He took all these travels into Arabia.

HB: Um-hum.

SM: You wrote on him in your dissertation?

HB: He was one of the people I wrote on. And I wrote on the work of the . . . one of the great painters.

RL: [Paul] Cezanne, right?

SM: There was the man who travelled to Arabia, the painter Cezanne. Were there other artists?

HB: Um-hum, [Johannes] Brahms. That's enough.

SM: I would like to read that. I know that you have a copy of that.

HB: I hope so. I don't know.

SM: I think so.

HB: I can look for it.

RL: You worked on that after you got out of the service and came back to Berkeley?

HB: That is when I really got to work on it, because I ceased to attempt to do academic work as it were and tried to dig into what it was that was possessing me, which lead me down the trail that I was following.

SM: Henry, is this correct that when you came back, the first year all you did was just fish?

HB: Of course. [laughter]

SM: You fished for a long time and then you were able to sit down and write your dissertation in about six weeks.

HB: I think so.

SM: I think that is very interesting.

RL: Henry, I want to hear something about your fishing stories. Where did you fish? Was it steelhead fishing or were you fishing for rainbow?

HB: Steelhead.

RL: Steelhead, mostly. And were you using a fly rod?

HB: As soon as the end of the steelhead season came, I quit fishing.

RL: But that was a month of steelhead fishing that you enjoyed?

HB: Yeah.

RL: Were you using a fly rod?

HB: Yeah I did.

RL: Because fly rod fishing for steelhead in those days was pretty experimental. And did you sustain yourself on the steelhead that you caught?

HB: Well, I didn't keep many, that is for sure. I gave a fish or two to the family that I was staying with.

RL: You were staying with a family.

HB: Ranchers lived up there. And they had prepared to make accommodations to people who had come there to stay with them and eat their meals there.

RL: You rented a place from them?

HB: Yeah.

RL: Ok. I suppose that you don't have any memory of the rod that you used when you fished that. Was it that old Winston?

HB: It was before that.

RL: It was before the Winston that I've seen you steelhead with so frequently. So then, after a month of fishing, you went back and wrote this dissertation inside of a short period of time.

HB: It took at least a month and a half.

RL: The muses must have sat on your shoulder during that time.

HB: I spent a lot of that time listening to my records.

RL: Classical music as you wrote?

HB: A lot of the time, I'd listen and then I'd write.

SM: Henry is not one who ever can listen to music that can ever be a background. When he listens to music, he is listening to music.

RL: He shuts it off, and then he writes.

HB: Um-hum.

RL: I see. And what happened after you completed the manuscript? What then occurred? You submitted to the university?

HB: I submitted it to my committee.

SM: Can I just ask one thing before we go on? Is it possible for you to talk at all about your dissertation? [pause] Maybe that's not possible. But I thought that I'd ask.

HB: To get back into the midst of it just wouldn't be the same.

SM: I know.

RL: [laughter]

SM: That's true of anything, of course.

RL: But it's there for us to read.

HB: But I sure got to work in it. I had a committee that I thought would never accept it. But they didn't raise any objection.

RL: I am very tempted to ask some very philosophical questions about that dissertation but I don't know.

SM: He's been retired.

RL: But I would like to know the connections you found between such people as Cezanne, Brahms, and . . . what was the name of the man who went to Arabia? Doughty?

HB: Charles M. Doughty.

RL: What kind of connection did you see between these apparently various folk?

HB: Well, very simply, the theme that I picked up on was that he spent four or so many years among the nomadic Arabians and he made it appear, made it clear that while he was there that he gave himself to the guidance of those who lived that life and who he trusted and who trusted him. They accepted him and they didn't try to fool him at all. They didn't try to take advantage of him in any way. They saw in him a man they could trust and that they would not betray him to any one. It was incredible.

RL: So how does this connect to your dissertation and your insights about Cezanne?

HB: It's a matter at the bottom of integrity.

SM: How did you come up with this "something"?

HB: These were men of the same reliability.

RL: In their commitment to what had . . . .?

HB: His relation with the natives whom he entrusted himself to and who accepted him in their trust.

RL: And he was claimed by that relation?

HB: Um-hum. Absolutely.

RL: And Cezanne?

HB: How Cezanne, what he stuck with.

RL: And he too, was claimed by his uttermost commitment to his work.

SM: And he painted that picture of the Chaîne de l'Etoile Mountains over and over and over again.

RL: Until he . . . well he never did get it right, right?

HB: Well, I don't know if he ever said he got it right.

RL: And Brahms, the same thing. Right?

HB: Yes.

SM: Could you say a little more about Brahms?

HB: That would be very hard to do.

RL: Well you know Henry, Brahms was a frequent visitor in the hall of the Wittgenstein's in Vienna.

HB: I know. They thought a lot of him. I became introduced to Wittgenstein through the repute at which he stood in the eyes of those who befriended them in their homes.

RL: Some of the original presentations of the works that he had written were in the household. And of course, Wittgenstein's brother, Paul, who lost his right arm during war, came back and wrote music for left-handed pianists

SM: That's interesting.

Way Stations: Reno, Stanford, Catham, Penn State

RL: I'm anxious to hear about your first teaching appointment. Where was it?

HB: I went to the University of Nevada at Reno. And while I
was there I got invited to come to Stanford, so I did not
continue teaching at the University of Nevada.

RL: But wasn't it at Nevada, you've told me this story on
numerous occasions, the one about the "caretaker"
Mr. Lewis?

HB: Oh, yeah.

RL: Was it there in Nevada that that happened?

HB: Yeah. There was a pond there and wild geese used to fly
into that pond and nobody disturbed them there including me. I used to take my lunch down and sit under the
willows by the pond and eat my lunch and enjoy the bird
water fowl. And I never disturbed them.

RL: But there was this caretaker . . .

HB: Right. He was in there. An inside man, I'd say, who
worked on a position that made him in charge of the
library, the university library.

RL: He was in charge of the library?

HB: Yeah. But mainly just as to see to it that no body stole
anything or took advantage of the opportunity that they
might have had there to cater to his own taste. His name
was Mr. Lewis. Everybody called him Mr. Lewis, even
if they were members of the faculty. Even if one was
a member of the faculty, one wasn't shit compared to
Mr. Lewis.

[laughter]

HB: So it was established. I think he kind of appreciated that
sense of the country there and he would leave a trail from
the pond outside the library all the way up and into the
door leading into the library.

RL: How did he build this trail?

HB: He just prepared . . . he just opened a hatch, actually a
door into the library.

SM: A trail of grain.

HB: Yes, he got some grain and started it in there and in due
time the geese became quite confident and they would
come in there. They would come in through the door and
make themselves at home in the basement of the library.

[laughter]

HB: And he was the man that was in charge.

RL: They assumed that it was Mr. Lewis.

HB: They thought that it was Mr. Lewis. He used to tell me, well. I remember asking him once if he ever did any prospecting and he said "oh yeah." I get a little need of money and go out pan some gold. And that's how I managed to guarantee a grub steak when I was working at the University of Nevada when I didn't have enough to make the expenses. Or I would talk to Mr. Lewis about it and he would tell me what his capacity was, and that he would like to go out and get a few results of mining.

RL: Gold.

HB: Gold. Yeah.

RL: So was it on a Thanksgiving that Mr. Lewis finally decided to harvest one of those geese?

HB: Well, it was right around there. I can't remember for sure when it was. The concession I made to myself was to providing Thanksgiving dinner or not. But, I arrived at a condition of confidence and I don't know if Lewis knew anything about how I followed his example to pocket a turkey.

RL: You mean that you took one too, Henry?

HB: Oh yeah!

[laughter]

HB: I took a turkey.

RL: This is a new twist of the story that I have heard many times. You'd always told it to me that Mr. Lewis got the turkey. Now it also comes clear that you also took a turkey.

HB: I took a goose.

RL: Right, not a turkey, but a goose. So these poor innocent geese would follow the trail of corn?

HB: One goose came in there . . .

RL: Into the basement of the library.

HB: They left the door to the library basement open and I stood behind it and the goose came in and I whacked him.

[laughter]

RL: What did you whack him with, Henry? Do you recall?

HB: I think I had a stick.

SM: Where was the custodian?

HB: He wasn't there. I was there all by myself and got myself my own goose.

RL: Can we say that this was your most memorable experience at the University of Nevada?

HB: Along with being impressed by the prestige of Mr. Lewis. He had a position that was sacrosanct. I never had any trouble with him, because I didn't mistreat any of the property of the University or the Library.

RL: Did Mr. Lewis know that you harvested this goose?

HB: I wouldn't be surprised.

RL: But you never spoke with him directly.

HB: I don't remember doing so. He didn't bother me any. He knew.

RL: And did you have this goose for Thanksgiving dinner?

HB: Sure did. I think so. I can't imagine that we didn't it eat.

RL: It must have been a memorable occasion. How long were you at the University of Nevada? Do you recall?

HB: Not more than two years.

RL: Then you went to Stanford?

HB: Yep.

RL: Can you put a date on your arrival at Stanford?

HB: No. I suppose that it would be possible to do so.

[laughter]

RL: I am sure it would. I guess will find that date some other way. But you went to Stanford? And what did you do that for?

[laughter]

HB: I couldn`t believe it when I was offered a position there.

RL: It wasn't because you could play tennis?

HB: No.

SM: Did you apply there? Or were you sought out?

HB: There were a couple of members of the philosophy department at Stanford who had found my work, and my thesis, and the kind of commitment I was involved in for that.

SM: How did they know you?

H: Through my relationship with other people in the Department of Philosophy at Berkeley. They knew the good people I had worked with on my committee there. They boosted me. Not that I think they did it all together. Though there was a little liability of collusion.

[laughter]

HB: They thought that I was an honest guy that was up to something that should be honored. They gave me my chance and I went a long with it.

RL: So how long were at Stanford?

HB: No more than a year.

RL: Really?

HB: Um-hum.

RL: A short tenure. You left Stanford to go to Harvard?

HB: Um-hum.

RL: And it was the invitation to join the Harvard faculty that drew you away from Stanford?

HB: Um-hum. I figured that I couldn't afford to miss that opportunity.

RL: Was it Harvard that you began *The Inward Morning*?

HB: Before I began to write *The Inward Morning*, I was already writing a lot—when I quit fishing and went to work. That's when I wasn't just teaching.

RL: *The Inward Morning* was about your stays in Nevada and Stanford.

HB: When I was at Stanford. I was really in it then.

RL: Were you actually writing things down?

HB: I think so. I don't know how or how effectively or how long a period of time. I was sure writing.

RL: Did they make any attempt, the people at Stanford, to keep you there.

HB: They did. They offered me an associate professorship [laughter] and I hadn't even taught one full year. I wasn't even a member of the faculty yet at Stanford.

Harvard

RL: But you turned that down, so you could go to Harvard as an assistant professor.

HB: I turned Stanford's offer down. I went to Harvard as an assistant professor.

RL: To Harvard?

HB: Um-hum. And I worked my butt off.

RL: Doing what?

HB: Preparing myself as a philosopher.

RL: To teach these courses?

HB: To work through the thoughts that were on my mind.

RL: How did you find Harvard to be?

HB: Well I found that it was wonderful. And I certainly did not have one complaint about the way I was being treated by my colleagues. They almost declared to me that "Well you know Henry, we can't put a person up for a tenure position in the department unless that person has prepared himself for that sort of position. As a tenured position. And you haven't published." I said," I know that. I've been expecting." [laughter] And you wouldn't be able to do anything about that. I think it is one of the greatest breaks I've had, when I had really four years. I had a five-year appointment and I worked it out, the whole of it.

RL: So you expected not to be tenured.

HB: Not at all. But they individually, each one of my colleagues, came to me and told me, some of them with tears in their eyes, that they hated like hell to see me have to leave because I hadn't been published yet. At just about that time, I finished the first paper I had published.

RL: Which paper was that?

HB: "A Moment of Obligation and Experience."

RL: Who were among those colleagues, Henry?

HB: At Harvard?

RL: At Harvard.

HB: Jacob Loewenberg who had refused to sign the oath. Remember that whole ordeal?

RL: Gosh, yes.

HB: The oath of loyalty to the United States. He was deeply respected because he refused to sign that oath that guaranteed that he wouldn't do something that would embarrass Harvard, or something.

SM: A loyalty oath?

HB: Yes, that's right. The McCarthy thing.

RL: Who were some of the other colleagues, Henry? Van Quine?

HB: Van Quine, Henry Aiken, and Donald Williams. Quine and I became the closest friends.

RL: Yes, I know that.

SM: He gave us a very nice thing [poem] for the guest room.

RL: Oh did he? Quine did? Wonderful!

HB: You should see it.

RL: I will, I will, no question about it.

SM: Very short but quite sweet.

HB: But he's not a gracious person.

RL: Oh no. If he can put it into an axiom, he will do it.

[laughter from all]

RL: Wasn't this about the time that Quine was assembling those essays that would later be known as "The Logical Point of View"?

HB: Yeah, I suggested that title.

RL: I know you did. And tell the story of how that came about.

HB: I told them all then that I had no qualms about offering him advice because we were such good friends. "Quine," I said, "I've thought up a title for your book." He said, "No! You did?" I said it came from a calypso song—I've forgotten how it goes.

RL: Was it a Harry Belafonte song that was popular?

HB: [trying to recall song]

SM: It'll come later.

HB: Yeah. All that I can ring up is a positivist's point of view.

RL: Quine's book was named at your suggestion?

HB: I don't even know if he remembers that it was.

RL: Actually in his introduction, he attributes that to Aiken.

HB: Well, Aiken made the most of it.

[laughter]

RL: But that was from Belafonte's calypso song?

HB: Oh yeah. It wasn't Henry Aiken who suggested that title. I think I only had proprietary commission with it.

RL: But while you were at Harvard, you began working on *The Inward Morning* in earnest.

RL: Did you complete *Inward Morning* while you were at Harvard?

HB: Well, it was being completed while I finished up there.

RL: At Harvard.

HB: Um-hum.

RL: They accepted it as a publishable piece of work.

HB: They never told me that. They told me that it would be a good idea for me to publish.

RL: But *The Inward Morning* was published after you left Harvard, was that correct?

HB: Um-hum.

RL: But nonetheless a substantial portion on *Inward Morning* was written while you were at Harvard.

HB: And even before. I wrote some of it when I was working in Stanford. But I'd have to do some research in order to reconstruct sequences.

RL: But you left Harvard because they were unable to provide you tenure there so the truth is, you had to leave because they were unable to tenure you?

HB: They told me gently, of course we can't put you up for promotion, for a tenure position. I had expected it.

SM: Where were you, as far as academics was concerned, was is at Harvard that you were asked to somehow speak about what you wanted to do there?

HB: I know what you're inquiring about. At Harvard they had a philosophy club and all graduate students were just about required to attend its meetings. They were as numerous as ours, here but a little more reasonable in spacing. But I remember when it came my turn introduce myself to the fellow students and faculty very early in the first year, I was very much immersed in Spinoza at the time. I wrote a little essay called "Good, Bad and Real." When it came to articulating a sense of reality, I was supposed to write about a chapter in *Moby Dick* where Ahab sets forth with the crew, excited for the chase to attack the white whale, who's Moby Dick. There's a paragraph at the end of that chapter which having detailed the make up of the whaling boat from which members of the crew would man it and go out with a harpooner and the helmsman with the steering oar and about maybe 6 men at the oars to move it. He elaborates the detail of instances that would be matters of life and death for members of a whaling boat's crew. After a lot of that is built into the ending of that chapter, Melville writes, "And if you be a philosopher, you will feel not one more whit of terror though seated in such a boat that you would be sitting by your fire of an evening with a poker rather than a harpoon by your side." I've always had the feeling that awe and terror of things that can invade one about matters that can strike one as unforgettably real, not only those that are good or bad but real. That sort of spelled out the alternatives. If you be a philosopher, irrespective

of where you're situated, you're not going to be any less
involved. Gripped by things that are matters of potential
life and death.

RL: Where did you go after you left Harvard?

HB: Chatham College.

RL: Chatham, all right. And you were at Chatham for several
years.

HB: Um-hum.

SM: One year.

RL: One year?

HB: Was it only one year?

SM: Um-hum.

RL: Was *The Inward Morning* published while you were at
Chatham?

SM: No, afterwards.

RL: Afterwards?

HB: In '58.

SM: I typed up the manuscript because I was at Chatham

RL: You were at Chatham, Sally?

HB: Of course she was. How do you think I began to learn so
much?

RL: And why did you leave Chatham?

SM: Why would you want to stay at Chatham?

Moving to Montana

RL: When you left Chatham, you came to the University of
Montana, Missoula.

HB: Um-hum.

RL: Why in the world, did you do that?

HB: Because I wanted to.

RL: I understand. But why did you want to?

HB: Well, I could teach the sort of thing, I was interested in
teaching and also I was extremely involved in the wilderness theme and the relation of that with the commitment that I found in my teaching.

SM: And you fell in love with this part of the country when
you were a boy and would come out here with your
family to a dude ranch in Wyoming, wasn't it?

HB: That was part of it, yeah.

SM: You always longed to live in the Rocky Mountains.

HB: Also, I worked in a hayfield there all summer.

SM: But those boyhood times in the Rocky Mountains were deeply imprinted upon you.

HB: Yep.

RL: But you recall those events when you were lured to Missoula Valley?

HB: Um-hum.

RL: How did you find it at the University of Montana, Henry?

HB: Well . . . I had a full time professorship.

RL: When did you become the chair of the Department of Philosophy at the University of Montana?

HB: My second year of teaching there.

RL: You became discontent Henry, shortly after you were made chair there, right?

HB: Yeah, but probably a total of a couple of years later.

RL: What happened?

HB: [long pause] I wasn't really discontent so much with the department or my teaching. I had the opportunity to teach what I wanted. I was very much taken with the idea of pursuing further than I had before teaching the history of philosophy. That was not a bad idea to get really grounded with that kind of preparation.

RL: But didn't you leave the University of Montana?

HB: Eventually. That was about a full four years later I would say, at least.

RL: What prompted you to do that?

HB: Well, as chairman, I thought that the commitment of this university made to me in coming to join them was not solid concerning the matter of the presupposition of the size of the department would be, and what the expectation of the members of the department were to be. We were not to be held to a lockstep advancement. In other words, we were supposed to teach no more than the equivalent of one full course a year. And we really had a toe-hold on the department that way.

RL: But the administration was not supporting you in the manner you felt was necessary in running a department.

HB: What we had agreed upon.

SM: They didn't stand by a written agreement, is that correct Henry?

HB: Yeah, that's the way I remember. I don't know. Where is there a copy of it?

SM: But what was the agreement, do you remember?

HB: That one full course a year would be the normal teaching agreement for teaching.

RL: Were all members of the faculty promised the same thing?

HB: If they did that kind of intensive work.

RL: Ok. So when you left the University of Montana, which would have been 1958–59 or so, what did you do?

Penn State and Lecture Tour

SM: I think that is when we went to the Pennsylvania State University.

RL: You went from the University of Montana to Penn State?

HB: Because it became apparent that the university wasn't going to back up there commitment to me as I had understood it.

RL: So you went to the Penn State?

HB: Um-hum. I was invited there by former colleagues and so on.

RL: Who were they?

HB: One of them was Dick Gotshalk. Another one was John Anderson.

RL: John Lawry remained at the University of Montana, is that right?

HB: For a year. Maybe more than a year . . .

RL: Yeah, because he was there when you came back.

HB: I read him a note after being there a full year that said I felt like I was bleeding to death. I couldn't stand being away from the mountains.

RL: So then you came back to Missoula.

HB: Um-hum. And I came without having a commitment to be taken back in.

SM: No job.

RL: But you did go on a lecture tour during those years?

HB: Yeah but that came after when I knew I didn't have a position of any sort.

RL: That's what I mean. You came back to Missoula and didn't have a job, so then you went on a lecture tour.

HB: Yeah. It was really all of the efforts of my friend, who I'd known already from Stanford.

SM: It wasn't Houston Smith, was it?

HB: Yes. Houston Smith was a very good friend.

SM: I know that, but was he the one that was responsible for your taking this tour?

HB: I don't know the extent of which he was. He and Jeffrey Smith had a big part in it.

RL: You travelled all over the nation?

HB: No.

RL: Where did you travel for these lectures?

HB: Oh those lectures. Well those were all around. Yeah.

RL: So you saw a lot of universities?

HB: Well, yes.

Intensive Humanities Program: University of Montana

RL: I always understand that that experience in that lecture tour taught you things that were integral in your belief in the soundness of the intensity of the humanities program upon what was organized at the University of Montana some years later.

HB: Yeah. Not very long later. Quite a lot of intensive humanities projection. It was getting into that that led me more closely into teaching in line with the sort of thing that we were taking up with in that program.

RL: You came back to the university in about 1966–67.

HB: Something like that, I suppose.

SM: Those three years he was on the road.

RL: Right. And now I begin to have good memories of all of this, because I soon came involved in 1967. You took over the chairmanship of the department; I know a number of people were hired because of that. And it was about in 1970 or 1971 that the intensive humanities program was instituted and I've been very anxious to give you the opportunity to talk about that. I know that it claimed you in an irrevocable sort of way.

HB: Irrevocable. Yeah.

SM: In other words irrevocable. [different syllabic stress]

RL: Irrevocable. [repeat of the above]

SM: Henry, was that your baby? Did you dream up that
program?

HB: No.

SM: Was it a collaboration?

HB: There were three of us that worked it out. Ray Lanfear,
and Tom Huff and I. Isn't that the way you remember?

RL: No. I didn't play much of a part in its inception. It was
Tom and you and maybe John Lawry. I became a part
of the program a year or two after it was in full gear.
What do you remember about the intensive humanities
program?

HB: Nothing.

RL: Nothing?! You are speaking with a forked tongue now.
I'm sure you do.

[pause]

HB: About how much we trusted ourselves to people to work
with certain books that we believed in. That we thought
were substantive in their character. And how we needed
to drive those students to take them really seriously. Trying to figure out what was going on in them.

RL: Henry, for the twenty-eight years I have known you,
I have always believed that the intensive humanities
program was perhaps the most important event in your
entire academic career.

HB: I thought so to.

RL: How come?

HB: Well, No one wants to participate in that program the
way we did. And the kind of teaching that we did when
we were participating in it. And I believed in that.

RL: What kind of teaching was that, Henry?

HB: The substance of it was the work we did. And that included every week that I had to tutor a student. And that
was a major commitment, those tutorials. As I remember
mine. They were weekly. One a week.

RL: So each student weekly.

HB: Um-Hum.

RL: For at least an hour.

HB: And they wrote a paper each week.

RL: Almost. But more importantly, they wrote a journal.
Remember the journal?

HB: Oh, yes.

RL: The journal kept track of their response with the reading.

HB: Um-Hum.

RL: You would give us that journal and we would read it and talk with them in advance and then you would talk with them in tutorial about how they were engaging with the class.

HB: That's right.

RL: Do you recall, Henry, how you and I meet in the department at five o'clock in the morning so we could talk with one another about the material?

HB: I sure do. That was absolutely fundamental in my attraction into that program that we shared it that way. And that we got up early so that we could get in that time before we had to teach. And then things began to unfold.

RL: Do you remember some of the students in your program?

HB: I ought to. I've since seen something of some of them ever since.

RL: Not many enrolled at the onset?

HB: No. You would have to look through the records and see how many enrolled in the program.

SM: Would it be pertinent at this point for you describe a little about what this program was?

HB: I'm very poor at it, aren't I?

RL: We don't think you are. You're very good. I could describe it, but I want to hear it in your words.

HB: [pause] . . . There was quite a bit of time invested in the program to begin with; it was based on what we considered to be foundational readings. It was absolutely essential to grapple with that stuff and not in a strictly academic way, but working with the students in a way that formed our own habits of study too. Our purpose was to not approach the texts in an overly scholarly manner but listen to the texts "with a brotherly ear."

Appendixes

Henry Bugbee remains to this day a revered member of the Montana community. His reputation stems from his roles as teacher, outdoorsman, and avid environmental advocate.[1] His testimonies at local wilderness hearings were "spectacular moments" that enriched and deepened discourse about nature and the wilderness forever.[2] It is interesting to note that when interviewing for the job of assistant professor of philosophy at the University of Montana in 1956 he confessed, "I didn't dare look at the hills or rivers for fear I'd be unduly influenced . . . So I stuck strictly to the business ahead during that interview."[3]

Curriculum Vitae: The Course of Life

Bugbee's *Vitae* is an interesting piece of writing for reasons extending beyond chronological record. Today a *curriculum vitae* is synonymous with a résumé, losing the original meaning of *curriculum vitae* as a *living* record of a *life* of learning. At a time when many philosophers are forced to resort to journeymen status—traveling to wherever the job happens to be—note how Bugbee refers to Missoula as "HOME for me from then on . . . [and] that Montana had claimed me and my fundamental loyalties of placement. . . . [T]his rocky Mountain country has sustained my work ever since, the two becoming more and more inseparable." On more than one occasion he remarked that being away from Montana was an experience of "internal bleeding."

Bugbee's comments about the Philosophy Department at Missoula are also noteworthy. As his CV indicates, he resigned from the University of Montana in 1961, returning to Missoula in 1967 *without* any formal offer of employment: "I was able to rejoin my department at the university of Montana under a new University Administration which supported our building a strong department, which I came to believe in as the finest department to teach in that I had ever known from experience."[4]

The CV also evidences the peripatetic nature of Bugbee's life and thought. His statement "I have walked these hills most days from 1963 to the present . . . ." is well-documented. At his memorial service on January 8, 2000, Cass Chinsky offered the following testimony:

> There's a trail that goes up to the toe of Mount Jumbo. Henry did that. It's his trail. I remember watching him for three or four years . . . And finally I said "who's that guy who was going up that one way?" And he was developing a trail, and it goes straight up. [S]o finally I saw this person going up and I live in the lower Rattlesnake so I thought, "I'm going to find out who that is." Well, it was Henry. And I met him at the top, and we talked about this and that, and usually it was about the wild things, the animals, the trees, the water, what was going to happen to all of it as things were disappearing. After he realized that his trail was even too steep for himself, we used to meet quite often on the north hills, up Waterworks Hill and such, and so today when you walk out that door and you're looking from the valley down up Mount Jumbo, there's this trail, and I guarantee you he did that. The trail was not there until Henry walked it every day for a long time.[5]

Henry Bugbee was a trailblazer.

Vita

Henry G. Bugbee
March 17, 1993

Born in New York City: February 19, 1915

Institutional Affiliations:

The Hotchkiss School, Lakeville, Connecticut: 1928–32.
Princeton University: 1932–36, high honors in Philosophy.
University of California, Berkeley: Graduate study and Teaching Fellow, Philosophy 1937–40; James Sutton Fellow 1940–41.

United States Naval Reserve: Ensign, Lieutenant (j.g.), Lieutenant 1942–45: minesweeping, anti-submarine warfare, Pacific.

University of California, Berkeley: PhD, Philosophy, 1946.[6]

University of Nevada, Reno: Assistant Professor, Philosophy, 1946–47.

Stanford University: Assistant Professor, Philosophy, 1947–48.

Harvard University, Assistant Professor, Philosophy, 1948–53.

George Santayana Post-Doctoral Fellow in Philosophy, 1953–54.

Chatham College, Pittsburgh, Pennsylvania: Associate Professor and Departmental Chairman, Philosophy, 1954–57.

University of Montana, Missoula: Professor, Philosophy, 1958–61. Resigned, June 1961. Had been brought to this university to build a strong Philosophy Department, but a change of the university administration did not support this understanding.

Pennsylvania State University: Professor, Philosophy, 1961–62; also Harvard University, same year: Research Fellow. Went on Adjunct Professorship at Penn State, 1962–67, largely in conjunction with its graduate program in Philosophy, and returned home to Missoula, which became HOME for me from then on. (I found that Montana had claimed me and my fundamental loyalties of placement.)

The Arts Program of the Association of American Colleges and the Danforth Foundation, Visiting Speaker at 55 colleges and universities in the United States all told: 1963–66.

University of Montana, Missoula: Professor, Philosophy, 1967 through retirement, June 30, 1979, as Professor Emeritus. Taught more and more in Humanities, especially in our Intensive Humanities Program, founded in 1969, and continued to the year of my retirement. Department Chairman, 1969–74. I was able to rejoin my department at the University of Montana under a new university administration which supported our building a strong department, which I came to believe in as the finest department to teach in that I have ever known from experience. And this Rocky Mountain country has sustained my life and work ever since, the two having become more and more inseparable. I have walked these hills most days from 1963 to the present . . . excepting:

A year at Mount Allison University, New Brunswick, when I enjoyed a year as a Visiting Professor with Humanities Faculty, including the philosophers; and walked the west shore at the head of the Bay of Fundy. That was in 1980–81.

My work has yielded some published outcomes too. I shall list here
only briefly two published works of mine which may serve as indicating a key trend and purport at issue in the others:

1) *The Inward Morning*, "a philosophical exploration in journal
   form," with an introduction by Gabriel Marcel, originally published by Bald Eagle Press, State College, Pennsylvania, 1958,
   but more likely available in the Harper and Row Colophon edition of 1976.
2) An essay originally published in the *Journal of the American
   Academy of Religion* under the title "Wilderness in America,"
   1974, but most recently republished in *New World Metaphysics*, "readings on the religious meaning of the American Experience," edited by Giles Gunn, New York: Oxford University
   Press, 1981, pages 455–63. This essay can provide an inkling of
   how I think of the potential of Mount Jumbo, and most closely
   for our community of Missoula, Montana.

Letter from C. I. Lewis (n.d. ca 1951)

Bugbee came to Harvard in 1948 upon the recommendation of Jacob Loewenberg. He served as assistant professor until 1953, at which time he was
awarded the first George Santayana Fellowship for the 1953–54 academic
year. The ruling oligarchy in the Philosophy Department consisted of W. V.
Quine, Morton White, and Henry David Aiken. The realist Donald C.
Williams was also a department member.[7] Clarence Irving Lewis, the most
senior member, retired in 1953.

Bugbee's Harvard experience reaped reward and challenge. While Harvard
provided fertile ground for philosophical development, the challenge was to
balance the pressures of a "publish or perish" mentality with living a life of
genuine reflection. In the end, emphasis was placed upon living a reflective
life. Bugbee would be denied tenure at Harvard for lack of publication.

Lewis, on the other hand, is most known for his pragmatic epistemol-
ogy and his work on symbolic logic. Bugbee asked Lewis to read his essay
"The Moment of Obligation in Experience."[8] Lewis's remarks are introspective, thoughtful, and interesting in their own right.

Lewis's first remarks that Bugbee's writing represents traces of what
used to make "philosophy *philosophy* in the past ages, and the complete
absence of which makes this period in philosophy contemptible." He cites
Royce's last writings as examples of philosophical writing's ability to exhibit "something universal and noble."[9] In 1953, the preeminent concerns
of academic philosophy were logical and linguistic analysis. Such concerns

logically eclipsed interest in the topic of the meaning of being *Überhaupt*: what it *means to be*. Bugbee's style of writing brought Lewis back to the spirit of the "golden age of American philosophy"—a period at Harvard from roughly 1860 to 1930, consisting of such figures as William James, Josiah Royce, Ralph Barton Perry, William E. Hocking, Alfred North Whitehead, as well as Lewis himself.[10]

Yet the fact remains that Bugbee's essay "fails to jibe" with Lewis's moral sensibility. Like many philosophers of his generation, Lewis was able to successfully compartmentalize his own private moral sense from his role as professional philosopher, concerned with the question of what it is *objectively* right to do.[11] As he states: "The subjective side of that can take care of itself. What you have put together, I would pull apart . . . For me, it doesn't come off."

Nevertheless, Lewis's concluding remarks imply the "drift and articulation" of Bugbee's thought may have left their mark upon Lewis when he says: "I wonder if what reaches the obtuse listener like myself is that he characteristically speaks of objective fact, open to commonplace inspection, and what goes deeper is between the lines instead of in them."

C. I. Lewis

Dear Henry,

I read your paper [The Moment of Obligation in Experience] through yesterday afternoon and this morning.

My first and strongest impression is that it bespeaks and expresses that elevation of mind which has made philosophy *philosophy* in past ages, and the complete absence of which at present makes this period in philosophy contemptible. I was reminded of those sheets which Royce left on his death at the last, and which in turn remind me of the spirit of the man I knew and his power to express, when he spoke and wrote at his best, something universal and noble.

As a thesis in ethics, it fails to jibe with my sense of the moral. First, because I am put together differently. Seligkeit and Selbstgufriedenheit [happiness and autonomy] don't occupy me. The stoic slant of there words come nearest to me; but a stoic who strains after stoicism is a comic figure, and I hope I have little of that. I choose to be independent; to grant other men a like independence I will respect. I will endure my loneliness and privation as best I may. There is no tragedy in that. The only tragedy is in what I have loved and lost, and that tragedy can know no healing and no sublimation. And love is by the grace of God alone.

All that is aside from such moral sense as I have. There I am occupied to determine what, objectively, it is right to do. The subjective side of that can take care of itself, for all I care. So what you have put together I would put apart.

As a piece of writing, you will have had, for this paper, the response of an audience far more indicative than any of mine. For me, it doesn't come off. I don't get either the continuity of mood or clarity of expression in the drift and articulation of your thought.

As suggested, your opening pages reminded me of Royce; and on this last point I think of Royce again. I wonder if what reaches the obtuse listener like myself is that he characteristically speaks of objective fact, open to commonplace inspection, and what goes deeper is between the lines instead of in them.

My poor best,
Clarence

Letter from John M. Anderson (August 9, 1950)

Bugbee met John Mueller Anderson[12] while studying at Berkeley in the 1940s. They became kindred spirits, exploring the mountains and streams of northern California whenever they found the opportunity. As mavericks, they viewed philosophy as a life of experientially grounded reflection and not an acquired skill in concept construction and formal analysis. They engaged in continuous correspondence.[13] Besides being a way of "catching up on things," the letters express shared concern over the existing climate of professional philosophy and what it *means to be* a philosopher.

This letter begins asking what it *is* that Bugbee finds in the philosophical tradition that *demands* his allegiance. This is a bold question. Anderson is skeptical of the existence of a universal tradition of philosophical wisdom—a golden braid connecting the history of philosophy from past to present. Recognizing that Bugbee "finds something there" worthy of investiture in philosophy, he asks him to consider what that something *is*, in hope that Anderson might also agree. Anderson recalls a meeting at Berkeley in 1936 when Bugbee brought key members of the Philosophy and English departments together to see what discipline he ought to offer his allegiance. Bugbee's opening *salvo* was: "Gentlemen, I have come out of the hills and a flower is just a flower to me." Apparently, at that time, Bugbee was struggling with the question as to which "discipline" he should commit to in order to realize the goal of a reflective life. Jacob Loewenberg, Bugbee's doctoral advisor, was apparently deeply moved by the commitment Bugbee expressed toward the *vocation* of philosophy. In the end, philosophy was chosen.

Anderson gets to the heart of the matter when he asks Bugbee how he could willingly enter into an arrangement—undoubtedly referring to Bugbee's decision to go to Harvard—where he "knew well enough that the pressure to write was fully equaled by the pressure of duties preventing that writing, and where the second pressures might well prevent you from becoming what you were" [*meant to be*]?[14]

Anderson is trying to explore the tension between commitment to philosophical wisdom per se and whether any possible combination of experience, reason, and imagination may result in a body of knowledge resembling anything similar to the term "*Wissenschaft*"[15]—a body of truth adhering to a constellation of formal disciplinary practices that are often contrary to one's deepest *philosophical* concerns. By the end of the letter, Anderson's doubts remain "deep" concerning philosophy's claim to universality. Anderson ends with an appeal to experience:

> I suppose the crux of the matter lies in intention and realization. To profess a theme is good, but only if it is really professed and not words alone. It takes words and the focus to make a profession; but not only the words, for the words must break through to positive expression. Break through to what? I expect to what walking already is sometimes, the glowing world of being. I have not yet forsaken my hope for the words as well, words which, like walking, *are*.[16] (emphasis added)

John M. Anderson

217 Sparks Bldg.
State College, PA
August 9, 1950

Dear Henry,

I might as well include a note with these letters—here's to your new home up there and the possibility of breaking a bottle with you all in it!

The next time we get together I'm going to ask you what you find in philosophy that demands your allegiance. I think you are right in saying that you find something there, and if so the motivation (formulated positively) must be a central theme of anything you have to say. I am not sure that, in answer to this question, I could do much more than say that philosophy seems to me the right to take my own position and so to preserve my own integrity and character. If this is so, then any field in which confusion and disagreement are as prevalent as philosophy would do as well, and any such field and medium which permitted me to state and evoke in others my concern with "thatness," would serve as well. What more could I say about being a philosopher by profession than that the accident of circumstance gave me that field because of so much less pressure there to cease and refrain from observing and dealing with the darkness of the world? I am not sure that I could claim that if my efforts to remake philosophy should succeed against the overwhelming opposition, I should be continuing any tradition in philosophy.

Viewing your past with somewhat more objectivity than I can bring to bear on my own, you seem committed to philosophy in a sense to which I cannot commit myself articulately. But since I am not sure of your articulation, I am also not sure that I am not also committed in fact as you seem to be. To mention two instances of your factual commitment; First, I recall that you once brought the English and the Philosophy departments together at California to determine whether you should move into the field of English. I recall that you began the discussion with a remark committing you to English or, at least, away from philosophy: "Gentlemen, I have come out of the hills and a flower is just a flower to me." But at the end of the discussion the results were otherwise, for Professor Loewenberg remarked that he hadn't realized how deeply you were interested in philosophy. Second, you went to Harvard where you knew well enough that the pressure to write was fully equaled by the pressure of duties preventing that writing, and where the second pressures might well prevent you from becoming what you were—I should think the only justification of this situation could be the inward belief that the statement of one's position and concern depended upon that explicit allegiance to philosophy that Harvard demands. Now when you say that "there are always good men in English departments," you suggest to me that a doubt remains concerning that formal settlement in 1937; and your revolt against the analytical philosophy represented by the better and the good at Harvard suggests the possibility that explicit allegiance to philosophy may not be possible.

Well, I want your answer one of these days. I suppose that the crux of the matter lies in intention and realization. To profess a theme is good, but only if it is really professed and not words alone. It takes the words and the focus to make a profession; but not only the words for the words must break through to positive expression. Break through to what? I expect to what walking already is sometimes, the glowing world of being. I have not yet forsaken my hope for the words as well, words which, like walking, are.

I think that I have put off the problem as long as I remain at Penn State. When I think of staying here I do so because I wish, primarily, to preserve my attitude and to know my own concern. I can know my own deepest concern in a private idiom and personal language so long as to be myself I do not have to speak publically; and I also argue that gradually I am transforming something which for so long was only felt and dreamed and muttered about into statements which can be heard by others and at least understood before being opposed. But this may not be philosophy, and I am not sure that I care. Does philosophy mean that others must agree and that one can demand of others not only understanding but also acceptance? Would explicit adherence to philosophy mean the use of argument as persuasion as well as expression? Is philosophy a claim to universality? Well, then, my doubts are deep. Loewenberg used to consider philosophical positions in terms of defensibility, I think many of those at Harvard still do; for myself, I would be clear, I would demand recognition but not acceptance.

This last paragraph got tacked on by momentum,

John

Journal Entry (February 11, 1957)

The journal entry of February 11, 1957, demonstrates the existential character of Bugbee's approach. An experience of recovering from a cold leads to his recognition of the difference between things "taking care of themselves" and "a forgetting of what is really going on." The self must live "in exile" in the sense that it must *act* with decision and integrity while remaining alert to the possibility of falling into the embrace of forgetfulness.

The "derivativeness" of finite being presents an undeniable stretch of facticity, indicating that the present is temporally thick and unified at the level of our existence. Lest we not forget that:

[There is an] absolute priority to the present, the present of this one man in this one life; a present which theoretical positing cuts free from; a present which brings all knowledge to the bar and absolutely questions it; a present which knows no man who will

not declare himself in, of, out of, and from it; not from what he
knows . . . but from *what he is*; even if he has nothing much to say.

∽

Something I am about to forget, and therefore better to be just indicated as it seems now.

After having been dragging along for about nine days on the verge
of a cold, too tired to make it when awakened one way or the other
early; this morning, after 5 ½ hours sleep came easily and wonderfully into consciousness steadily in the present moment and flow
of my life. My work was going on by itself, and I could tell beyond
any possibility of mistake that what I would do with the way things
are shaping up is just more or less hit or miss, largely a forgetting of
what is really going on, an ante-room affair compared with what is
going on in the central locus of the work. One's position is not to be
confused with what one posits; this is established every time one is
open to the level at which things are "taking care of themselves."
The carry-over into waking life should be at least sufficient to keep
one more or less consciously "in exile," and to occasion presence
of mind about not knowing the true version from which, now and
then, decision and integrity become possible. The conscious self is
the agent of what is inscrutably at work in one's life. If the conscious
self can go along with this, it is well. If not, it is what Kierkegaard
calls despair.

I remember especially the conversation with Van [Quine] in which
I kept speaking of the derivativeness of finite being as fundamental
for me, but without being able to say anything illuminating about
this. Now it seems that apart from present living, all notions treating this derivativeness must roam about at loose ends, or worse,
pictorialize the matter. In particular, theories of "the unconscious"
must not be permitted to supplant or undermine the absolute priority of the present, the present of this one man in this one life; a
present which theoretical positing cuts free from; a present which
brings all knowledge to the bar and absolutely questions it; a present which knows no man who will not declare himself in, of, out of,
and from it; not from what he knows—and not, therefore, contrary
to what he knows—but from what he is; even if then he has nothing
much to say.

"Henry"—A Tribute

Albert Borgmann was Bugbee's longtime colleague in the Department
of Philosophy at the University of Montana. Borgmann read *The Inward
Morning* with care and with an abiding respect for Bugbee's genius. Borgmann's heartfelt obituary in tribute to Bugbee was published in *Proceedings and Addresses of the American Philosophical Association*.[17]

Borgmann captures the personal and intellectual timbre of the man
Bugbee was known to be, describing him as exhibiting the *rarest* form of
genius—one filled with radiance and grace—whose speech and manner
displayed unmistakable and unforgettable immediacy, depth, and resonance. Speaking as a philosopher, Borgmann should be taken at his word
that *The Inward Morning* "helped to redirect philosophy in this country"
toward a greater degree of awareness of the philosophical value of everyday experience. The compelling nature of Bugbee's work has succeeded in
humanizing many "beyond the [Philosophy] Department and beyond this
University . . . And this, in fact, is true of Henry's life."

Albert Borgmann

As a humanist one lives off the capital accumulated by people of genius. Hence I am not unfamiliar with such people. But there is only
one person of genius I have known and learned from personally; I
mean Henry, of course.

Geniuses seem to fall into one of two groups. Members of the first
suffer from the burdens of their talents and make their friends and
next of kin bear part of that burden through the self-centeredness
that we sometimes think is the genius's prerogative. The members
of the other group are so filled with the radiance of their that they
naturally and generously share their grace with others. This was and
is Henry's way.

Henry's genius is publically most evident in his great book that
has gone through three editions and, in a manner both inconspic-
uous and consequential, has helped to redirect philosophy in this
country. And yet the more powerful and captivating aspect of this
extraordinary man is in the immediacy of speech and conversation.
Henry never speaks but that there is a depth, resonance and grace in
what he says at once unmistakable and unforgettable.

A major source of Henry's inspiration was the great literature of
the West and the East. Henry is a humanist *par excellence*. He lives
with and out of the great texts, and through his example he has made

humanists out of analytically trained philosophers and scientifically oriented researchers. His imprint has been most forceful here in the Philosophy Department, but it has gone beyond the Department and beyond this University.

It has done so through his public addresses and most impressively, perhaps, through his testimonies at wilderness hearings. These were spectacular moments where audience, accustomed to the idiom of economics and recreational resources, came to realize that there is a kinship between the eloquence of nature and the eloquence of art. Henry has enriched and deepened our discourse about nature and the wilderness forever.

Henry's most ambitious and devoted enterprise on behalf of the humanities was the Intensive Humanities Program, a year-long course of studies that was dedicated to reading the great literature in a way that honored this heritage. It was designed for first year students who spent almost all of their time during that year in this intensive humanist setting. I never taught in the program, but I could unfailingly identify the students who had come out of it into my classes. They were extraordinarily thoughtful, well-spoken, and of course well-read. In the late seventies, neither the students, nor the faculty at the University were equal to the rigors of the program any longer. But it stands as a monument of the highest humanist aspiration and practice.

And this, in fact, is true of Henry's life.

Albert Borgmann

The Splendor of Rock Creek

Henry Bugbee was a "fishermen's fisherman." He began fly-fishing at the age of six. He often recounted the story of how the fish came to be his totem animal. The following is an excerpt from an interview with Henry Bugbee (HB) conducted by his wife, Sally Moore (SM), and fellow-colleague and friend, Ray Lanfear (RF).

SM: You had a governess when you were little that was oriented completely towards pleasing your parents?

HB: And I was to perform in a play that my sisters were the principles in. They looked down upon me and always tried to consolidate their sense of superiority, being older than I, and they resented the fact that they thought that our parents were unfairly partial to their little son.

SM: This was a German governess?

HB: It was a play to be about the time of Christmas in which I was to play a chimney sweep—to prepare the chimney so Santa Claus could come down without "sooting" himself up, which was a "fatuous" assumption.

SM: And so what did she do to you?

HB: She tried to incorporate me into this little play that she prepared for my sisters and me to play.

SM: And what did she do to prepare you for that?

HB: She sooted me up! She put soot all over me, so as to make me look like I had been down a chimney.

SM: How did that strike you?

HB: I didn't feel that was my natural self. I didn't want to be anything I wasn't.

SM: I remember one time I read your description of that incident and the thing you emphasized was "This was not me." And "I can't stand not being me."

HB: And people presuming to give me a place that I should occupy as if it were me.

SM: What did you do?

HB: Well, I ran away from home. I went down in the local town, Bronxville, in New York, near where my father's hospital was—where he worked. There was a constructed pool with some plants in it and goldfish. I zeroed in on the goldfish and they found me. What I was doing was watching these fish swim in that pool. I don't remember who found me.

SM: What were you thinking or feeling as you watched these fish?

HB: Just that what I later constructed as a sense of what I was seeing as my totem animal in there swimming around.

RL: Henry, was this the first time that you were relatively mesmerized by a fish?

HB: True, pretty close.

For Bugbee, fly-fishing was a vocation—as natural as breathing. To behold him fly-fishing was a supernatural experience and many who fished with him went as much to watch him fish as to fish themselves. The angler's task is to spot and cast to riffles—short, relatively shallow lengths of course-bedded stream over which the water flows at a slower velocity but a higher degree of turbulence. Lower velocity and heightened turbulence cause ripples to serve as feeding lanes as fish tend to spend their time holding within seams between fast and slow currents funneling food into narrow chutes of water. Larger fish hug the bottom. When insect activity is peaking in summer months, feeding occurs at or near the surface, and pools or runs with moderate to strong flows, due to greater amounts of forage contained within the drift. For Bugbee:

> Fly-fishing is an activity by which you become integral with all that surrounds you. You become steeped in the surroundings, the flow of the water itself. It has a musical feel to it; that sound of the moving water and the grasses, and maybe the sounds of the birds that like to be in that place, and the rhythm of casting. It's possible to fish all day long and not catch a fish yet come away with a sense of fulfillment.[18]

Bugbee was also a diehard steelhead fisherman—a "steelheader." The "steelhead" is an anadromous species of rainbow trout that migrates to coastal waters. Steelheads are known for their torpedo-like body and the effort required to land them. The following is a realistic account of the *Lebenswelt* of steelheading:

> It is a vexing business, this chasing of the steelhead. As if sensing their power over us, the fish time their return for the least inviting times of the year. Still we come. The feed capriciously or not at all, and still we spend days deliberating over the flies that we carry. Steelhead fishing is full of long, wet cold hours of toil, often punctuated by crushing moments of the darkest despair. More than once, fly-fishers must face the reality that they may cast ten thousands more times without experience so much as a tug ever again.[19]

Bugbee possessed an acute sensitivity to the ways of fish. "Upper Clark Fork: Rock Creek Fishing" captures Bugbee's autochthonic appreciation of the flora and fauna of the region.

Upper Clark Fork: Rock Creek Fishing

Rock Creek is generally clear and it is fast—above all a natural Rainbow stream, though many good Browns run in the lower ten miles. Eastern Brook, Cutthroat, and Bull trout are also to be found. The streambed is extremely slippery, and the trout require a rather careful and delicate approach.

Natural reproduction and an abundant food supply keep up a large population of fine trout. Especially where the bottom is dark with algae, it crawls with various hellgrammites and caddis larvae. This sets the basic pattern of the fishing. A hellgrammite fisherman with the touch is always at home here. And the splendid hatches make Rock Creek at truly great stream.

Until salmon fly hatch it's pretty hard to do much with flies. Thus hellgrammites and worms lead off—to remain effective all season. Usually after the runoff peaks, during the first two weeks of June, the salmon fly hatch is working its way upstream. Hair imitations are then in order, floated or sunk. As the waters continues to drop small spinners and lures begin to take fish. By late June the Pott flies (the "Mites"), Bucktail Royal Coachman, Royal Wulff, and the Wooly Worms begin to serve. For about three weeks, usually the last three in July, the hatch of spruce bud moths is on. Be on the water as the sun rises, and bring something like the following: Blonde Wulff, Ginger Quill, Wickham's Fancy, Adams, Renegade, Apple Green. By now the creek has dropped down to a trot and can be waded and covered thoroughly. Leaders should be longer (say 9 feet) and as fine as your nerves can stand. For this writer this is the time of dry-fly delirium.

With August come the grasshoppers (try Joe's Hopper, fished wet or dry) and the caddis begin to emerge, culminating with a last major hatch of large, dark caddis in September. Add caddis imitations to the flies already mentioned—which continue to be useful (sizes 12 to 8 average about right). Once heavy frosts set in, the Wooly Worm, fished like a nymph, seems the best among flies. But from mid-August on, Browns are running in the lower reach of the creek from the Clark Fork, and the Muddler Minnow is a favorite for them.

Rock Creek trout average from half a pound to a pound and a half. A Rainbow, particularly, of three pounds is large for this water, but even the two-pounders here can leave you flat-footed and amazed.

Ranches border much of the lower ten miles of the creek. Owners appreciate being asked permission. The dirt road continues up along some forty miles of beautiful water, where timbered slopes and rock slides plunge close to the creek, and here and there a flat or a meadow affords a good campsite.

The Bugbee Nature Preserve

A few miles outside of Missoula, Montana, along Rattlesnake Creek is an eight-acre nature preserved named for Henry Greenwood Bugbee, M.D. (1879-1945)—Bugbee's father. The parcel was at risk of being developed.

Henry G. Bugbee Jr. borrowed the money to procure the property in 1975. His bequest was for "the property to be forever preserved in its natural state and that it be named for his father, a New York doctor who first introduced his son to the mountain west and fly fishing, irresistible lures to his future Missoula home." Bruce Bugbee, Henry Jr.'s son, has provided an informative narrative capturing the circumstances surrounding the creation of the Bugbee Nature Preserve.

Bugbee Nature Preserve—Named for Henry Greenwood Bugbee, M.D. (1879–1945)

Bruce Bugbee

Rattlesnake Creek, a place of mystery made no less so by the possibility of its namesake. Actually named for the sound of rushing creek waters blended with wind in cottonwoods and pines, Henry's home was by this stream for many years.

Change came to this place in the form of subdivision development and the attraction of homes fronting on the creek, something that would require cutting the trees and filling the low streamside to create building sites. This eight-acre creek-side forest became a remnant surrounded by development and was soon to follow the fate of its neighbors as it was purchased by developers. In 1975, Henry borrowed the money to buy this place from the developers. Loan payments over several years took their toll.

At that time I was a graduate student attending the University of Montana studying environmental planning. Dad faced me one morning over a cup of his stout hobo coffee and with a grimace asked me to figure out how the fewest of home sites might be placed, the sale of which could pay off his debt and the remaining area kept in its natural state.

As serendipity would have it, the Nature Conservancy was making its way into Montana from its then-Portland regional office looking for demonstration projects. They formed a partnership with the local land trust and we worked out an agreement that had the county purchase the property for a natural preserve. Henry agreed to sell the property for enough to pay off his debt. The property had almost doubled in value since his purchase so he made a gift of the remainder to the Conservancy for which he received an unexpected tax benefit. In that transaction I also found my professional calling,

which has sustained me to this day, facilitating land transactions that have conservation outcomes.

Henry asked for the property to be forever preserved in its natural state and that it be named for his father, a New York doctor who first introduced his son to the mountain west and fly fishing, irresistible lures to his future Missoula home. Visitors may find their way along winding paths among cottonwood and pine trees, leading to the fresh rushing creek and its marvelous sound. And, to a lichen-covered boulder with the following inscription:

> ". . . in attending to this *wilderness*, I knew *myself* to have been *instructed* for life . . . "

The Bugbee Nature Preserve is part of a system of parks, preserves and trails along Rattlesnake Creek, connecting downtown Missoula to the Rattlesnake National Recreation and Wilderness.

"Philosopher"—A Poem by Gary Whited

Gary Whited is a poet, philosopher, and psychotherapist living in Boston. He first met Henry Bugbee in 1967 in the context of a class in Oriental Philosophy:

> I remember being struck by three things: his eyes that were so alive, his gray hair and his ever present pipe. At the time I began to wonder if philosophy was for me and was I up to the venture and the work that philosophy required. What happened in that class, in short, was that a whole new experience of inquiry and of doing philosophy opened up. I was so moved and excited by whatever Henry was doing up there in front of the class that I remember my entire body vibrating. . . . Such was the power of Henry's teaching.[20]

Whited later had the opportunity to backpack and to fish with Bugbee: "As I look back on all of these encounters, so much of what I remember about Henry was his capacity simply to be present; and out of that presence to allow whatever the world was offering to unfold in action, in spoken word or in silence."[21]

Gary Whited

Words keep falling out of his chest,
tumbling as birds from a nest

who find their wings, feather
the tattered sky.[22]

"For Henry"

(February 19, 1915–December 18, 1999)

A memorial service was held on January 8, 2000, on the campus of the
University of Montana. Many attended—there were not enough seats for
everyone. Bugbee had requested Bach's "Air" from Orchestral Suite No. 3
in D major be played. A total of sixteen statements were read by children,
students, colleagues, friends, and admirers. "For Henry" is a poem by Bruce
Bugbee—Henry's son—that speaks to the enduring presence of his father.

Bruce Bugbee

Born into a time when rivers flowed unchecked
Learning the way of the water
Nurtured by mountain adventures
Maturing at sea, during war
Disciplined artist, teacher to many, seeker of beauty, husband,
    father, grandfather, and friend
More than could be asked for, less than needed
His essential self knowing the way
His way upstream through pools, riffles, tumbling water, and
    uprooted cottonwoods
With every last strength and fiber of will
Slowly stripped of mind, then flesh
He returns home and dies.

Bugbee Annual Lectures

After Bugbee's retirement, a lecture series was created in his honor as
a tribute to his legacy as teacher, philosopher, and outdoorsman. The
impressive list of lecturers confirms the ongoing nature of Bugbee's
importance. This list was compiled with the assistance of Albert Borgmann, Professor of Philosophy at the University of Montana.

1st Annual Bugbee Lecture
1989—Stanley Cavell
Professor of Philosophy
Harvard University
Lecture Title: "Emerson's Constitutional Amending On Reading 'Fate'"

2nd Annual Bugbee Lecture
1990—Alasdair MacIntyre
Professor of Philosophy
University of Notre Dame
Lecture Title: "Colors and Culture"

3rd Annual Bugbee Lecture
1991—Annette C. Baier
Professor of Philosophy
University of Pittsburgh
Lecture Title: "Trusting People"

4th Annual Bugbee Lecture
1992—Willard van Orman Quine
Professor Emeritus of Philosophy
Harvard University
Lecture Title: "In Praise of Observation Sentences"

5th Annual Bugbee Lecture
1993—Gordon G. Brittan, Jr.
Professor of Philosophy
Montana State University
Lecture Title: "Autonomy and Authenticity"

6th Annual Bugbee Lecture
1994—Lecture postponed until spring of 1995.

7th Annual Bugbee Lecture
1995—Lecture cancelled.

8th Annual Bugbee Lecture
1996—Hubert Dreyfus
Professor of Philosophy
University of California at Berkeley
Lecture Title: "Motorcycles, Feasts, and Highway Bridges: Pirsig, Borgmann,
    and Heidegger on How to Affirm Technology"

9th Annual Bugbee Lecture
1997—Edward F. Mooney
Professor of Philosophy and Humanities

Sonoma State University
Lecture Title: "When Philosophy Becomes Lyric"

10th Annual Bugbee Lecture
1998—Andrew Feenberg
Professor of Philosophy
San Diego State University
Lecture Title: "Zen Existentialism: Bugbee's Japanese Influence"

11th Annual Bugbee Lecture
1999—Richard Gotshalk
Professor of Philosophy
Pennsylvania State University (1957–77) and University of Montana
   (1982–95)
Lecture Title: "Fishing, Philosophy, and Contemporary Life"

12th Annual Bugbee Lecture
2000—Edward S. Casey
Professor of Philosophy
State University of New York at Stony Brook
Lecture Title: "Finding Face in the Environment in the Wake of Emmanuel
   Levinas"

13th Annual Bugbee Lecture
2001—Bruce Wilshire
Professor of Philosophy
Rutgers University
Lecture Title: "Henry Bugbee: Philosopher of Intimacy"

Addenda from Albert Borgmann

2002—Hilary Putnam
Cogan University Professor Emeritus of Philosophy
Harvard University
"The Relevance of Philosophy to Life"

2003—David Chalmers
Professor of Philosophy
University of Arizona
"The Matrix as Metaphysics"

2003—Susan Haack
Professor of Philosophy
University of Miami
"Coherence, Consistency, Cogency, Congruity, Cohesiveness, &c.: Remain
   Calm! Don't Go Overboard!"

2005—Elliot Sober
Reichenbach Professor and William Vilas Research Professor of Philosophy
University of Wisconsin, Madison
"Morgan's Canon"

2006—Robert Bellah
Professor of Sociology Emeritus
University of California, Berkeley
"Ethical Politics: Illusion or Reality?"

2007—Michael Ruse
Lucyle T. Werkmeister Professor of Philosophy
Florida State University
"The Evolution-Creation Struggle: An American Story"

2007—Jonathan Lear
Distinguished Service Professor, Committee on Social Thought
University of Chicago
"Dignity, Integrity, and Courage in the Face of Cultural Attack"

2009—Albert Borgmann
Regents Professor of Philosophy
University of Montana
"Politics and the Pursuit of Excellence"

2010—Alexander Nehamas
Edward N. Carpenter II Class of 1943 Professor of Humanities
Princeton University
"Because It Was He, Because It Was I: The Good of Friendship"

2011—Cora Diamond
William R. Kenan, Jr. Professor of Philosophy Emerita
University of Virginia
"The Problem of Impiety: Is Anything off Limits for Us?"

2011—Amelie Oksenberg Rorty
Lecturer, Department of Social Medicine
Harvard Medical School
"The Use and Abuse of Morality"

2012—Alan Wood
Ruth Norman Halls Professor of Philosophy
Indiana University
"Marx on Equality"

2014—Avishai Margalit
Professor of Philosophy
Hebrew University
"The Arab Spring and the Israeli Spring"

Notes

Introduction. Being in Nature: The Experiential Naturalism of Henry G. Bugbee Jr.

1. *Hotchkiss Record*, January 21, 1954, p. 3.

2. Personal correspondence [with DWR] dated September 15, 2015: "There are two great books, the greatest in fact, that have come out of American philosophy. Both are truly American as they are great. One is John Rawls's magisterial *A Theory of Justice*. It needs no plea. The other is Henry Bugbee's *The Inward Morning*. It is a stunningly profound and innovative book—both an astute and incisive critique of early analytic philosophy and a break-through in opening up the depths of the world of concrete experience, of nature, and of art for philosophical reflection. The history of its publication is an indication of the enduring and also sporadic effect it has had. But its crucial time is still to come, or rather it is now— as the world of commanding presence is in danger of being eclipsed by the glamorous fog of information and communication technology. Henry's gift of observation and eloquence is our best hope of making the fog lift."

3. Henry G. Bugbee Jr., "In Demonstration of the Spirit" (undergraduate thesis, Princeton University, 1936).

4. See also Henry G. Bugbee Jr., *The Inward Morning, A Philosophical Exploration in Journal Form*, Introduction by Gabriel Marcel (1958; repr. Athens: University of Georgia Press, 1999, with a new introduction by Edward F. Mooney), 131–32. "Every time I retrace the course of my reflections since 'their beginning' in my undergraduate years I discern as central this preoccupation with [the] 'somewhat absolute' in experience, with a kind of unconditional meaning which always introduces a harmony and simplicity into the complex and otherwise inconclusive."

5. The reader is encouraged to consult John M. Anderson's letter contained in the appendix Letter from John M. Anderson (August 9, 1950).

6. Interview with Henry G. Bugbee Jr. Part IV. At Harvard, Bugbee met intellectuals ranging from W. V. Quine to Paul Tillich and D. T. Suzuki.

7. Bugbee was denied tenure in the spring of 1953. He was awarded the Santayana Fellowship for the period 1953–54. In the preface to *The Inward Morning*, he stated that its "pages . . . rounded out in the fall of 1953" (9). The reflections included in *The Inward Morning* had been "in the winds," gestating, prior to the formal tenure decision. At the risk of overstatement, the Harvard experience helped contribute to a profound moment of "inward morning" for Bugbee, both professionally and personally.

8. Bugbee, *The Inward Morning*, 10.

9. Bugbee, *The Inward Morning*, 107. See also p. 80: "The point is that a person must make known where he stands. And if it be philosophy he is engaged in, he must speak out. In so far as he fails to do this he loses reality and he loses his community."

10. Ibid, 92.

11. Paul Tillich, *Systematic Theology*, vol. 1 (Chicago: University of Chicago Press, 1951), 102.

12. Bugbee, *The Inward Morning*, 139.

13. Bugbee, *The Inward Morning*, 141.

14. "The Sense and the Conception of Being." Lest the reader be tempted to dismiss "The Sense and the Conception of Being" as a failure, which it clearly is not, it should be noted that Bugbee maintained "[T]he experience with which this thesis is so largely concerned cannot be shaken" ("The Sense and the Conception of Being").

15. See William James, "The Ph.D. Octopus," *William James: The Essential Writings*, ed. Bruce W. Wilshire (Albany: State University of New York Press, 1984), 343–48.

16. Gabriel Marcel, "Introduction," *The Inward Morning*, 18.

17. Thomas M. Alexander, *The Human Eros: Eco-Ontology and the Aesthetics of Existence* (Bronx, N.Y.: Fordham University Press, 2013), 17, 18. It is interesting in this context to note Dewey's adamant claim that "Not safely can an 'ism' be made out of experience" (see John Dewey, *Experience and Nature* [Chicago: Open Court Publishing Company, 1925]: 4).

18. Alexander, *The Human Eros*, 106. While Alexander chooses "eco-ontology" as the appropriate title of his account of nonreductive account of naturalism, John Ryder advocates for the title of "pragmatic naturalism." See John Ryder, *The Things of Heaven and Earth: An Essay in Pragmatic Naturalism* (Bronx, N.Y.: Fordham University Press, 2013), 22: "For the naturalist . . . the central category is nature, and experience is an aspect of it . . . [T]he thrust for Dewey, as for James and other pragmatists, is that experience is the constitutive context in which nature takes its shape." The positions of Alexander and Ryder are largely in keeping with Bugbee's version of experiential naturalism.

19. Bugbee, *The Inward Morning*, 141.

20. Bugbee, *The Inward Morning*, 139. For an example of Bugbee's peripatetic approach to life see Janice Downey, "Streamside Philosophy," *Montanan*, Spring 1991, 14–15.

21. A classic treatment of this issue is contained in John Searle's, "How to Derive 'Ought' from 'Is,'" *Philosophical Review*, vol. 73, no. 1 (January 1964): 43–58. Searle attempts to bridge the gap between descriptive and prescriptive "facts" linguistically: "[T]o state an institutional fact [such as to make a promise] is already to invoke the constitutive rules of the institution. It is those rules which give the word 'promise' its meaning" (57–58).

22. John E. Smith, "The Experience of the Holy and the Idea of God," *Phenomenology in America: Studies in the Philosophy of Experience*, ed. James M. Edie (Chicago: Quadrangle Books, 1967), 299.

23. Ibid. Emphasis added.

24. Henry G. Bugbee, Jr., "The Moment of Obligation in Experience," *Journal of Religion*, vol. 33 (1953): 3.

25. Henry G. Bugbee Jr., "A Point of Co-articulation in the Life and Thought of Gabriel Marcel," *Philosophy Today*, vol. 19, no. 1 (1975): 65.

26. Bugbee, "The Moment of Obligation in Experience," 6–7. Bugbee's experience at sea provided a source for this insight.

27. The German word *"Augenblick"* conveys this sense of momentary illumination.

28. Bugbee, *The Inward Morning*, 52, 53. The self *"de*-mands" because the self is "demand-*ed* of"—occupying a gossamer-like frontier between secular and sacred existence.

29. "A Point of Co-articulation in the Life and Thought of Gabriel Marcel," 65. See. Bugbee, *The Inward Morning*, 182: "Concrete reality dwells in the sinew of decisive action."

30. See David Strong, *Crazy Mountains: Learning from Wilderness to Weigh Technology* (Albany: State University of New York Press, 1995) and David James Duncan, *The River Why?* (New York: Bantam Books, 1984) for rich accounts of the natural world reflecting principles of Bugbee's experiential naturalism.

31. See Bugbee, *The Inward Morning*, 140: "[I]n attending to this wilderness . . . I knew myself to have been instructed for life . . . ." This quotation is inscribed on a rock along Rattlesnake Creek in The Bugbee Nature Preserve in Missoula, Montana—a wilderness area created under Bugbee's direction and named in honor of his father, Henry Greenwood Bugbee, M.D. (1879–1945). The genesis of the wilderness area is explained in the appendix, The Bugbee Nature Area.

32. An excellent example of this elevated transition from one level to another is the movement from acquaintances with objects at the "visible" level, to the intelligible perspective of "knowing through" afforded by *dianoia* in Plato's "Divided Line."

33. Ralph Waldo Emerson, "New England Reformers," *Essays*, Second Series (Boston: Houghton, 1876), 284.

34. Bugbee, "Thoughts on Creation," *Essays in Philosophy*, ed. Penn State University Philosophy Department (University Park: Penn State University Press, 1962), 138–39. See also Bugbee, *The Inward Morning*, 222: "The truly creative deed of man seems that of which he becomes lucid to himself as a creature of creation; and the very deed in which his to be is clarified is itself creaturely participation in creation."

35. Henry G. Bugbee Jr., "The Philosophic Significance of the Sublime," *Philosophy Today* vol. 11, no. 1 (1967): 57.

36. See Keith H. Basso, "'To Give up on Words': Silence in Western Apache Culture," *Southwestern Journal of Anthropology*, vol. 26, no. 3 (1970): 213-230. Bugbee was well familiar with Max Picard's profound study, *The World of Silence* (Chicago: Regnery/Gateway, 1952), and the rich modalities of silence that remain despite an increasingly "public" world. David James Duncan writes: "We hear nothing so clearly as what comes out of silence" ("Five Henry Stories," *Wilderness and the Heart: Henry Bugbee's Philosophy of Place, Presence, and Memory*, ed. Edward F. Mooney [New York: Bantam Books, 1995], 256).

37. The German word *"gelichtet"* captures this sense of reflexive illumination.

38. Bugbee, "The Philosophic Significance of the Sublime," 59.

39. See "A Point of Co-Articulation in the Life and Thought of Gabriel Marcel," 66. See also p. 62: "At work in all of Marcel's reflective writings, the force of what he meant by 'recueillement' had come to seem pivotal for me. And now, the more I become acquainted with him in daily life, the more I was struck by the *consonant* note of 'accueil' which he imparted to it." "Le Recueillement et L'Accueil," is Bugbee's French translation of "A Point of Co-Articulation in the Life and Work of Gabriel Marcel" and can be found in *Les études philosophiques: organe officiel de la Société de études philosophiques* (1975): 47–54.

40. Bugbee, *The Inward Morning*, 128. The theme of homecoming (*Heimkunft*)—an experiential return to the source of one's origin—is also prevalent in the philosophy of Martin Heidegger. See Robert Mugerauer, *Heidegger and Homecoming: The Leitmotif in the Later Writings* (Toronto: University of Toronto Press, 2008). As Alexander rightfully points out, "The Greek injunction *Gnōthoi Seauton* 56 meant more 'remember who you are'—i.e. a mortal; *gnōsis* is an intimate bringing of oneself back to one's existence rather than a formalized a formalized teachable knowledge like *epistēmē*" (Alexander, *The Human Eros*, 56).

41. Bugbee, *The Inward Morning*, 35, 229. The phrase *"In statu nascendi"* connotes a sense of active participation in the process of being (re)born.

42. See Martin Heidegger, *Aus Der Erfahrung Des Denkens* (Pfullingen: Neske, 1954), 13.

43. Bugbee, *The Inward Morning*, 37.

44. Annie Dillard, *Holy the Firm* (New York: Harper & Row, 1977), 16. See also p. 1: "Every day is a god, each day is a god, and holiness holds forth in time. I worship each god, I praise each day splintered down, splintered down and wrapped in time like a husk, a husk of many colors spreading, at dawn fast over the mountains split." Dillard's works align nicely with Bugbee's philosophy.

45. Elie M. Adams, "Reinstating Humanistic Categories," *Review of Metaphysics*, vol. 55, no. 1 (September 2001): 21.

46. Bugbee, *The Inward Morning*, 221 (emphasis added).

47. Michael Palmer, "Memorial Service for Henry Bugbee," January 8, 2000.

48. Henry David Thoreau, *A Week on the Concord and Merrimack Rivers, Walden; or, Life in the Woods, The Maine Woods, Cape Cod* (New York: Library of America, 1985), 587. See also Bugbee, *The Inward Morning*, 91.

1. In Demonstration of the Spirit (Selections)

1. [Henry G. Bugbee Jr., *The Inward Morning, A Philosophical Exploration in Journal Form*, Introduction, Gabriel Marcel (1958; repr. Athens: University of Georgia Press, 1999, with a new introduction by Edward F. Mooney), 131–32. —Ed.]

2. [See Warner Fite, "The Impersonal Point of View and the Personal," in *Contemporary American Philosophy*, vol. 1, ed. G.P. Adams and W.P. Montague (New York: Macmillan Company, 1930), 357, 360: "A mind without prejudice—it may be a *tabula rasa*, a mirror, a cinematograph, or any of those contrivances which psychologists substitute for mind, but it will see nothing . . . . [F]or me, only persons are real and only persons are significant. All impersonal things, including the objects presented by science, are abstractions, constructions, fancies." For a brief account of Fite's philosophical importance, see Charles W. Hendel, "Warner Fite" in *Proceedings and Addresses of the American Philosophical Association*, vol. 29 (1955–1956), 113–14. —Ed.]

3. [See Edward F. Mooney, "Death and the Sublime: Henry Bugbee's *In Demonstration of the Spirit*," in *Lost Intimacy in American Thought: Recovering Personal Philosophy from Thoreau to Cavell* (New York: Continuum, 2009), 56–57: "'[D]emonstration'" is not accomplished by blackboard proofs or Hegelian dialectics. It will come by way of displays or evocations . . . [of] an experiential, viscerally known reality . . . [as one] increasingly attends to the *things of creation*—in their bounteous unfolding." —Ed.]

4. [Cyril Edwin Mitchinson (C.E.M.) Joad (1891–1953) was a British philosopher and radio personality who wrote popularly and prodigiously. Sadly, he is not included in Paul Edward's *The Encyclopedia of Philosophy* (New York: Macmillan, 1967) or the 1996 *Supplement* edited by Donald M. Borchert. —Ed.]

5. [See C. E. M. Joad, *The Return to Philosophy: Being a Defence of Reason, an Affirmation of Values, and a Plea for Philosophy* (New York: E. P. Dutton, 1936), 31: "I believe that intuition . . . rightly used, is capable of exhibiting to the mind's awareness aspects of reality which are inaccessible to logical reason. . . . [T]his intuitive awareness of reality confers the most valuable experiences which the human mind, at its present level of evolutionary development, enjoys." —Ed.]

6. ["Ears brotherly and holy" [*Aures fraternae ec piae*] is a phrase taken from book 10, chapter 34 of Augustine's *Confessions* See Augustine, *Confessions*, books 9-13, trans. William Watts (Cambridge, MA: Harvard University Press, 1912):168. Cf. "In Demonstration of the Spirit," where Bugbee refers to the possibility of "recreative experience"—implying the human capacity for creative reappropriation of existence. —Ed.]

7. And on this ground may lay just claim to the title of "Realism."

8. Cf. Fite, "The Impersonal Point of View and the Personal."

9. Cf. Fite, "The Impersonal Point of View and the Personal"; also, Warner Fite, *Moral Philosophy* (New York: Dial Press, 1925), 268: "Experience of truth is the experience of a satisfied critical imagination."

10. T. M. Greene, "Notes on Systematic Introduction to Philosophy of Art." First Term, 1935–36.

11. Cf. Joad, *The Return to Philosophy*, 31—"This intuitive awareness of reality confers the most valuable experience which the human mind, at its present level of evolutionary development, enjoys."

12. Cf. Warner Fite, "The Philosopher and His Words," *Philosophical Review* (March 1935): "Emotion without thought is mere digestion; thought without emotion is mere words."

13. For the expression and understanding of this as well as other moral values, I will suggest the paramount importance of the media supplied by art (in the next chapter).

14. Would it not be in accord with the greatest good for the greatest number to "act so as to treat humanity, whether in thine own person or in that of any other, in every case as an end withal and never as a means?"

15. That is, recreative approach.

16. Or "construction"; cf. Stace.

17. Cf. Greene, "Notes on Systematic Introduction to Philosophy of Art."

2. The Sense and the Conception of Being (Selections)

1. ["Experience, Memory, Reflection: An Interview with Henry Bugbee," Part IV. See also Bugbee, *The Inward Morning*, 140–41. —Ed.]

2. [See Edward F. Mooney, "Death and the Sublime: Henry Bugbee's *In Demonstration of the Spirit*," in *Lost Intimacy in American Thought: Recovering Personal Philosophy from Thoreau to Cavell* (New York: Con-

tinuum, 2009), 64: "For Bugbee, Being is not an onto-theological abstraction but fundamentally experiential, something *sensed* rather than only conceptualized or system driven." —Ed.]

3. [Jacob Loewenberg (1882–1969) earned a PhD from Harvard in 1911 with a dissertation on Hegel supervised by Josiah Royce. George P. Adams (1882–1961) also received his PhD from Harvard in 1911, developing a position largely influenced by Royce. Stephen C. Pepper (1891–1972), most known for his work on aesthetics, took his PhD from Harvard in 1916. —Ed.]

4. [Bugbee later developed this idea in the context of Gabriel Marcel's conception of *l'exigence ontologique.* See Henry G. Bugbee Jr., "L'Exigence Ontologique," in *The Philosophy of Gabriel Marcel, The Library of Living Philosophers*, vol. 17, ed. P. E. Schilpp and L. E. Hahn (Chicago: Open Court Publishing, 1984), 81–93. —Ed.]

5. [Norman Maclean, *A River Runs Through It* (Chicago: University of Chicago Press, 1976), 92. —Ed.]

6. A very discerning criticism of this confusion, with special reference to Hume and Kant, is expressed by Professor Norman Kemp Smith in the 1931 Philosophical Lecture before the British Academy: "Is Divine Existence Credible?"

7. As Professor Kemp Smith says of the awareness of the Divine: "Potentially any situation may yield an immediate awareness of the Divine; actually there is no situation whatsoever which invariably yields it." Op. Cit., p. 24.

8. *Metaphysics*, 982b, 12–13.

9. We might say, then, that metaphysics is concerned with saying "the first words" in formulating our knowledge, rather than "the last words"; this point is well stated by Professor F. J. E. Woodbridge in his *Essay on Nature*, and *Nature and Mind.*

10. *Metaphysics*, A, 983a, 16–17.

11. Ibid., A, 983a. 13–15.

12. *Metaphysics*, A, 982b, 17–19.

3. A Venture in the Open

1. [Henry G. Bugbee Jr., *The Inward Morning, A Philosophical Exploration in Journal Form*, Introduction, Gabriel Marcel (1958; repr. Athens: University of Georgia Press, 1999, with a new introduction by Edward F. Mooney), 52. Bugbee's conception of inward morning is derived from Thoreau's poem "The Inward Morning" contained in *A Week on the Concord and Merrimack Rivers.* —Ed.]

2. [Henry G. Bugbee Jr., "A Venture in the Open." A 1958 conference paper delivered in Brussels, Belgium, and published in *Colloque Orient-Occident: Entretiens International* (Bruxelles: Snoeck-Ducaj, 1958). —Ed.]

3. [Henry G. Bugbee, Jr., "The Philosophic Significance of the Sublime," *Philosophy Today*, vol. 11, no. 1 (1967): 58. —Ed.]

4. [Henry G. Bugbee, Jr., "Thoughts on Creation," *Essays in Philosophy*, ed. Penn State University Philosophy Department (University Park: Penn State University Press, 1962), 134.]

5. [Bugbee, *The Inward Morning*, 79. —Ed.]

6. [*Pour ceux qui plongent dans la réalité des choses, pour ceux qui vivent penchés sur ce qui se passé à tout moment dans le monde, les considerations sur les différences fondamentales qui existent entre la façon dont historiquement telle ou telle civilization est née dans télle ou telle contrée, de la façon dis-je dont diffère l'appreciation du temps ou des choses qui intéressent certainement l'intellectuel qui a la temps,les loisirs, le confort de se livrer à des speculations gratuities et agréables, mais pour l'homme qui vit dans la réalité le temps, le nombre et l'espace sont précisement les cadres de cette cruelle réalité.* (Translation DWR) —Ed.]

7. G. P. Malalasekara, "Vie active et Vie contemplative," *Syntheses*, Numero Special (#150), consacré au Collogue Orient-Occident, Bruxelles, 1958 (November 1958).

4. Thoughts on Creation

1. [See Henry G. Bugbee Jr., *The Inward Morning, A Philosophical Exploration in Journal Form*, foreword, Gabriel Marcel (1958; repr. Athens: University of Georgia Press, 1999, with a new introduction by Edward F. Mooney), p. 170: "Thinking dedicated to essential truth seems consummated only as it is *graced*." Cf. Joseph Grange, "The Generosity of the Good," *Review of Metaphysics*, vol. 62, no. 1 (September 2008): 115: "[The Good] is superior to being in every way, and without it there would be no cosmos at all. Again, what is first and foremost is the act of giving which is the very nature of the good. . . . What then does the good do? It gives reality and truth and thereby gives intelligibility to objects of thought and the power of knowing to the mind. . . . [T]he power of the good resides in the strength of its organizing force." —Ed.]

2. [Henry G. Bugbee Jr., "Thoughts on Creation," *Essays in Philosophy*, ed. Penn State University Philosophy Department (University Park: Penn State University Press, 1962), 134. —Ed.]

3. [Ibid, 135. —Ed.]

4. [Bugbee, *The Inward Morning*, 55. —Ed.]

5. [Gabriel Marcel, *The Mystery of Being*, vol. 1, *Reflection and Mystery*, trans. G.S. Fraser (Chicago: Regnery, 1950), 167. —Ed.]

6. [Annie Dillard, *Living by Fiction* (Harper & Row, 1983), 55. —Ed.]

7. [Bugbee, *The Inward Morning*, 39. See Jeanne Parain-Vial, *Gabriel Marcel et les niveaux de l' experience* (Paris: Seghers, 1966) for treatment of Marcel as both "watchman" and "awakener" to forms of transliminal experience. —Ed.]

5. Wilderness in America

1. [Henry G. Bugbee Jr., "Wilderness in America," *Journal of the American Academy of Religion*, vol. 42, no. 4 (1974): 614-20. —Ed.]
2. [Ibid. —Ed.]
3. [Ibid. —Ed.]
4. [Ibid. —Ed.]
5. [Ibid. Emphasis added. —Ed.]
6. [Ibid. —Ed.]

6. The Revolution in Western Thought: Another Step (1962)

1. [Huston Smith, "The Revolution in Western Thought," *Saturday Evening Post*, August 26, 1961, 28–29, 59–60. Bugbee and Smith were close friends and Smith was instrumental in helping to secure funding for Bugbee's extensive (fifty-five) college and university lecture tour from 1963 to 1967. The lectures were sponsored by the arts program of the Association of American Colleges and the Danforth Foundation. —Ed.]
2. [Ibid., 29. —Ed.]
3. [Ibid., 59. —Ed.]
4. [Nicholas de Cusa recognized this element of post-Copernican "aftershock" when he indicated that the universe is a sphere of which the center is everywhere, and the circumference is nowhere. See Alexandre Koyré, *From the Closed World to the Infinite Universe* (Baltimore, Md.: Johns Hopkins University Press, 1957) for an informed treatment of the importance of Cusa. —Ed.]
5. [Smith, "The Revolution in Western Thought," 59. Emphasis added. —Ed.]
6. [Ibid., 59. —Ed.]
7. [Ibid., 60. —Ed.]
8. [See Smith, 60: "Having labored in the shadow of rationalism during the modern period, contemporary theology . . . has [reaped] two gains. One is new realization of the validity of Pascal's 'reasons of the heart' as distinct from those of the mind. The other is a recovery of the awe without which religion, as distinct from ethical philosophy piously expressed, is probably impossible." —Ed.]

7. Nature and a True Artist (n.d.)

1. [A yet to be explored topic in Bugbee studies is the importance of fine art and music in Bugbee's philosophy. For example, in the bibliography of "In Demonstration of the Spirit," he writes:
"A personal library including sixty-two volumes of recorded music from Bach, Beethoven, Brahams, Brückner, Chopin, Dvorak, Franck,

Haydn, Lalo, Mozart, Rachmaninoff, Schubert, Sibelius, Richard Strauss, Wagner, and a few others has contributed more to the experience and conviction I have expressed than any other 'bibliographical' factor." The bibliography of "The Sense and the Conception of Being" lists over twenty works of classical music. —Ed.]

8. A Way of Reading the Book of Job (1963)

1. [For an insightful look into the relationship between the experience of the holy and the concept of God, see the following comment of John E. Smith: "The transition from the Holy to God, while not logically necessary, is nevertheless not without some ground; it is rooted in a mediating concept which we may call the general *concept* of God derived from reflective analysis of recurrent experience and presupposed as part of the meaning of every specific religious doctrine of God. The topic calls for more extended treatment but one essential point can be elucidated. The term 'God' need not be restricted to use as a name (although there are contexts in which it so functions) but stands as well for a concept that finds its basis in philosophical reflection on the world and ourselves. The concept embraces the idea of a supremely worshipful reality which gives being to and controls the final destiny of all finite realities. If the term 'God' were merely a name, significant exclusively within the confines of a special religious tradition, there would be no intelligible connection between the experience of the Holy and God. But because there is a concept of God available for our use, it is possible to connect the concept of God with the experience of the Holy in which we become aware of the dependence of our being upon a power that is at once the supremely worshipful being, and that upon which we depend for our final worship and destiny" (John E. Smith, "The Experience of the Holy and the Experience of God," in *Phenomenology in America: Studies in the Philosophy of Experience*, ed. James M. Edie [Chicago: Quadrangle Books, 1967], 305–6). —Ed.]

2. [Job 42:3–6 (Revised Standard Version). Herbert Fingarette prefers "Therefore . . . I melt away" to "Therefore . . . I repent in dust and ashes." See Herbert Fingarette, "The Meaning of Law in the Book of Job," in *Revisions: Changing Perspectives in moral Philosophy*, ed. A. MacIntyre and S. M. Hauerwas (South Bend, Ind.: University of Notre Dame Press, 1983), 270: The original Hebrew may be read as saying something more just and true to the situation: "I melt away and I repudiate my words." —Ed.]

9. Notes on Objectivity and Reality (n.d.)

1. [Cf. Martin Heidegger's remarks on meditative thinking in *Gelassenheit* (Pfullingen: Neske, 1959). —Ed.]

10. Experience, Memory, Reflection: An Interview with Henry Bugbee

1. [Bugbee's father shot an Albino caribou, "a rare and beautiful creature with white skin and pink eyes," in the Canadian Rockies. —Ed.]

2. [See Henry G. Bugbee Jr., *The Inward Morning, A Philosophical Exploration in Journal Form*, foreword, Gabriel Marcel (1958; repr. Athens: University of Georgia Press, 1999, with a new introduction by Edward F. Mooney), 45-51, for Bugbee's reflections on John Schultz and the experience of rowing at Princeton. —Ed.]

Appendixes

1. [The reader is strongly encouraged to consult David James Duncan's "Five Henry Stories," in addition to the other fine essays collected in *Wilderness and the Heart: Henry Bugbee's Philosophy of Place, Presence and Memory*, ed. Edward F. Mooney (Athens: University of Georgia Press, 1999). —Ed.]

2. [Albert Borgmann, "Henry" infra. —Ed.]

3. [Janice Downey, "Streamside Philosophy," *Montanan*, Spring 1991, 14. —Ed.]

4. [See "Streamside philosophy," p. 15, where he claims the department developed into "the strongest teaching department I've ever been privileged to work in." —Ed.]

5. [Cass Chinsky, memorial service, January 8, 2000. Note Bugbee's reference in his CV to the fact that while teaching at Mount Allison University in 1980–1981, he "walked the west shore at the head of the Bay of Fundy." No small accomplishment. —Ed.]

6. [While the CV lists the date that PhD was awarded as 1946, the date of the dissertation defense was January 25, 1947. —Ed.]

7. [See Donald C. Williams, "Realism," *Journal of Philosophy*, vol. 42, no. 21 (1945): 577. Bugbee included Williams's poem in Henry G. Bugbee Jr., *The Inward Morning, A Philosophical Exploration in Journal Form*, foreword, Gabriel Marcel (1958; repr. Athens: University of Georgia Press, 1999, with a new introduction by Edward F. Mooney), 93. —Ed.]

8. [Henry G. Bugbee Jr., "The Moment of Obligation in Experience," *Journal of Religion*, vol. 33, no. 1 (1953). —Ed.]

9. [Lewis referring to Royce's brief piece referred to as "The Cult of the Dead." In 1916 "two or three nights before his death, he slipped downstairs unnoticed, set his customarily disarranged desk in order, burned many papers and this unfinished writing on his desk" (J. Harry Cotton, *Royce on the Human Self* [Cambridge, Mass.: Harvard University Press, 1954], 7). The piece is also contained in *Josiah Royce's Later Writings: A Collection of Unpublished and Scattered Works*, ed. Frank M. Oppenheim, S. J. (London: Thoemmes Press, 2001), 34. —Ed.]

10. [The classic account of this period is Bruce Kuklick's *The Rise of American Philosophy: Cambridge Massachusetts, 1860-1930* (New Haven, Conn.: Yale University Press, 1977). Lewis is actually considered part of the "silver age" of philosophy at Harvard, the period immediately following, but he was a student at the height of the "golden age." —Ed.]

11. [After reading Gabriel Marcel's *The Mystery of Being*, vol. 1, *Reflection and Mystery*, trans. G.S. Fraser (Chicago: Regnery, 1950), Bugbee's ethical orientation became increasingly Socratic, emphasizing the importance of *being* the same person in public as in private. See Plato, *Apology*, 33a. —Ed.]

12. [To learn more about Anderson's philosophy, see *Being Human in the Ultimate: Studies in the Thought of John M. Anderson*, ed. N. Georgopoulos and Michael Heim (Amsterdam: Rodopi, 1995). —Ed.]

13. [A sizable collection of letters that Bugbee received from Anderson is contained in Bugbee's philosophical papers. Sadly, Bugbee's letters to Anderson were destroyed after Anderson's death in 1999. —Ed.]

14. [Lest the reader come away with a less than positive impression of Bugbee's time at Harvard, several points must be kept in mind. In *The Inward Morning*, Bugbee acknowledges his gratitude to the Philosophy Department, especially to Quine. Bugbee was awarded the Santayana fellowship after spending three years in the department, *and* he returned to Harvard as a research fellow in 1961–62. Bugbee once recounted that some members of the department broke into tears when he left in 1954. —Ed.]

15. [See Socrates's comments in the *Apology*. After implying that he possesses "human wisdom, perhaps" (20d), he concludes "What is probable, gentlemen, is that in fact the god is wise and human wisdom is worth little or nothing" (23a). —Ed.]

16. [See Thoreau's *Walking* for a celebration of the peripatetic nature of philosophical reflection: "So we saunter toward the Holy Land; till one day the sun shall shine more brightly than ever he has done, shall perchance shine into our minds and hearts, and light up our whole lives with a great awakening light, so warm and serene and golden as on a bank-side in Autumn" ("Walking," in *Excursions: The Writings of Henry David Thoreau*, ed. J. J. Mauldenhauer [Princeton, N.J.: Princeton University Press, 2006], 222). Cf. Daniel W. Conway, "Answering the Call of the Wild: Walking with Bugbee and Thoreau," in *Wilderness and the Heart: Henry Bugbee's Philosophy of Place, Presence, and Memory* (Athens: University of Georgia Press, 1999), 6: "Walking is not merely a callisthenic propaedeutic to the heroic labors of philosophizing. Rather walking functions as an engine of immersion . . . ." —Ed.]

17. [Albert Borgmann, "Henry Bugbee, 1915-1999," *Proceedings and Addresses of the American Philosophical Association*, vol. 73, no. 5 (May 2000): 246–47. —Ed.]

18. [Downey, "Streamside philosophy," 15. Bugbee once remarked while fishing that "The fish will probably make known if and when they

come when they are ready, but meanwhile I have to cast ceremoniously any way a bit." When asked "what is going through his mind while fly-fishing on Rock Creek," Bugbee answered: "I'm steeped in what's going on, the life there. All the creatures, they're fellow creatures to me so they are not separate from human life. They're not identified with it, but they are fellow creatures. They articulate the lived world. When you see a place that you've known with wild creatures in it and then they're gone, it's dead, it has no voice of the sort that you've been accustomed to hear. And when you're fishing you're drinking that all in . . . Fly fishing has certainly been a long and central strain in my life and my sense of it is that rivers call on me, fish call on me. Whenever I'm near water, I go to it and I usually hang around until I see a fish rise. And then I feel, ah, he's acknowledged me as belonging there with him. I love that sort of relationship with the country and the land. It fills out the meaning of creation for me: The beings around me are fellow creatures." —Ed.]

19. [Troy Letherman and Tony Weaver, *Top Water: Fly-Fishing Alaska, The Last Frontier* (Woodstock, Vt.: Countryman Press, 2004), 11. A wonderful book. —Ed.]

20. [Memorial address, January 8, 2000. —Ed.]

21. [Ibid. —Ed.]

22. [Gary Whited, *Having Listened* (Stonington, Conn.: Homebound Publications, 2013), 72. —Ed.]

Bibliography

Adams, Elie. "Reinstating Humanistic Categories." *Review of Metaphysics* 55, no. 1 (September 2001): 21–39.

Alexander, Thomas M. *The Human Eros: Eco-Ontology and the Aesthetics of Existence.* New York: Fordham University Press, 2013.

Allard, James W. Jr. "Bugbee on the Ground of Unconditional Affirmation." *The Pluralist* 6, no. 2 (2011): 35–53.

Anderson, Douglas R. "Wilderness as Philosophical Home." In *Philosophy Americana: Making Philosophy at Home in American Culture.* New York: Fordham University Press, 2006.

Anderson, John M. *The Individual and the New World.* State College, Pa.: Bald Eagle Press, 1955.

———. "Sketch for a Phenomenology of the American Experience." In *Selected Studies in Phenomenology and Existentialism.* Edited by C. O. Schrag and W. McBride. New York: State University of New York Press, 1983.

Armstrong, J. H. S. "*The Inward Morning—A Philosophical Exploration in Journal Form* by Henry G. Bugbee, Jr." *Mind* 72, no. 287 (1963): 457–58.

Augustine. *Confessions.* Books 9–13. Translated by William Watts. Cambridge, Mass.: Harvard University Press, 1912.

Basso, Keith H. "'To Give Up on Words': Silence in Western Apache Culture." *Southwestern Journal of Anthropology* 26, no. 3 (1970): 213–30.

Borgman, Albert. "Bugbee on Philosophy and Modernity." In *Wilderness and the Heart: Henry Bugbee's Philosophy of Place, Presence, and Memory.* Edited by Edward F. Mooney. Athens: University of Georgia Press, 1999.

———. "Henry Bugbee, 1915–1999." *Proceedings and Addresses of the American Philosophical Association* 73, no. 5 (May 2000): 246–47.

Brittan, Gordon G., Jr. "Autonomy and Authenticity." In *Wilderness and the Heart: Henry Bugbee's Philosophy of Place, Presence, and Memory.* Edited by Edward F. Mooney. Athens: University of Georgia Press, 1999.

Brockelman, Paul. "The Miracle of Being: Cosmology and the Experience of God." *Human Studies* 20 (1997): 287–301.

Bugbee, Henry G., Jr. "From an American Philosophical Journal." *Yale French Studies* no. 16 (1955): 89–95.

———. "In Demonstration of the Spirit." Undergraduate Thesis. Princeton University, 1936.

———. *The Inward Morning, A Philosophical Exploration in Journal Form.* Introduction (1958) Gabriel Marcel, with a new introduction by Edward F. Mooney, repr. Athens: University of Georgia Press, 1999. First published by Bald Eagle Press, 1958.

———. "L'Exigence Ontologique." In *The Philosophy of Gabriel Marcel. Library of Living Philosophers*, vol. 17. Edited by P. Schilpp and L. Hahn. Chicago: Open Court Publishing, 1984.

———. "Le Recueillement et L'Accueil," *Les études philosophiques: organe official de la Sociéte d'études philosophiques*, 1975: 47–54.

———. "Loneliness, Solitude and the Twofold Way in Which Concern Seems to Be Claimed." *Humanitas* 10, no. 3 (1974): 313–328.

———. "The Moment of Obligation in Experience." *Journal of Religion* 33, no. 1 (1953): 1–15.

———. "On Starting with Love." *Humanitas* 2, no. 2 (1966): 149–63.

———. "The Philosophical Significance of the Sublime." *Philosophy Today* 11, no. 1 (1967): 55–59.

———. "A Point of Co-Articulation in the Life and Thought of Gabriel Marcel." *Philosophy Today* 19 (1975): 61–67.

———. "The Sense and the Conception of Being." PhD Dissertation. University of California, Berkeley, 1947.

———. "Thoughts on Creation." *Essays in Philosophy*. Edited by Philosophy Department of the Pennsylvania State University. University Park: Penn State University Press, 1962.

———. "Une Exploration de l'Inconnu" [A Venture in the Open], *Colloque Orient-Occident*: Entretien International. Bruxelles: Snoeck-Ducaj, 1958.

———. "Wilderness in America." *Journal of the American Academy of Religion* 42, no. 4 (1974): 614–20.

Bunge, Robert. *American Urphilosophie: An American Philosophy Before Pragmatism*. Lanham, MD: University Press of America, 1983.

Casey, Edward S. *The Fate of Place: A Philosophical History*. Berkeley: University of California Press, 1997.

———. *Getting Back into Place: Towards a Renewed Understanding of the Place World*. Bloomington: Indiana University Press, 1993.

Cavell, Stanley. "Finding as Founding." *The New Yet Unapproachable America*. Chicago: University Chicago Press, 2013. First printed by Living Batch Press, 1989.

Clarke, Orville. "On Starting with Love." In *Wilderness and the Heart: Henry Bugbee's Philosophy of Place, Presence, and Memory*. Edited by Edward F. Mooney. Athens: University of Georgia Press, 1999.

Conway, Dan. "Answering the Call of the Wild: Walking with Bugbee and Thoreau." In *Wilderness and the Heart: Henry Bugbee's Philosophy of Place, Presence, and Memory*. Edited by Edward F. Mooney. Athens: University of Georgia Press, 1991.

———. "The Wilderness of Henry Bugbee." *Journal of Speculative Philosophy* 17, no. 4 (2003): 259–269.

Crites, Stephen. "The Narrative Quality of Experience." *Journal of the American Academy of Religion* 39, no. 3 (September 1971): 291–311.

Dewey, John. *Experience and Nature*. Chicago: Open Court Publishing Company, 1925.

Dillard, Annie. *Holy the Firm*. New York: Harper & Row, 1977.

———. *Living by Fiction*. Harper & Row, 1983.

Doughty, Charles M. *Travels in Arabia Deserta* vols. 1 and 2. New York: Random House, 1937.

Downey, Janice. "Streamside Philosophy." *Montanan* (Spring 1991): 14–15.

Duncan, David James. "Five Henry Stories." In *Wilderness and the Heart: Henry Bugbee's Philosophy of Place, Presence, and Memory*. Edited by Edward F. Mooney. Athens: University of Georgia Press, 1999.

———. *River Teeth*. New York: Bantam Books, 1995.

———. *The River Why?* New York: Bantam Books, 1983.

———. "Six Henry Stories." *My Story as Told by Water*. San Francisco: Sierra Club Books, 2001.

Edwards, James C. *The Plain Sense of Things: The Fate of Religion in an Age of Normal Nihilism*. University Park: Penn State University Press, 1997.

Emerson, Ralph Waldo. "New England Reformers" *Essays*, Second Series. Boston: Houghton, 1876.

Feenberg, Andrew. "Zen Existentialism: Bugbee's Japanese Influence." In *Wilderness and the Heart: Henry Bugbee's Philosophy of Place, Presence, and Memory*. Edited by Edward F. Mooney. Athens: University of Georgia Press, 1999.

Fingarette, Herbert. "The Meaning of Law in the Book of Job." In *Revisions: Changing Perspectives in Moral Philosophy*. Edited by A. MacIntyre and S. M. Hauerwas. Notre Dame, Ind.: University of Notre Dame Press, 1983.

Fite, Warner. "The Impersonal Point of View and the Personal," *Contemporary American Philosophy*, vol. 1. Edited by G. P. Adams and W. P. Montague. New York: Macmillan Press, 1930.

———. *Moral Philosophy*. New York: The Dial Press, 1925.

———. "The Philosopher and His Words." *Philosophical Review* 44, no. 2 (March 1935): 120–37.

Fowles, John. "Seeing Nature Whole." *Harper's Magazine*, November 1979, 49–68.

Friskics, Scott. "Dialogue, Responsibility, and Oil and Gas Leasing on Montana's Rocky Mountain Front." *Ethics and the Environment* 8, no. 2 (2003): 8–30.

Georgopoulos, N., and Michael Heim. *Being Human in the Ultimate: Studies in the Thought of John M. Anderson*, vol. 23. Value Inquiry Book Series. Amsterdam: Rodophi, 1995.

Gotshalk, D. W. *Structure and Reality: A Study of First Principles*. New York: Dial Press, 1937.

Grange, Joseph. "Being, Feeling, and Environment." *Environmental Ethics* 7 (Winter 1985): 351–64.

———. "The Generosity of the Good." *Review of Metaphysics* 62, no. 1 (September 2008): 111–21.

———. "The Roads of Maine: Pathways and Highways." *Religious Humanism* 10, no. 3 (1970): 98–99.

Gray, J. Glenn. "Splendor of the Simple." *Philosophy East and West* 20, no. 3 (July 1970): 227–40.

Gunn, Giles, ed. *New World Metaphysics: Readings on the Religious Meaning of the American Experience*. New York: Oxford University Press, 1981.

Harris, James F. "An Empirical Understanding of Eternality." *Philosophy of Religion*, vol. 22, no. 3 (1987): 165–83.

Heidegger, Martin. *Aus Der Erfahrung Des Denken*. Pfullingen: Gunther Neske, 1954. *Gelassenheit*: Pfullingen: Gunther Neske, 1959.

Hendel, Charles W. "Warner Fite," *Proceedings and Addresses of the American Philosophical Association* vol. 29 (1955–1956): 113–14.

Henderson, David Graham. "Bugbee's Wilderness: Metaphysical and Montanan." *The Pluralist* 8, no. 3 (2013): 46–54.

Hofstadter, Albert. "The Tragicomic: Concern in Depth." *The Journal of Aesthetics and Art Criticism* 24, no. 2 (1965): 295–302.

Jackson, John Brinkerhoff. *A Sense of Place, a Sense of Time*. New Haven, Conn.: Yale University Press, 1994.

James, Williams. "The Ph.D. Octopus." *William James: The Essential Writings*. Edited by Bruce W. Wilshire. Albany: State University of New York Press, 1984.

Joad, C. E. M. (Cyril Edwin Mitchinson) *Return to Philosophy: Being A Defence of Reason, An Affirmation of Values and A Plea for Philosophy*. New York: E. P. Dutton, 1936.

Karnos, David D., and Robert G. Shoemaker. *Falling in Love with Wisdom: American Philosophers Talk About Their Calling*. New York: Oxford University Press, 1993.

Koestenbaum, Peter. "*The Inward Morning: A Philosophical Exploration in Journal Form* by Henry G. Bugbee, Jr." *Philosophy and Phenomenological Research* 20, no. 1 (1959): 126–28.

Koyré, Alexandre *From the Closed World to the Infinite Universe*. Baltimore, Md.: Johns Hopkins University Press, 1957.

Krutch, Joseph Wood. *The Grand Canyon: Today and All Its Yesterdays.* New York: William Morrow, 1957.

Kuklick, Bruce. *The Rise of American Philosophy: Cambridge Massachusetts, 1860–1930.* New Haven, Conn.: Yale University Press, 1977.

Larson, Gerald James, and Eliot Deutsch, eds. *Interpreting Across Boundaries: New Essays in Comparative Philosophy.* Princeton, N.J.: Princeton University Press, 1988.

Lawry, John. "God and Temporal Being." *Philosophy Today* (Spring 1984): 83–98.

———. "Henry Bugbee's Interpretation of the Book of Job." In *Wilderness and the Heart: Henry Bugbee's Philosophy of Place, Presence, and Memory.* Edited by Edward F. Mooney. Athens: University of Georgia Press, 1999.

Leopold, Aldo. *A Sand County Almanac and Sketches Here and There.* New York: Oxford University Press, 1949.

Letherman, Troy, and Tony Weaver. *Top Water: Fly Fishing Alaska, The Last Frontier.* Woodstock, Vt.: Countryman Press, 2004.

Luce, A. A. (Arthur Aston) *Fishing and Thinking.* UK: Hodder and Stoughton, 1959.

MacIntyre, Alastair. "Foreword." In *Wilderness and the Heart: Henry Bugbee's Philosophy of Place, Presence, and Memory.* Edited by Edward F. Mooney. Athens: University of Georgia Press, 1999.

MacLean, Norman. *A River Runs Through It.* Chicago: University of Chicago Press, 1976.

Malalasekara, G. P. "Vie active et Vie contemplative," *Syntheses*, Numero Special (#150), consacré au Collogue Orient-Occident, Bruxelles (November 1958): 55–57.

Marcel, Gabriel. Gabriel Marcel, *The Mystery of Being*, vol. 1, *Reflection and Mystery.* Translated by G. S. Fraser. Chicago: Regnery, 1950.

———. "Introduction." To *The Inward Morning, A Philosophical Exploration in Journal Form.* Repr. Athens: University of Georgia Press, 1999, with a new introduction by Edward F. Mooney. First published by Bald Eagle Press, 1958. 131–32.

Martin, Calvin Luther. *The Way of the Human Being.* New Haven, Conn.: Yale University Press, 1999.

Marx, Leo. *The Machine in the Garden: Technology and the Pastoral Idea in America.* New York: Oxford University Press, 1964.

Matthews, Gray. "Reality as Sacred Place: The Parallel Insights of Thomas Merton and Henry Bugbee." *The Merton Annual* 17 (2004): 88–120.

McKibben, Bill. *The End of Nature* (New York: Anchor Books, 1990).

Mooney, Edward G. *Lost Intimacy in American Thought: Recovering Personal Philosophy from Thoreau to Cavell.* New York: Continuum, 2009.

———. *Wilderness and the Heart: Henry Bugbee's Philosophy of Place, Presence, and Memory.* Edited by Edward F. Mooney. Athens: University of Georgia Press, 1999.

Mugerauer, Robert. *Heidegger and Homecoming: The Leitmotif in the Later Writings*. Toronto: University of Toronto Press, 2008.

Nash, Roderick. *Wilderness and the American Mind*. 3rd ed. New Haven, Conn.: Yale University Press, 1982.

Oelschlaeger, Max. *The Idea of Wilderness: From Pre-History to the Age of Ecology*. New Haven, Conn.: Yale University Press, 1991.

Ong, Walter S. J. "*The Inward Morning: A Philosophical Exploration in Journal Form* by Henry G. Bugbee, Jr." *The Modern Schoolman* 37, no. 1 (1959): 67–69.

———. "Personalism in the Wilderness." *Kenyon Review* 21, no. 2 (1959): 297–304.

Palmer, Michael D. "A Burden Tender and in No Wise Heavy." In *Wilderness and the Heart: Henry Bugbee's Philosophy of Place, Presence, and Memory*. Edited by Edward F. Mooney. Athens: University of Georgia Press, 1999.

Parain-Vial, Jeanne. Gabriel Marcel et les niveaux de l' experience Paris: Seghers, 1966.

Picard, Max. *The World of Silence*. London: Harvill, 1948.

Plato. *Plato I: Euthyphro, Apology, Crito, Phaedo, Phaedrus*. Cambridge, Mass.: Harvard University Press, 1999.

Quine, Willard Van Orman. "In Celebration of Henry Bugbee." In *Wilderness and the Heart: Henry Bugbee's Philosophy of Place, Presence, and Memory*. Edited by Edward F. Mooney. Athens: University of Georgia Press, 1991.

Rodick, David W. "Finding One's Own Voice: The Philosophical Development of Henry G. Bugbee, Jr." *The Pluralist* 6, no. 2 (2011): 18–34.

———. "Martin Heidegger and Bill McKibben: On the End of Nature." *The Maine Scholar: A Journal of Ideas and Public Affairs*, vol. 7 (Autumn 1994): 153–63.

———. "Poetic Dwelling and Deep Ecology." *Call to Earth: Journal of the International Association for Environmental Philosophy* 2, no. 1 (March 2001): 2–7.

Rothenberg, David. "Melt Snowflake at Once! Toward a History of Wonder." In *Wilderness and the Heart: Henry Bugbee's Philosophy of Place, Presence, and Memory*. Edited by Edward F. Mooney. Athens: University of Georgia Press, 1999.

Royce, Josiah. "The Cult of the Dead." In *Josiah Royce's Later Writings: A Collection of Unpublished and Scattered Works*. Edited by Frank M. Oppenheim, S. J. London: Thoemmes Press, 2001.

———. "The Problem of Job." In *Studies of Good and Evil*. New York: D. Appleton, 1898.

Ryder, John. *The Things in Heaven and Earth: An Essay in Pragmatic Naturalism*. New York: Fordham University Press, 2013.

Seamon, David. *Dwelling, Seeing, and Designing: Towards a Phenomenological Ecology*. Albany: State University of New York Press, 1993.

Schmitz, Kenneth L. "Natural Imagery as a Discriminating Element in Religious Language." In *Experience, Reason, and God*. Edited by E. T. Long. Washington, D.C.: Catholic University Press of America, 1980.

Schrag, Calvin O. "The Structure of Moral Experience: A Phenomenological and Existential Analysis." *Ethics* 73, no. 4 (1963): 255–65.

Schweber, Nate. "Former UM Philosophy Chairman Dies." *Montana Kaiman*, January 25, 2000, 7.

Searle, John. "How to Derive 'Ought' from 'Is.'" *Philosophical Review* 73, no. 1 (February 1964): 43–58.

Shenk, Robert. *Authors at Sea: Recollections of Modern American Authors of Their Naval Service*. Annapolis, Md.: Naval Institute Press, 1996.

Smith, Henry Nash. *Virgin Land: The American West as Symbol and Myth*. New York: Vintage, 1957.

Smith, Huston. "The Revolution in Western Thought." *Saturday Evening Post*, August 26, 1961, 28–29, 59–60.

Smith, John E. "The Experience of the Holy and the Experience of God." In *Phenomenology in America: Studies in the Philosophy of Experience*. Edited by J. M. Edie. Chicago: Quadrangle Books, 1967.

Stace, Walter T. *Time and Eternity*. Princeton, N.J.: Princeton University Press, 1952.

Steele, Joel Dorman. *Barnes' Centenary History: One Hundred Years of American Independence*. New York: A. S. Barnes & Company, 1876.

Strong, David. *Crazy Mountains*. Albany: State University of New York Press, 1995.

———. "The Inward Wild." In *Wilderness and the Heart: Henry Bugbee's Philosophy of Place, Presence, and Memory*. Edited by Edward F. Mooney. University of Georgia Press, 1999.

Thoreau, Henry David. *Walking* in *Excursions: The Writings of Henry David Thoreau*. Edited by J. J. Moldenhauer. Princeton, N. J.: Princeton University Press, 2007.

———. *A Week on the Concord and Merrimack Rivers, Walden: or, Life in the Woods, The Maine Woods, Cape Cod*. New York: Library of America, 1985.

Tillich, Paul. *Systematic Theology*, vol. 1. Chicago: University of Chicago Press, 1951.

Toole, David. "As We Take Things, So We Have Them: Reflections on the Fragility of Nature." In *Wilderness and the Heart: Henry Bugbee's Philosophy of Place, Presence, and Memory*. Edited by Edward F. Mooney. Athens: University of Georgia Press, 1999.

Tuan, Yi-Fu. *Space and Place: The Perspective of Experience*. Minneapolis: University of Minnesota Press, 1977.

Webb, Steven E. "Presence, Memory, and Faith: Passages from a Notebook on *The Inward Morning*." In *Wilderness and the Heart: Henry Bugbee's*

Philosophy of Place, Presence, and Memory. Edited by Edward F. Mooney. Athens: University of Georgia Press, 1999.

Welch, Cyril. "Henry Bugbee as Teacher." In *Wilderness and the Heart: Henry Bugbee's Philosophy of Place, Presence, and Memory*. Edited by Edward F. Mooney. Athens: University of Georgia Press, 1999.

Whited, Gary. *Having Listened*. Stonington, Conn.: Homebound Publications, 2013.

———. "Henry Bugbee as Mentor." In *Wilderness and the Heart: Henry Bugbee's Philosophy of Place, Presence, and Memory*. Edited by Edward F. Mooney. Athens: University of Georgia Press, 1999.

Williams, Donald C. "Realism." *Journal of Philosophy* 42, no. 21 (1945): 577.

Williams, George Hunston. "Wilderness as Wasteland and Paradise." In *Wilderness and the Heart: Henry Bugbee's Philosophy of Place, Presence, and Memory*. Edited by Edward F. Mooney. Athens: University of Georgia Press, 1999.

Wilshire, Bruce. "Henry Bugbee: *The Inward Morning*." In *The Primal Roots of American Philosophy*. University Park: Penn State University Press, 2000.

———. "Henry Bugbee: Philosopher of Intimacy." *Fashionable Nihilism: A Critique of Analytic Philosophy*. Albany: State University of New York Press, 2002.

gROUNDWORKS|

ECOLOGICAL ISSUES IN PHILOSOPHY AND THEOLOGY

Forrest Clingerman and Brian Treanor, series editors

Forrest Clingerman, Brian Treanor, Martin Drenthen, and David Utsler, eds., *Interpreting Nature: The Emerging Field of Environmental Hermeneutics*

Bruce V. Foltz, *The Noetics of Nature: Environmental Philosophy and the Holy Beauty of the Visible*

Martin Drenthen and Jozef Keulartz, eds., *Environmental Aesthetics: Crossing Divides and Breaking Ground*

Louise Westling, *The Logos of the Living World: Merleau-Ponty, Animals, and Language*

Brian Treanor, Bruce Ellis Benson, and Norman Wirzba, eds., *Being-in-Creation: Human Responsibility in an Endangered World*

Henry Bugbee, *Wilderness in America: Philosophical Writings*. Edited by David W. Rodick